What They All Said
MANIFESTOS OF MAJOR POLITICAL PARTIES OF INDIA

What They All Said
MANIFESTOS OF MAJOR POLITICAL PARTIES OF INDIA

Surojit Mahalanobis

ANMOL PUBLICATIONS PVT. LTD.
NEW DELHI - 110002 (INDIA)

ANMOL PUBLICATIONS PVT. LTD.
4374/4B, Ansari Road, Daryaganj,
New Delhi-110 002 (India)

Waht They All Said Manifestos of Major Political Parties of India

First Edition 1997

ISBN 81-7488-526-9

PRINTED IN INDIA

Published by J. L. Kumar for Anmol Publications Pvt. Ltd. New Delhi and Printed at Mehra Offset Press, Delhi.

This book is dedicated to my loving parents whose silent blessings are always the courage to me in difficult times.

Preface

POST-INDEPENDENT India's political scenario has offered myriad hues of the society. If we draw a dividing line for better understanding of it, we might have to take the sixties as the transition period for evaluation. During the initial era of Independence we were, and even today, we partly remain, well bred in thoughts of great thinkers of modern India like Swami Vivekananda, Mahatma Gandhi, Netaji Subhash and Pandit Nehru and hundred others down the line. Brilliant ideas of Tagore continue to inseminate in us love for humanity even today, beyond the divide of sixties, after fifty-five years of his death (1941). While all these influences of post-Independent India's heritage roused our spiritual sensibility of truth and ethos of life, the approach to political ideas took rather the bylanes of life, and gradually discarded what was initially ingrained in value systems. If the initial systems were directed to offer the best confort to life, the byproduct of the post-sixties political thoughts has decidedly found ways to attain quick and enormous mundane benefits guided by opportunistic designs of self before service. However, the catchword has remained better than all earlier bests of comforts of life which eventually has turned out to be mere hollow pretexts, to the common man. The complacence of the initial decades had of course blinded our mind's eyes as it soon neutralised the advantages which several of our modern thinkers had earned for us and had entranced the entire humanity as audience. Our thinkers of yesteryears had offered theories not merely to solve our nascent problems but of "world-historical problems" (Prof Pantham). Situations after the first decade started changing.

The scenario from the second decade, from the sixties precisely, when we had to compromise our economic advantages to meet the Chinese war liabilities, had a number of surprises in Indian political life. Parties started becoming more centrifugal and began to assert their egotism and hero-dominated bravadoes. Nation-building process was subjected to and governed by more individualistic exercises of democracy and for personal fames. Egoes dominated decisions offering abundant contradictions, stresses and strains onto the polity. The political parties expressed themselves in various alignments along caste, religion, social groupings and agrarian solidarity. What was sharp and clear divide between the right of the Centre and the Left, gradually brewed forth heterogeneous interest groups—demolishing the very sanctity of healthy relations between Government and the Opposition.

Situations further worsened in eighties. It was turbulent eighties for India. Earlier divides in parties and multifarious compositions in different broader thoughts like those of Congress, Socialist parties, Indian Communism and the Indian Nationalism — all took differential strokes, as if from a master painter's brush, and colours changed so frequently. Present day political activism is generally looked down upon as if tepid exercises of the disgruntled, or of the corrupt self-seeker. The nexus between the criminal and the politician (which eventually encompasses the administration as well), always haunt our mind today. We, the common man, would most often wish to draw away from the humdrum of political assertions. But we cannot. Almost every year now we are sharply drawn into democratic processes, which we have ideally adhered to so dearly. Most often we are confronted by a new problem — emergence of numerous vote-seekers. New parties, newer lobbies, and even newer faces propping up out of the millions, eagerly trying to assert their claims. Almost all of them claim to tell something new, which all think are novel. A conscientious voter only passes it as trifle, over-democratised expression of yet a different ego. The voter has to be choosy today, about his likes and dislikes; he has to be firm in decisions, choices and rejections. He has to identify what he is and is not. The present book is an impartial attempt towards the goal of offering collective thoughts of all major Indian political parties.

Efforts have been made to accommodate all national parties. There are some parties which can claim their 'national' prestige — such as Revolutionary Socialist Party of Bengal, Telugu Desham Party of Andhra Pradesh, Akali Dal of Punjab, All-India Dravida Munnetra Kazagham or Dravida Munnetra Kazagham of Tamil Nadu, Assom Gana Parishad Mulayam Singh Yadav's Samajwadi Party or the like, but all these parties have not been taken for consideration because they are active only in their respective regions, and donot have much common interest to serve in the all-India arena. Besides, almost all important standpoints of each of these parties are equally well expounded by the major national parties also, and in many of such cases these parties unite with a national platform and serve the common ends. The lone question lies, however, in the inclusion of All-India Forward Bloc that belongs to the Left Front. AIFB has been accommodated with the sole purpose to discuss its policies vis-a-vis what Netaji Subhash Chandra Bose had envisioned for the free India. For, it is Netaji whose brainchild was the original Forward Bloc, which now is non-existent.

There are dearth of books on post-Independent Indian political thoughts. There are indeed a few great books on individual thinkers and political leaders, thought, yet majority of these are rather tilted expressions, while most of other flatter their ways to personal ends. It is well justified by Professor Thomas Pantham, a Fulbright senior scholar in universities of Princeton and Massachusetts (1981) and a professor of Political Science in M S University of Baroda, in his introduction to *Political Thought in Modern India*: "when it comes to a book dealing with the whole or nearly whole of the political thought of modern India, the available books seem to be disappointing to us. They donot maintain a uniformly high level of treatment or movement in India."

This book was intended to appear before the hustings for the eleventh Lok Sabha were to start. The idea had to be dropped as things were changing fast in flude dimensions offering points and probable counter-points. I decided to wait and watch till the activities settled down to, what is the crux of the matter, the governance of the State. Also, there were enough indicators to justify the anxiety that no party was going to record absolute two-third majority in the Parliament. Eventualities were therefore rife to concentrate over a probable coalition Government consisting of (well, calling the spade a spade) parties with contradictory principles. For, the basic purpose of this book is to offer a non-committal picture of principles of all major political parties.

Target readership of this book are millions of new voters who are not bred in politics, and for whom a stable government means progress in life. Besides, this book should serve as reference adjuvant to the purposes of research by political scientists in the country and the like readership. Labour put in for last few months would be well justified, if the book becomes a handy reference for general knowledge of the prospective polity.

While planning this book, initial thoughts were to find out political history of each component of nation-building activities by the parties. However, that would have given it unnecessary bulk. This apart, talking of political manifestos is more like talking in their terms of reference and become a silent indirect spokesman. Hence, the best way to keep away from committing to any mind-set and express a non-committal voice is to tell under inverted commas; and I have done so, silently. The secondary thought over planning, therefore, became more dominating. Efforts in this book is to inform indeed the psychic patterns of think-tanks of all parties, which modulated their activities during and after hustings. This pattern would, by all probability, remain even in future times, perhaps in modified versions. The backgrounders in this book hence are not the backdrops from which these parties were born, but how their think-tanks worked to brave up themselves to face the polity. This mind-set might even become a trend-setter in future democratic processes in India as well. It seems well indicated by elements of historicity, if I am not mistaken.

The task is immense and not hassle-free. My approach is towards writing the political history in the specified time. And here lies the basic intriguing question. What exactly is the history of time? Is it which are recorded in the day-to-day reportage in broadsheet newspapers? Or is it the culled up blob of spicy details of life from the news kitsch of tabloids? Or, is it the meticulous effort to discern the trend of the society, and truthfully recording it? The question perhaps would continue to remain unaddressed by a political scientist even in near future, as long as the trend of hustings would not be able to read future beyond sentimentalism. For, history of time is indeed the history of contemporary life of the polity, which has at least one thing as essential pre-requisite—that is, necessity to record.

How far have I been able to tread the road to success I cannot gauze. However, I am lucky to have constantly my inner worlds at my side—my wife, the daughter, the son, the parents—who give me courage and succours of understanding, and research. After all writing an impartial book on truth Indian political parties or suggesting untilted views is not a cakewalk in Indian journalism today. At the same time this book would not have been a possibility without prompt cooperation by members of Anmol Publications Pvt. Ltd., New Delhi. I express my gratitude to everybody concerned with publishing it.

Surojit Mahalanobis

Contents

Preface vii

1. Backdrop 1
2. Backgrounder: Manifesto: BJP 24
3. Backgrounder: Manifesto: Congress 101
4. Backgrounder: Manifesto: Janata Dal 146
5. Backgrounder: Manifesto: Janata Party 189
6. Backgrounder: Manifesto: Left Front 206
7. Backgrounder: Manifesto: All-India Indira Congress (Tiwari) 259
8. Backgrounder: Manifesto: Bahujan Samaj Party 291
9. Poll Reforms 329
10. Common Minimum Programmes: United Front Government as Declared After Election 331

1
Backdrop

ELECTIONEERING for the Eleventh Lok Sabha has proved to become important in Indian political life mainly because of its record values. For a political scientist and students of political science it has revealed myriad characteristics of the Indian polity and has also developed at least three essentially new features which need analysis. It is necessary for the sake of political history of this polygenic nation that these novel traits be properly discussed while people remain enthralled at the time of and complacent after the hustings. For that, to begin with, we can find out in depth what exactly these parties want to convey. This apart, the political parties being the essential players in the mechanism of democracy, have to have clear-cut face which might give people enough confidence in the democratic processes.

Of these novel features, the first one is quite apparent—that is, absence of any kind of sentimentalism this time that might have swept the popular mandate in favour of any particular political party. The second novelty is to be discernible now and not quite manifest like the first — it is, voters' perplexities at amalgam of issues oddly mixed up where they are not supposed to have been in the first place. The third novel feature is, indeed, a unique but mute agreement over one salient issue — economic liberalisation, that has given teeth to almost all noteworthy contenders seeking the high place of power. The last novelty confirms the transition of Indians' political mind from conservative to rational.

Novelties

For a nation emerging after long alien subjugation, to embark upon the task of boosting up its economy becomes the paramount task. The most dominating feeling indeed is how best to give comforts to the polity and have entirely human face at every aspect of the life. Sentimental or personal appeals from the leaders in power to the polity play the magic always. For men is essentially drawn to himself, a self lover who wants only that which directly consummates his needs, his dear feelings and his ambitions. He is generally an in-grown player who loves to create a choice domain always exclusively his own. To satiate what he longs so dearly in his heart, he wants to put each of his prospective candidates in the fray for power into acid tests. However, when something is very commonly appealing to all and sundry, which stokes the fire of his own compassion, he ignores the reasons of plus-points and counter arguments. Modern scenario is entirely different from what was during the first two terms of Lok Sabha.

Looking Back: Populism in Last Elections

Fifty years ago, the tryst with the nation having been fulfilled, the spirit was high with surging patriotism for nation-building process. People's zeal was indomitable as they were nursing centuries-old wounds at self-esteem and economy by the alien rule. Their fight against them to attain what they sincerely believed their birth right was live in their mind. Memoirs of such epochal leadership as Netaji's and the Mahatma's make their feelings welled up along with the surviving companions of their beloved leaders and would cast their votes in one single choice. Their mind and intellect were successfully groomed up by such heart-rending culture of oration by Pandit Jawaharlal Nehru and his fellow politicians. That was onset of the futuristic pattern of suffrage in India.

What was initial fervour from pent-up zeal indeed got soon transformed to imbibe them with poised determination to cement what was first achieved. Our Second Five-Year Plan began with happy notes of success from the first, which in fact was more than expected success. The First Plan (1951-56) was dependent upon rational hypothesis and national zeal with emphasis on agriculture, irrigation, power and transport boosted by two grand harvests during the last two years. The total outlay for the First Plan was Rs 2378 crore and the newly instituted Planning Commission had to start both from noval experience and adjustment according to needs. It had mostly to coorelate the activities from different government departments often ending up in incorporating patchworks of isolated projects.

The Second Plan (1956-61), therefore, had a better beginning. And what a great leap forward was it for the nascent economy. It ushered in a new concept of industrial self-sufficiency. Truly, India was not curving even a needle those days. Special stress was given on basic and heavy industries and developing public sector industries with the Plan-year targets. Though foreign aids were required for the first time to set up the avowed projects, and forex reserves were to be used, the step was necessary for future plans. A nation whose economy was ravaged and which had to work out speedy progress to be able to ward off future foreign onslaughts definitely needed Plans that would make it self-sufficient in short period. It was obviously in the mind of the nation planners to strengthen domestic small-scale industries and private enterprises during further programmes, which would have been much an easy task to accomplish once basics of both agriculture and industries were rooted. At the same time it was also very much in programmes to update instrumental renovations and scientific research—a job for which nation was dependent on the posterity. With an ambition to establish real democracy where majority views grow with nation's prosperity the planners stressed on an economic programme whereby have-nots be economically developed. This is in conformity with principles of democracy, the guiding principles of Indian Plannings, being strictly derived from Directive Principles of State Policy. The new-found ecstasy from the First Lok Sabha proved catalyst for newer ventures in nation's capabilities. At the same time charismatic pull of Pandit Jawaharlal Nehru, who epitomised both as a freedom fighter and an administrator, had built up firm confidence in the polity, despite controversial Pakistan policy of the government.

However, the genesis of Kashmir problems lay inherent in the government's myopic and complacent Pakistan policies of the time and was so much dormant that the defects did not seem existing. Polity was much drawn towards the successes of the government, read here the economic successes, that the first sign of defects in the government's Pakistan policy was apparent only in 1962 when China invaded into India's northern sector. A nation that is dragged into wars cannot hope to step up growth-plan, nor can retain savings or ensure whopping up revenues. As eventual consequence the economy has to flop, which it did, as we know.

The Third Plan (1961-66) rode on high expectations following overall growth of the Indian economy, resulted from first two Plans, wanted to establish self-sustaining measures for which it had also to incur foreign loans. This perhaps could have been well handled sooner, had there not been two wars—first with China (1962) and then for the second time with Pakistan (1965). Constraints on domestic finances and rising prices added up to the stangant per capita income and the gross domestic products. Growing trade deficits was recorded along with debt obligations which continued to mount. Had these wars not been there, sure enough India could have improvised upon its agricultural enterprises, renovated and updated its heavy industries installed in the second Plan-years, developed its projected small-scale industries, and the private sectors could have been allowed to play bigger roles. A nation for which the immediate priority was to give succour and comfort to its teeming poverty-stricken millions, could not afford to okay unrestrained economic power to the limited few in the private sector unless basic ground work was prepared through spread of education, literacy, and positive administrative consolidation. Scenario of the fifties and sixties were not what we find today. After all we are polygenic, and not one race like the Japanese or the Germans.

People's mandate for the Indian National Congress for the Second Lok Sabha, therefore was a foregone conclusion, as we can find today. Who would be fool enough to throw away the government which did the spadework earlier foreign rulers never tried? Sentimental wave influencing the polity hence went on unabated even for the Third Lok Sabha (1962-67), in which Congress was elected in 361 out of 494 seats for which polls were taken. Pandit Nehru's pivotal leadership of the country got the first blemish during this Lok Sabha, in 1962, when China attacked India on 19 September. It was a blow to his statesmanship as the Chinese aggression proved a trend-setter in the post-Nehru politics in the subcontinent. The aggression was a naked mockery of that country's erstwhile slogan "Hindi-Chini bhai bhai" — a concept Pandit Nehru indeed dreamt of. The shock from the deceit, and insult from our unpreparedness of defence had their toll on the great mind of contemporary India, who never recovered from his illness (May 27, 1964).

With his successor, Lal Bahadur Shastri, the priority became defence and not economic growth. He had to gear up ingrown national military abilities more than anything else alongside constant efforts to put back the sluggish agriculture on rail in which he did not much succeed. However, he maintained the urge of the masses by a dynamic slogan, "Jai Jawan, Jai Kisan, Jai Brarat." For, he was well aware of the fact that Chinese aggression was just not an offshoot of Chinese empirical design. It was instead a part of long-standing foreign conspiracy against India as a sovereign nation, richly endowed with natural resources—a reality which has made it an alluring pasture for alien attacks, historically. Soon, a few years after there was the second war with Pakistan that India had to fight.

Shastriji was a sad man, often criticised for delays in taking decisions. Some personalities like Vijaylakshmi Pandit would even call him "a prisoner of indecision". But Shastriji's problem was more acute than one could appreciate from the outset. For he had to inhere a sluggish war-ravaged economy as he took up the reins at one of the most crucial times for India. The shock from indecisive Tashkent agreement with Pakistan at the behest of United Nations and under sponsorship of erstwhile USSR was much acute and unbearable for him. He died in Tashkent itself on 11 January 1966, and cemented a permanent place for himself in Indians heart. The populist wave therefore remained seething in the country for the Congress. During that Third Lok Sabha (1962—67) India saw death of two Prime Ministers, and swearing-in of the third Smt Indira Gandhi.

The fourth general elections, which were to install the Fourth Lok Sabha, (1967-72) was important yardstick an Indian politics to judge outcome of charismatic Pull. Congress fared poor comparatively, and for the first time in two decades after the Independence nation witnessed its popularity in the wane. It secured only 283 seats out of total 520, and no doubt that was again on sympathy wave. For Indira Gandhi, who had learnt politics from her dynamic statesman father and who had acclimitised herself from her very younger days in international diplomatic environs, responsibility of the Prime Minister were both novel and thrilling. So were her days amidst rivalries, opposition and loyalties of myriad faces of Indian politicians, mostly her father's contemporaries. It was a seat she had been given to fill by arts, she was yet to muster. Smt Indira Gandhi was under tremendous compulsion to continue despite strong adversaries from other hopefuls of the PM's seat, who were not the choice of the High Command. From this compulsion, perhaps, she got her strength and powerful resolve to consolidate her determination. Soon she endeared herself to the masses by series of populist measures, irrespective of consequences on the economy. These populist measures were directed to keep grassroots in romantic humours more than any solid revenue-spinning foundation.

The Third Plan had already gone away, the fourth was

overdue, as by normal process a Five Year Plan has to be formulated and drawn by the end of the last year of the previous Plan tenure. With the economy degenerated by then, stop-gap arrangements were made for three consecutive annual Plans for 1966-67, 1967-68 and for 1968-69, slating the Fourth Plan tenure from 1969 to 1974.

Meantime, a crafty game of politics swung into action. Most of the confirmed freedom fighters, Congress oldguards, oldtime champions of Nehru - Gandhi principles joined tacit hands of rebellion against the populist policies of Indira Gandhi. One of the intriguing points of dissent was the general expectation that though Indira Gandhi should consult her seniors in politics for all her decisions yet she would rarely do that, and also that she would lean more towards Left-oriented politics of class consciousness, than allow rightist, affluents and centrists play decision making roles. Her decision to nationalise 14 commercial leading banks annoyed her adversaries the most. This apart, in most of the key government high places she would work out plans to place her own choices, who would fit in Mrs Gandhi's purposes, which angered her seniors in the Congress.

In 1969 Congress party split, and Mrs Gandhi formed her own Congress under symbol of 'hand' which eventually turned out to be seeking hands of help of the teeming millions of the "garib." Her call "Garibi Hatao" thereafter became a clarion call for the masses. The loss of seats in different states in the fourth general elections gradually seemed would return to the new Congress (I) fold. Her adversaries had challenged in the Supreme Court the President's Ordinance nationalising the 14 commercial banks in late 1969, which the apex court ruled as illegal in February 1970. However, President had revalidated the decision by yet another Ordinance.

For Indira Gandhi her tryst with the populism and grassroots continued, while her old Congress companions and the estranged Congressmen spearheaded concerted efforts to dislodge her from the post. The internecine and extra-party rivalry soured the atmosphere to such extent that the Fourth Lok Sabha had to be dissolved, and interim Mid-term Poll had to be ordered. Populism is a gameplan that pays, so it did pay Smt Indira Gandhi. Her Congress (India) was returned to power with thumping majority winning 350 out of 518 seats. Charisma and sympathy wave thus consolidated power absolutely.

As we know the most trend-setting incident in the Fourth Lok Sabha was the major split in Congress (1969), Indians later years were in for a startling scenario of realpoitick. It was the genesis of series of divergent happenings, that would influence politics of India even in the nineties. As the situation was tense and speculations rife then, we saw yet another stunning case of desertion by a veteran Congress oldguard, Babu Jag Jivan Ram, who was the President of the Congress (India) and who served the nation by sterling administrative acumen in various ministries in all cabinets ever since. He joined the rebel camp to form Janata Party later.

In 1971 was further Indira Gandhi's position solidified as two very special steps she took to beef up people's faith in her. The first was her decision to nationalise yet another leading insurance company in the country, the General Insurance, and the second was her prompt decision to recognise the nationhood of Bengali East Pakistan as Bangladesh, soon as that country appealed to Indian government asking for the military help in their fight for freedom, by joining hands and imparting military training with their Mukti Bahini. It was all the way a winning war for her. However, as nature would have it absolute consolidation of power at hand gradually and silently started eroding, thanks to her over-confidence.

The Fifth Lok Sabha (1971-76) witnessed series of conservative and populist steps taken by Indira Gandhi's government, after registering India's victory over Pakistan in Bangladesh. Four states were created (Manipur, Meghalaya, Tripura and Sikkim). Two regions were put to Union Territory status (Arunachal Pradesh and Mizoram). Bonus Act was amended increasing the minimum bonus to employees from erstwhile 4 per cent to 8.33 per cent, (September 17, 1972). A tradition of supersession at high places for promotion was started by appointing Justice Ajit Nath Roy as the Chief Justice of the apex court, which was viewed by her stauch adversaries as a measure more to a design to build up absolute power base than one to reward the most talented. She dedicated the Farakka barrage to people—a measure that amused people always.

Adversary to Indira Gandhi gradually became so much intensified at home especially after her constant rise to popularity and Jayprakash Narayan's "Citizens for Democracy" animation against her corrupt bureaucracy, that time became hard for her. On one hand, she had no stomach to ignore JP's annoyance, nor was she able to anger people on whom she had no other alternative but to depend. The absolute power she had mastered politically was fast losing grounds due to corrupt and chauvinistic managers of her departments. Topping of all these were non-stop groupism by her adversaries' over restrained socio-economic prescription for Indian society and her constant actions to give more powers to her government thereby closing the economy. The scenario of the Indian political arena had turned to be one of chaos and confusing. Mrs Indira Gandhi now had but one option at her disposal, inflicting internal Emergency in the country. This was done on 15 June 1975 by Presidential Ordinance, to be relaxed only on January 18 of 1977 to permit electioneering and subsequently revoked on 21 March same year.

Above all these populist measures, was the Prime Minister's idea of 20-point programmes aired during the state of Emergency, which indeed took the downtrodden by storm. What people didnot know that time was that the entire 20-point programmes were based on conservative economic principles governed by tremendous control over entrepreneurship. Efforts were not to be made to decontrol economy which were in turn considered enough for generation of employments. The power was more allowed to be wielded by the government, and Indian entrepreneurs were rigidly subjected to vigils by officers who have already indulged themselves to corrupt habits. Growth of the economy as devised by Indira Gandhi's government was rather backtracked due to these self-seeking officialdom against whom old freedom fighter from Bihar Jaya Prakash Narayan had waged his undaunted war.

Mrs Indira Gandhi was, on the contrary, much mused in her game of populism, than considering resons behind the latest animation against her corrupt bureaucracy. As a consequence of that she went on bringing in drastic socio-politico laws by banning communal and parochial societies like Jamat-e-Islami, RSS, Ananda Marga and 23 other of such hues. Simultaneous to these steps she also instituted Conservation of Foreign Exchange and Prevention of Smuggling Activities Act (COFEPOSA). Maintenance of Internal Security Act (MISA), got Parliamentary approvals for making election of President, Vice-President, Prime Minister and the Speaker of the Lok Sabha beyond the scrutiny of the Judiciary and had the Rajya Sabha members successfully consider extend immunity of the Prime Minister to criminal and civil proceedings. She also successfully appealed for the Presidential ordinance abolishing Bonded Labour practice. The old guards promptly named these measures as 'draconian'.

During the Emergency life of the Lok Sabha was extended by one year more, making it a six-year term, by the 42nd Amendment to the Constitution. This extension was annulled by the 43rd Amendment to the Constitution in 1977 and the old term of five years was restored. This was done after the first Janata Government came to power under Nehruvian and his contemporary freedom fighter Morarji Desai's stewardship. Trend of nation's political thoughts during these days of upheaval was more expressed in exercise of powers. Clashes took place between the state power energised by politics of populism and opposition power working in combination to uphold free mind for prosperity by help of wit, intelligence and moral qualities, shunning short-cut idyllic life dependent on others talent and labour. The opposition was working hard to quell conservatism and trying hard to stop the nation falling under Marxist protectionism. While Indira Gandhi was drawing satisfaction from protective economic principles, the opposition mustered courage from broader futuristic outlook of liberty, perseverence and free economic life. The scenario (during Emergency upto the Sixth Lok Sabha), was fit for Indian political activists as what Aristotle had said about the man in politics "Man when perfected is the best of animals, but when separated from law and justice is the worst of all, since armed injustice is the most dangerous, as he is equipped at birth with arms of intelligence and wit, moral qualities which he may use for the worst ends." As for Indira Gandhi, she seemed to have acted as what Machiavelli suggested for a prince. The prince, Machiavelli said, must combine the strength of a lion with the cunning of the fox; he must always be vigilant, ruthless and prompt striking down or neutralizing his adversaries without warning. And when he does an injury it must be total.

These years during the Sixth Lok Sabha (1977-1981) had witnessed surges of two different kinds of populism which affected the voters' sentiment and reason. On one side it was the combined Opposition's antagonising of the State which culminated in the Emergency. They took majority of conscientious mind into their stride and advocated free mind and free economic life. This was outcome of aversion created in the minds of the common man by corrupt elements of Indian society who thrievd historically under-world by doing odd job for their patrons in power. For man now started thinking in terms of anti-corruption drives which Jaya Prakash Narayan had spearheaded to rouse. The other side of the public mind had got deeply entrenched while supporting Mrs Gandhi's charismatic populism. The latter surged again in favour of Mrs Gandhi soon is she was sent to jail. The Morarji Government had successfully got her arrested and released on unconditional bail on 5 November of 1977. This was the first cause that quelled aversion accumulated towards the excesses during her earlier rules. The second sympathy wave she started gaining ground soon as she was sentenced by the Lok Sabha on 19 December of 1978 to imprisonment for a term lasting until its prorogation. All these are the prices she paid for Emergency measures and also for not towing the lines of Congress oldguards. Some members from her "Syndicate" also sabotaged her efforts just on ego clashes. However, it is said, absolute consolidation of power corrupts absolutely, and this came much true in her case. Nevertheless, the fact that Indira "Priyadarshini" was turned to become a lady in disgraceful distress was enough to rouse sympathy in the masses belonging to downtrodden, SCs, STs, OBCs and lower-middle class and even aspiring higher middle and upper classes. For the most of these polity economic liberalism and free mind had no relevance. This ensured gradual development of popular opinion in her favour, as a consequence of which she was released by the Lok Sabha on the 26th of the same month. The absolute majority of the Janata Party which took 296 seats out of 542 against Congress (I)'s 153 in hustings for the Sixth Lok Sabha could not contain surging popular opinion in favour of Mrs Indira Gandhi.

Stage was set for her come back. In 1979 the nation witnessed fierce scenario of floor-crossing and heterogeneous swichings of allegiance. Stage was fast being set for the Seventh Lok Sabha by end of 1979, which indeed took place in January of 1980. Morarji Desai had to relinquish his post bowing to Janata Partymen's wrangles for power; out of sheer disgust he withdrew from active politics once for all. The Deputy Prime Minister Mr Charan Singh took up the reins to head the Janata (S) and Congress coalition government which did not last long. Scenario turned such messy and inconsistent that President had to dissolve the Parliament and ordered for year-end General Election. Popular sympathy and faith was by then fast swerving towards Mrs Indira Gandhi.

The Seventh General Election in 1980, returned Mrs Indira Gandhi once again by abolute majority pollings. Her Congress (I) not only mustered two-thirds of seats in the fray (542), but also gained 200 additional seats more than the Sixth General Election. The Janata party got relegated to only 109 seats.

This time her task was two-fold, to live with the nation-building process by keeping her "garib" voters in good humours with rosy pictures of gain from conservative economic principles, and to bring the law and order situations under her crafty control. Sikh terrorism which was allowed, rather stoked, to emerge to nasty heights during this term was one of the instances which is much complained about. Nation's mind was readily divided about her exact policies, for there was no let up of continued insurgencies and terrorism in states like Punjab, Jammu and Kashmir and particularly in the north-east of India. The disgruntled section gradually reconsolidated and the culmination was in her assassination in 1984. Eighties were the days for her when she indeed had no wise connsellor to her side. The syndicate comprising such matured contemporaries of her father as Mr CB Gupta, Mr SK Patil, Mr Kamraj, Mr Morarji Desai, Mr Jag Jivan Ram, Mr Nijalingappa and Mr Sadiq Ali, who were her constant guide when she took to politics and from whom she learnt politics of post-Independent India had all deserted her long. They were replaced by people who had more personal aspirations and sycophant demeanour in them that the real qualities required for matured politics. Mrs Gandhi's assassination was the saddest commentary of individualistic power game Indians played till recently. However, the incident took the eighties by storm and turbulent days were set loose upon the polity. One very common thing nevertheless happened, that is, sympathy wave for the family, which Congress (I) utilized wisely by putting up Rajiv Gandhi, newly inducted into politics by his mother, into the mantle of Mrs Indira Gandhi.

Rajiv Gandhi, the sixth Prime Minister of the country led the Government in the Eighth Lok Sabha. The General Election was swept by his party absolutely on sympathy wave which was an expression of love of the teeming millions to the fallen leader, Mrs Indira Gandhi. Many of her adversaries too this time had opted to support her son, and might have even voted for him. For Rajiv it was a seat of thorns, he had to prove his competence once the wave settled down to crass reality. He was found quite often asking his ministers work correctly and fast with results positive, for he had only "four years" more to prove. The swiping mandate for him, 401 seat out of 508 constituencies where electioneering took place for the Eighth Lok Sabha, began to wane from startling revelations about Bofors and Fairfax deals over artilary and submarines. People were started by hitherto unimaginable thought that even the post of Prime Minister cannot be taintless. Their doubt got further base in Rajiv Gandhi's constant opposition to his Finance Minister VP Singh's penchant for ordering several kinds of tax raids and administrative enquiries into various entrepreneurs and high placed people. Rajiv was more intrigued by embarrassment of his close aides who included both partymen and ministers in his cabinet, and friction between him and VP Singh went on unabetted. Situation worsened for him, with popular support fast eroding, soon as VP Singh resigned his finance minister's post in protest against corruption at such high places as prime minister, especially in case of Bofors gun deal and the alleged kickback. Corruption abounded in this cabinet and noises were being made systematically which ultimately paved for Rajiv's debackle in hustings for the Ninth Lok Sabha (1989-93).

Sentimental wave once again went awry for Nehru family this time. The General Election was fought by the parties with allegations and claims both by the Opposition spearheaded by VP Singh and other allies of the Janata Dal, and Congress of Rajiv Gandhi. Of the 543 seats this time 523 seats were on poll and for the second time Janata variation took up the reins. This time VP's party had to depend on outside supports from BJP as the hustings produced the nation's first "hung" Parliament. Sympathy wave having been absent once again parties were put on hard realities of real politic, with State exchequer condition precarious and foreign exchange position almost nil.

Fall of VP's government was to hasten the mid-term poll in 1991, in which was yet another "hung" Parliament. Of 516 seats contested out of 543 Congress secured 224 seats, with the nearest runner BJP at a distant 119 and Janata Dal farther away at 53 seats.

However, VP's was not to survive long as his cabinet got involved soon more in heterogeneous non-economic issues than real nation-building process. First, it was egotist approach to politics by Haryana leader and Deputy Prime Minister Mr Devi Lal and his son OP Chautala. The senior patriarch wanted the Prime Ministerial post but had to yield to coaxing appeals by other National Front leaders. The second squeeze for VP came from Chandrashekhar who disagreed with the Government's New Industrial Policy. Third was controversial issue of OP Chautala's taking over of Harayana chief ministership after questionable electoral practices. Three union ministers — Arun Nehru, Arif Muhammad Khan and Satpal Malik — resigned over the Chautala issue and the political crisis culminated as VP offered to resign over it, on the very next day (on 14 July 1990). V P's term was always intrigued by one non-economic problem after another, indeed never really he managed to settle down to the crass job of the Prime Minister. On August 1 of 1990 the Harayana patriarch Mr Devi Lal, country's Deputy Prime Minister, was dropped from the cabinet. When the situation was such fluid about the real work for the nation-building, came the issue of Mandal Commission recommendations, which VP's Government immediately took up and accepted, as if to show its eagerness to get rid of National Front constituents' internecine wranglings. Mandal Commision Report on SCs, STs and OBCs was long dusted during Congress rule, and never was sincerely taken up. VP's government indeed provided the issue by which perhaps they thought would be able to acquire greater political mileaye. Sadly it proved defferent. Soon it was to be National Front Government's, especially VP's, nemesis. Popular faith in him began to dwindle soon upper caste poor students agitated against implementation of the Mandal Commission recommendations reserving 27 per cent of jobs for the backward class candidates, despite Cabinet committee's decision to put 10 per cent reservation of Government jobs for the economically weaker section among upper class job-seeker, on 27 August. A number of serious cases of self-emolation and heavy burns from self-emolation bids wrecked the nerve of the people and popular opinion on VP Singh's Government fell sharply. Supreme Court stayed the implementation of the Mandal Commission recommendations on 1st October, though on 21 of the previous month it had refused to stay it.

Amidst the chaos over Mandal Commission recommendations nationwide, came BJP's yatras over Ram Janmabhumi issue at Ayodhya. After a few successful ones, Mr LK Advani's Rath was held in Samastipur by Laloo Prasad Government of Janata Dal in Bihar and Mr Advani was subsequently arrested on charges of ignoring administrative order of section 144. This prompted BJP withdraw its support to the National Front Government at the Centre. Disunity with BJP culminated in violent episode by administration and BJP's karsevaks in the bid to storm Ram Janmabhumi structure wherein died many karsevaks. Popular support fast swang away from VP's sail, and Janata Dal quickly split in the very first week of November with Chandrashekar as the dissident group's leader, Congress (I) supporting. This hastened V.P. Singh Government's loss of popular support and fall.

The new Prime Minister, Chandrashekar, on control having mustered support from 58 MPs other than his dissident group and of Congress from outside, Indian political mind has earned dubious distinctions, both compromising and opportunistic. There was a bent to offer totalitarian life for the polity, though the real players of the game wanted only power and access to the nation's kitty. Mr Chandrashekhar had also claimed before that the hustings for the Tenth Lok Sabha was to be declared. During his short Prime Ministerial life Mr S Chandrashekhar wanted to solve many of intriguing issues and even solved one of them, the Punjab tangle. However, all he did was to earn a political mileage in the Tenth General Electioneering. People's sentiment was always an issue in the back of his mind, and he did a record of sorts by evacuating largest number of Indian immigrants in Gulf prior to the Gulf War. Two things demolished Mr Chandrashekhar's efforts to earn a good political mileage despite his earnest efforts to sit down to deal with impending issues concerning nation's economy boosting. The first was the anti-defection law which Rajiv

Gandhi had earlier got passed. Five of Mr Chandrashekhar's cabinet colleagues were found guilty under the law and was subsequently disqualified by the Speaker Mr Rabi Ray. Those ministers later resigned, but allowed by the Prime Minister Mr S Chandrashekhar to continue until election. The second irritant for him was Congress threat of non-cooperation to the Government if the Government didnot stop supplying US war planes get fuel in Indian soil to fly thereafter over to Iraq for bombarding that country. Matter instantaneously turned very hot for Mr Chandrashekhar who promptly assured he would do as Congress wanted (17, February 1991), the very next day. However, the fall of his Government came in March 1991 (on the 6th) as Chandrashekhar offered to resign complaining Congress non-cooperation over issue of two Haryana policeman espying on Rajiv Gandhi, and for keeping surveillance on Rajiv Gandhi's residence. Before the present Prime Minister could generate popular sentiment towards his candidature in the ensuing hustings for the Tenth Lok Sabha, he had to resign, President Mr R Venkataraman declared dissolution of the Lok Sabha and ordered for mid-term poll.

It was the time, on 21 May 1991, when Rajiv Gandhi was assassinated. He was on his scheduled election tours to Tamil Nadu's Sriperumbudur, when his entourage was demolished by highly sophisticated human bomb. That was yet another scenario in the Indian political life after the Independence, which was destined to take the Indian polity by storm. Congress came back to power however, this time without two-thirds majority. For the mid-term poll was not quite affected by assassination of and sympathy to Rajiv Gandhi thereby, during the first phase of the polling (May 20, 1991). But there was this upswing in sympathy of Rajiv, after his assassination on 21 May, that hustings on 15 June that year, that Congress returned as the single largest party. The Opposition was once again sharply divided on issues which was half dealt with on merit, leaving other half on sentimental pulls.

The eventual Prime Minister, Mr Narasimha Rao's term was then destined to be one where every aspect of state-running would be weighed in cross evaluation. In the first Phase of the pollings, that is on 20 May, popular mind was engrossed in rigid analyses of style of functioning of the political parties. Consequently, out of 211 seats on the fray that day Congress was found victorious only in 55 seats. However, after-assassination electioneering being the second day for hustings for remaining 294 seats, Congress swung back to win 169 seats, just like a swindle of the magic wand. Such is Indian mind.

The new Prime Minister was well aware of popular sentiment and has been successful in harnessing it to his party's benefit. It started where exactly Mrs Indira Gandhi had left the mooted point — anti-poverty programmes. It claims to have assisted 115 lakh families under integrated rural development programmes, having dug 8.12 lakh wells under a million wells scheme, constructed 28 lakh houses for the downtrodden, 260 villages covered under rural drinking water supply scheme, constructed 21 lakh sanitary latrines, distributed 421 lakh tools to artisans, benefited 1.2 lakh groups of people under Development of Women and Children in Rural Areas Scheme, trained 13 lakh youths for self-employment, 7837 projects approved with release of Rs 160.85 crore for 16,000 voluntary agencies and many more. Rao government claims success at every department of each of the ministries, particularly in boosting up the economy. It claims to have restored the forex reserves to Rs 60,000 crore from all time low of Rs 2,100 crore. Truly, it should rightly claim the restoration of Eighth Five Year Plan, which the previous Governments had abandoned and depended on borrowed money. It claims to have checked the rising inflation rates, revived the industries, boosted up agricultural incentives effecting higher growth rates every year during last five years. Claims are, many and most of them are factually not incorrect. However, this Government did some glaring mistakes which went wrong with the same populism. This time the Corruption charges leveled against Rao Government, one after another, went rather deterrent in people's mind. Whatever success the Government, claimed and recorded, to people's mind they were only respected. Corruption charges are not. People donot like the corrupt at the core of heart. Populism in Mr Narasimha Rao case flowed through reverse direction, to submerge him and his fortune perhaps for ever.

Electioneering for the Eleventh Lok Sahba therefore assumed very special importance because people today are more conscientious. With all probability, sentimentalism will not again rule the ballot. Mr Deva Gowda's Governement will have to show results in crass realism.

Second Novelty

For the first time in the country people has been aroused into reckoning the hypocrite and the rational. Before the electioneering began issues intriguing people's mind were oddly mixed up. Priorities were needed to be emphasised. New affairs of men in power had surged up with newer terms. Common man never really knew if share scam could at all be possible. Nor the polity would have ever thought so explicitly how unauthorised transactions of Indian rupee against foreign currency could have affected the nation's exchequer. These economic terms were novel wonders for the common man. Their perplexities were further admixed by such sentimental issues like religion and future identity, economic and academic security and hazards which are unseen today but might take up the shape of frankenstine.

Never before the polity was as much confused as today. They cannot trust anybody, especially when two consecutive Congress Prime Ministers have been indicated on corruption charges, the last in multiple charges. Never the polity had seen executive to the status of Governor can be asked to resign on charges as heinous as duping a few thousands homeseekers, before being put up the laws of the land. Faith and charismatic pull towards a political party would soon take back seat in the memory of the polity, whether rich or poor, no matter if he has resources or he doesnot have. Today's popular zeal oscillates round absolute success in life in whatever a person does. The party that will ensure him of his ambition, he will go in for that party. Eleventh Lok Sabha therefore is a historic yardstick for Indian political history that should be marked as its second step towards realism.

Third Novelty

When nation started its economic resurgence with its First Five-Year Plan, it had come to a halt in sixties with the Chinese aggression. The Third Plan which was destined for 1961-66 had gone awry owing to wars and consequent failure from expected self-sustaining economy with internal resources having been strained to its limits. Overstrained by the excessive borrowings from International Monetary Fund, it was vehemently suggested by many that Plan holiday be announced, which was agreed to both by the Planning Commission and the Government. However, interim plannings were suggested and annual Plans continued from 1966 to 1969 for each single year—1966-67, 1967-68, 1968-69.

Mismanagement of the economy continued even on the Fourth Plan (1969-74). What was planned never was attained, as expected growth and stability projects always failed to meet the required target. The Nation indeed was staggering far behind its declared perspectives.

Fifth Plan (1974-79) was another flop. The Perspective Plan had offered 'Garibi Hatao' as its pivotal slogan, with long-term growth that economy was supposed to achieve by help of self-sustaining efforts constantly, was put at 6.2 per cent of the GDP per annum. Delay in approval of the perspectives ate up the advantages on premises, which waned, and the overall outlay had to be increased to Rs 39,303 crore from Rs 37,463 crore. With the fall of Congress Government of Mrs Indira Gandhi and enthronement of the first Janata Government in the Centre, the Plan got scrapped. The new Government rehauled the concept of Planning and declared that objective of planning onwards would be Growth for Social Justice and not Growth with Social Justice. This was a prospective ambition which India needed right from the Third Plan years, after its first two Plans objectives were quite satisfactorily attained, and opportunities created. The concept had a novel angle of thought. It aimed at taking one-year Plan. After attaining the objectives, its fruitfulness would be assayed and rectifications to be incorporated in the seen one-year Plan perspectives. They called it Rolling Plan. Strangely, the new Government started with the terminated Plan for 1974-79 by the Congress Government and put its Plan (Rolling Plan) for 1978-79 on the same rail.

Following two Plans, sexth (1980–81, 1984-85) and the seventh (1985-90) had nothing special among them. With the rise of population and pressures for never ventures in the economy, the revenue to the Exchequer came surprisingly from the secondary and tertiary (service) sectors, mainly while the major sector, the public sector units returned sickness and stagnation. The growth on average of the both Plans were nearly 5.3 per cent of the GDP. Of this 4 per cent was contributed by the secondary and service sectors. This confirmed that nation was not having any healthy/growth from the agriculture Public Sector Units which otherwise should have been the main torch-bearers of growth.

The polity today is conscious about it, as it puts everything on mute evaluation.

The Eighth Plan was obviously to be regenerated on the equal verve as the two initial plannings were recorded. It started belatedly from a Plan term 1992 to 1997, interim years 1990-91 and 91-92 having the one year votes-on-accounts only. Indeed the Eighth Plan started from an encouraging backdrop of resurgence in industrial growth during the eighties, at a higher rate even than majority of nations. Emphasis had been on deregulating system that was initiated in the recent past. The Plan term began from the growth rate of 5.6% of the GDP and industrial growth rate had been low at 7.5 per cent against 8.5 per cent of the Seventh Plan. The estimated rate of 8.02 per cent is largely unattainable and likely to end up in 8 per cent, which again will be lower than the Seventh.

Areas of concern hence remains for the polity, who are much conscious today. Constant educating of PSU disinvestment projects have further boosted up their conscientious morale which Indian politicians should have done at least twenty years ago.

The Eleventh Lok Sabha hence has enough promises to keep, umpteen hearts to boost up and many devils to slay. The policy of growth for the economy and the have-not is what the real economy should have implemented today. The third "Hung" Parilament this year is yet another indicator towards mixed reaction to rationale of free market and fair competition concept, which Indian leaders have to restart to educate. Polity is aware of pitfalls modern leaders are likely to fall in, so are the leaders in the Parliament, for whom hasty risks would be too bold treading to succeed.

Eleventh Lok Sabha has been installed presently. The drama was as was destined with parties joining hands in gloves on fake Machiavellian ruthlessness to throw away the most talented and adore the mediocre. As we have witnessed, BJP, despite being the largest single party with brilliant programmes to build up the nation long off-railed by pseudo populism, had to yield place to the combine who have myopic views on nation-building. The growth for the masses has been suitably compromised on unholy desire of the powergame that should have been stopped once for all. What India needs today is committed work on every aspect of functioning in every department of economic life, without which no nation can record success. Indian politicians today should have reasons to guide them and not the got-up interest groups, who in the past never allowed the nation to grow. The 13-party coalition Government, unifying themselves under one banner, United Front, have in their strides Janata Dal, Janata Party, Communist Party of India (Marxist), Communist Party of India, Telgu Desham, Tamil Mannilai Congress, Dravida Munnetra Kazhaghem, All India Forward Bloc, Assom Gana Parishad, All India Indira Congress (Tiwari), Revolutionary Socialist Party, Madhya Pradesh Vikash Congress and Samajwadi Party. Irony is, even after combining in their utmost bid to deprive the BJP, they had to seek outside support from Congress which the latter did, as if settling score for unraveling umpteen number of major and minor corruption episodes. It is necessary today that Indian Parliament should have one decision-making party to run the Government with free mind, open heart, foresight for the teeming millions, and stable approach to address issues of the nation. The concept of free market economy should have been guiding principles in economic decisions of that party in power. Indians have still to wait. For, as goes the oft-repeated cliche though true and relevant, many cooks might of course spoil the broth.

To effect blemish-free polling in future, as was done this time, the Election Commission has ordained strictures of Poll Reform which has been incorporated in this book for general information. The new Government's Common Minimum Programme, a wise step however in addressing the national problems and heterogeneous programmes of the parties, has also been incorporated to guide the readers about what they all said and how they have planned to address their programmes.

Before we envision what tomorrow's political life is likely to be the nation should have let us analysis what our National Political Parties have to assure in their own terms. In the process we will also highlight what they claim to have done already.

2

Backgrounder: Bharatiya Janata Party

OUR VISION, OUR FAITH, OUR COMMITMENT

"It is out of the past that the future is moulded. It is the past that becomes the future. . . ."

Swami Vivekananda

Even as this century draws to a close and the millennium turns, India stands at a critical crossroads of history. Centuries old hopes and aspirations of our people yearn for a true expression. The detiny of our land and its people cries for fulfilment. At such crucial turns historical choices are made and instruments of change adopted. That destined vehicle of change is the Bharatiya Janata Party.

Never before in the long history of our land has the country been governed by such a morally rudderless and financially corrupt regime. Seldom have our trusting people been duped by a base band. With the people's hopes belied and their aspirations thwarted, our ancient land stands today face to face with the option of a real change, a chance for a true departure from the last 50 years of Congress misrule, an alternative and an option: The Bharatiya Janata Party.

Our people are looking towards the BJP to become just this instrument of change. The party is ready to shoulder this great duty and responsibility. The task is nothing short of rekindling the lamp of our eternal *'Dharma'*, that *Sanatan* thought which our sages bequeathed to mankind—a social system based on compassion, cooperation, justice, freedom, equality and tolerance.

To realise this goal, the BJP will launch a new social, economic and political order. It will strive to transform the existing system of governance, to make it responsive and answerable to the concerns of our citizens. It will strive to make the economy cater to the largest demands of the largest number. The party will endeavour to place in the service of the nation a political organisation that is conscientous and clean. Above all, the BJP will secure for India a place in the comity of nations which befits its vast cultural, intellectual, economic, scientific and human wealth.

We realise that correcting the mistakes of the last 50 years of Congress misrule, of piecing togethter the shattered dreams of our citizens, of restructuring our polity which has been delivered a body blow by the present regime, of restoring the state's authority and reviving faith in the Govenment, is by no means an easy task. But we also realise that only the BJP has the ideological commitment, moral conviction and political courage to shoulder this task and gently guide our nation into the next millennium. The present millennium began with the subjugation of our ancient land; let a reinvigorated, proud, prosperous and strong India herald the next millennium.

In this noble mission, we shall be guided by our Manifesto—it contains our commitments to the nation and its citizens. Our State Governments in Uttar Pradesh, Himachal Pradesh, Madhya Pradesh, Maharashtra, Rajasthan, Gujarat and Delhi have demonstrated that for the BJP, these commitments constitute a sacred covenant with the people. We do what we say. This Manifesto shall be the covenant of our Government.

With a BJP Government at the Centre, the next five years will be devoted to implementing our Manifesto based on the four concepts of *Suraksha, Shuchita, Swadeshi and Samrasata. Hindutva,* or cultural nationalism, shall be the rainbow which will bridge our present to our glorious past and pave the way for an equally glorious future; it will guide the transition from *swarajya* to *surajya.* Our Manifesto reflects the application of these four concepts in good governance and their role in moulding the nation we dreamt of on the dawn of Independence—a prosperous and strong India, a country where every citizen regards this land of ours, this Bharatbhoomi, that stretches from the Indus to the seas, as his sacred motherland.

The BJP believes in one nation, one people, one culture. We are, therefore, committed to promoting social reconciliation rather than conflict. We are resolved to put an end to the politics of competitive communalism, of appeasement, and of casteism. The politics of pitting caste against caste, community against community and class against class has torn asunder our social fabric. The BJP will reweave this fabric into a harmonious pattern.

To translate this Manifesto into reality, to fulfil our destined role of leading India into the next millennium, the Bharatiya Janata Party seeks the support and cooperation of all our citizens.

A New Direction, A New Dispensation

Nearly half a century of Congress misrule has all but shattered the internal polity of the country. There is not one institution of the Republic left that can be said to now be in a state of total health. The Legislature, the Executive, unfortuantely the Judiciary, and even the media have been afflicted by the mindlessness of the Congress' exploitation and loot of our country.

The Bharatiya Janata Party well recognises that to correct this great wrong of the past five decades requires the skill and commitment of a Vishwakarma. With humility, we address ourselves to this task.

The first is to restore to our state its authority. Perhaps never since the scourge of the Pindaries has the writ of our state been as enfeebled as by this Congress misrule. The primary task, therefore, is to restore to the state, and to governance, its honour and its prestige—'izzat' and 'iqbal'. For this the BJP will institute a set of measures. This is a challenge that is principally moral and only then functional. The BJP commits itself, therefore, to :

1. Addressing purposefully to the many challenges being posed to us in Jammu & Kashmir and in the North-East of India. We are of the view that in both these strategically important border regions of the country, misgovernance, neglect and emotional separation from India lie at the root of the problems. Terrorism and challenges to the state will be met forthrightly; changes in law where warranted will be brought about expeditiously; the approach will be firm but always fair.
2. Launching a major nationwide drive to identify influx of illicit arms and their possession. Proliferation of small arms affects directly the law and order in the country as also the security of the nation. We recognise that narcotics smuggling and narco-terrorism are linked. The country must be rid of both. The law in this regard will be made more effective and implemented.
3. Toning up the administration (as enumerated subsequently) and reforming its functioning, accountability and responsiveness.
4. Rationalising the number, structure, composition and role of paramilitary forces, including recent initiatives like National Security Guard (NSG), Rapid Action Force (RAF) and Special Protection Group (SPG). We will review the personal security arrangements: We believe that the security of the high dignitaries of the country is the responsibility of the state. This security, however, should neither be exaggerated nor intrusive. It should not ever be at the cost of the collective convenience of the citizens of the country. The BJP will reform this.

Electoral Reforms

The BJP carries a conviction that amongst the many causes that have brought the state of our polity to its present plight, a major factor is faulty elections. We will, therefore, immediately on assuming office, implement various electoral reforms.

Corruption and Its Cure

The BJP treats this affliction as the single greatest wrong that Congress misrule of the past 50 years has brought about on our land. The corruption that now corrodes our country is of the spirit, it is moral, and it is also financial. The challenge thus to governance is principally of setting an example — of impeccable probity and unimpeachable accountability of all public men and women. This must not cover simply the elected representatives of the people but also the executive, the police and, indeed, even the judiciary, where the touch of corruption can already be felt. The BJP will address itself to this challenge and task, by adopting measures that are mentioned hereunder. We do not claim that this is either the ultimate blueprint for the reduction of corruption or the last word on it. It is an expression of our commitment; a first step to setting right a very great wrong of many years' malignancy; a beginning and that, too, with ourselves.

Shri Rama Mandir at Ayodhya

The BJP is committed to the concept of one nation, one people, one culture — our nationalist vision is not merely bound by the geographical or political identity of India, but defined by our ancient cultural heritage. From this belief flows our faith in 'Cultural Nationalism' which is the core of *Hindutva*. That, we believe, is the identity of our ancient nation — *Bharatvarsha.*

Hindutva is a unifying principle which alone can preserve the unity and integrity of our nation. It is a collective endeavour to protect and re-energise the soul of India, to take us into the next millennium as a strong and prosperous nation. ***Hindutva*** is also the antidote to the shameful efforts of any section to benefit at the expense of others.

We hold that only by recognising the limitless strength of cultural nationalism, can the nation be moulded. When the BJP joined the movement for the construction of the Shri Rama Mandir at Ayodhya, it was to strengthen just these foundations.

On coming to power, the BJP Government will facilitate the construction of a magnificent Shri Rama Mandir at Janmasthan in Ayodhya which will be a tribute to ***Bharat Mata***. This dream moves millions of people in our land; the concept of Rama lies at the core of their consciousness.

Economic Growth and Employment Through Swadeshi

Four decades of Congress misrule have ruined the economic creativity of our country; these decades failed to place the country on a sound economic footing, befitting India's stature as the largest democracy in the world. The experiments of the Congress, with vastly divergent models, have brought the country, from time to time, to the brink of crisis. The passive victim of all these experiments has been the long suffering Citizen of our country; even as under-nourishment, malnutrition, illiteracy and deprivation afflict a large percentage of them; even as the quality of life gets fractured between India and Bharat.

We commit ourselves to bringing certainty in economic policy. The Bharatiya Janata Party is proud of India's heritage and has an abiding faith in the creative genius of every Indian. We are committed to an economy that enables India to achieve its destiny in the forefront of the nations of the world.

In 1991 the present Government claimed that it inherited an economy which had a slender foreign exchange reserves. Accepting IMF conditionalities, it initiated a programme of deregulations of industry, trade and exchange rate policies, a radically different approach to foreign investment. The consequential foreign exchange reserves that it will be leaving, as a legacy to the successor government are, however, fragile, being composed mainly of quick-sand component of foreign institutional investment and FCNR deposits. Foreign direct investment (FDI) is only a minor component of them. An enormous $ 7 billion becomes ripe for debt servicing in 1996-97 itself. In its zeal to contain fiscal deficit — a task in which it failed, the fiscal deficit continuing around 7% of GDP — it pruned development expenditure beyond acceptable limits, in consequence constraining growth.

Despite the proclaimed deregulation, over the past five years, all earlier structures and institutions of the Licence-Quota- Permit Raj remain intact. Social infrastrcuture has been neglected and the lot of the poor and deprived has further deteriorated. The country's defence requirements were also neglected, thereby putting the nations' security in jeopardy.

The neglect of infrastructure by this Government has left a legacy of a fractured physical infrastructure—roads, railways, post, power, telecom—are grinding to near immobility, in the process constraining growth elsewhere in the economy. In its methodology for containing the budget through limits on monetisation of the deficit, this Government has compulsorily resorted to heavy borrowings, which in turn has resulted in illiquidity to the rest of the economy and a heating up of the interest rates. Our domestic industry, starved of liquidity, is in danger of slipping into recession.

In totality, this Government will leave an economy more fragile and shattered than what it inherited in 1991. The challenges thus, to us in our bid at governance, are formidable.

A society such as ours has to innovate its own strategy, to adapt itself to the high-tech challenges of a supposedly borderless world, without the attendant social stresses, economic instability and the abandonment either of its identity or of its own socio-cultural ethos. This is the essence of our Swadeshi approach: A self-reliant India, asserting its national economic interests, not as autarchy, but as a pre-requisite to meeting the challenge of globalisation; of preserving our identity without compromising our sovereignty or self respect. We reject unbridled consumerism and believe in adherence to sustainable consumption and growth.

Foreign investment will be required and encouraged for world class technology. But when foreign savings have to supplement and assist the economy in circumstances where domestic savings are inadequate, we compromise with the nation's long term interests. While many countries which started late but arrived much earlier than India, managed their growth on savings levels around 35-40% of GDP, the Indian domestic savings rate has steadily declined to a low level of 20% of GDP during Congress rule. This is grossly inadequate for even the current level of investment, let alone the levels required for a faster growth of the economy. Not only have private savings declined, more worrisomely, governmental savings are now virtually nil.

We recognise two immediate priorities—first, providing the physical and economic infrastructure that is appropriate for the stipulated growth in our GDP; second, providing the required social infrastructure for a minimum sustainable quality of life.

To attain these and yet contain fiscal deficit requires a different approach. The BJP will work towards pruning non-developmental expenditure; minimise the commercial activities of Government; severely cutting back on bureaucracy; shedding the structures of controls and regulation; and re-equipping itself for its new role of providing a framework for free market operations for growth, accentuating programmes for poverty eradication and social infrastructure.

Fiscal Reform and Taxation

We believe that taxation alone cannot be the base for revenue. A stable and fast growth is possible only through a high order of investment matched by an appropriate level of domestic savings. The present Government has done a great disservice by encouraging avoidable consumerism and diverting the depleted savings into speculative rather than safe and productive channels.

Price Stability and Consumer Protection

It is our firm belief that the price level can be controlled only through maximisation of production and a minimisation of costs of production. This is to be achieved through technology upgradation, economics of scale and free competition. Towards this end, the BJP will ensure an efficient, low-cost, corruption-free public distribution system (PDS), so that there is a regular, assured, timely and adequate supply of commodities to consumers in rural, tribal, remote and backward areas of our country.

Black Money and Corruption

Starting from its Jana Sangh days, the BJP has been waging a relentless battle against the twin evils of corruption and black money. We are committed to rooting out corruption, thus also the malignancy of black money.

Infrastructure

We hold that power, telecommunications, transport (surface, sea and air) constitute the basic building blocks of our development. With hardly 50% of the roads surfaced, about 40% of the traffic volume is handled by the National Highway System (NHS) which constitutes hardly 2% of the road network.

- We need to actively develop a National Waterways network.
- To meet our minimum needs, a staggering 10,000 MW have to be added annually for the next 15 years. Irrigation needs press upon our resources. All these call for large investments.
- We propose, therefore, to lay the foundations of a strong bond market in the country which can take care of the massive financial requirements. We invite foreign capital in the field of infrastructure.
- We will initiate a framework which will facilitate quick redressal of the acute infrastructure crisis based on international cooperation and partnership.
- We will strive to confine the role of the state to that of a facilitator, withdrawing in favour of suitably structured independent regulatory authorities.

Public Sector

Currently the policy relating to public sector is in disarray. In the case of disinvestment from ailing, non-profitable or sick public sector undertakings, the BJP will constitute a Disinvestment Commission for taking care of disinvestment from the country's public sector.

Foreign Trade and Capital

Foreign Trade Policy has in the past degenerated into one of providing palliatives. It has now become necessary to strengthen the interface between industry and trade.

The BJP welcomes foreign investment, because we hold that it supplies knowledge, technology and know-how and sharpens the quality and competitive edge of our economy.

Industrial Policy

Industry in India has to be enabled to become more productive, more innovative. Only then will it fulfil its main role:

Enhance the national wealth, provide greater employment in ever increasing numbers and thus assist the growth of other sectors, including agriculture. For, we recognise this inseparable interdependence. Our exports must compete with the best in the world, add to our resources and fiscal health, and thus enable India to achieve the status that we believe is its destiny. The BJP assures all about creating a healthy investment and industrial environment.

The BJP believes in the continued role and relevance of the small-scale sector. This important segment of our national economy, which has been entirely ignored by the Congress and whose very existence is threatened by the present policy of economic liberalisation, will receive all encouragement and help from a BJP Government.

The following principles will guide the industrial policy of the BJP.

A. Economic Sovereignty

The party regards the preservation of the nation's economic interests as a component of our external economic relations. Globalisation, to us, is not a synonym for the obliteration of national economic interests. Indeed, in the ensuing global competition we need to be constantly mindful of preserving them.

B. Modernisation

BJP stands for a modern and progressive India, open to new ideas, new technology and fresh capital. A modern India to the BJP is not a Westernised India; a pale copy of the Western economic models.

C. Decentralisation

We stand for a decentralised economic order. The BJP stands for political as well as economic democracy. The role of the Government must change from the restrictive to the supportive and encouraging.

Creating Jobs and Opportunities

Apart from employment which will be created in the normal course by the growth of the economy, special employment schemes will be undertaken by the Bharatiya Janata Party to eradicate unemployment.

The BJP proposes to introduce a scheme of voluntary National Service to undertake the task of national reconstruction and also in order to instill a sense of discipline and nationalism among the youth of the country. This service will aim at reclaiming waste land for commercial use—for instance, after reclaiming the waste land, it will be used for horticulture, social forestry or any other purpose that will provide the youth involved in the reclamation with continued income. Similarly, the National Service will be used for river management schemes.

Government Employees

BJP will set up a permanent Employees Welfare Board with a view to resolving the long-standing problems related to:

1. Time scale promotion;
2. Revision of pay scales and award of bonus;
3. Implementation of awards;
4. Housing; and,
5. Social welfare measures and travel concession of retired personnel.

Harnessing Nature for Human Welfare

The BJP believes that science and technology must play its due role in transforming India into a prosperous and strong country. The BJP will apply appropriate scientific and technological methods for increasing productivity, eradicating poverty, hunger and disease and providing meaningful employment along with the basic amenities of life. We believe that science and technology need to be harnessed to improve the lot of the vast section of our population living below the poverty line. We hold that science is not merely harnessing nature for material wealth but is as well for liberating and enriching the mind and enlarging the human spirit. The BJP will use science in the service of the poor and develop technology that has a humane face.

India, the New Millennium, the World

In a post-Cold War world India will be confronted by many new challenges and opportunities. To meet them, to benefit from the opportunities, mindful of the existing global disequilibrium and in consonance with India's national interests, our foreign policy in the emerging decades will be based on the human values of peace, equality and cooperation.

The BJP holds that a departure from the recent past, Indian diplomacy should be conducted in tune with India's position as a strong power and a major player in the world arena. A billion people who do not depend upon anyone for feeding or clothing themselves are a power which cannot be ignored. Our nation needs to regain its lost pride and the BJP alone can undertake this task. While we believe in partnership with everyone, we reject the very thought of patronage by anybody.

The BJP stands committed to peace amongst all nations; prosperity for all the peoples of the world; and, an international role for India that befits this great and ancient nation.

Protecting Our Country

The BJP accords the highest importance to the security of our Nation, our Society and our Citizens. We charge the present Government with imperilling our security, internal and external, as never before.

Our defence expenditure has been cut steadily in real terms during the Narasimha Rao regime. This has seriously compromised our combat effectiveness. The present Congress Government has been functioning without a full-time Defence Minister for over three years, and this negligence of India's sword arm has begun to affect the morale of our gallant forces.

The BJP will correct this damaging imbalance. We will accord due importance to all security-related issues—the emerging global realities and regional complexities demand this as the very minimum response from our Government.

Internal Security

The nature of the state and its relationship with society has a direct bearing on the level of the citizens' national commitment. An insensitive and uncaring state erodes the citizens' allegiance to the nation. The BJP will restore national commitment to its rightful place by establishing a harmonious relationship between state and society.

Jammu & Kashmir

The absence of political far-sightedness and clarity of national objectives has resulted in our nation continuing to have to pay a price even 50 years after Jammu & Kashmir became a part of the Republic. The failure of successive Congress Governments to formulate a Jammu & Kashmir policy that takes into account the State's internal problems has led to a situation where this strategic border State has emerged as the principal challenge to Indian nationhood. The BJP realises the magnitude of the challenge and dedicates itself to the task of not only solving the internal problems of the State but also reclaiming the portion of our territory which has been illegally held by Pakistan for nearly five decades.

North-East

The north-eastern States of our country continue to suffer from the violence perpetrated by insurgency and ethnic strife. Poor governance, a callous administration, seepage of development funds, and Congress' politics of manipulation have contributed to the alienation of the people and the growth in insurgency. In Assam, ULFA and Bodo militants are often in news striking with regularity; in Nagaland and Manipur the NSCN continues with its depredation; and, in Tripura, militant tribal outfits have once again reared their ugly heads. The tide of illegal immigration from Bangladesh has only worsened the situation. The BJP will address itself to the problems of our north-eastern States and institute a grievance redressal system monitored from Delhi.

Himalayas

Over the past five decades, our Himalayan bastions have been strategically pierced. Despite that, the attitude of successive Congress Governments has remained unchanged Strategically, the Government has failed to restore a balance there, leave alone regain the initiative. In the process, we have also lost large national territories to the People's Republic of China, thus demonstrating an absence of strategic thought about our Himalayan bastions. The BJP will evolve a security policy for the Himalayas so that India's national interests are fully safeguarded.

External Security

We believe that pro-active diplomacy, especially defence diplomacy, coupled with adequate preparedness of our armed forces, is the key to securing our frontiers against aggression. This requires both strategy and tactics.

Jai Jawan

The BJP is rightly proud of our valiant soldiers who have dedicated their lives to defend our nation from external aggressors and internal subversives. We believe it is our duty to take care of our serving jawans and look after those who have retired from service, as well as their families.

Illegal Immigration: Demographic Invasion — A Threat to our Security

We believe that illegal immigration from our neighbouring countries, especially Bangladesh, has a direct impact on our nation's security and has an unsettling effect on our demography. Given the sheer dimension of numbers — there are as many as *1.7 crore illegal immigrants, the bulk of them Bangladeshis, living in various parts of the country — illegal immigration is not only transforming the geography, but the sociology, the economy, indeed even the politics of this country.* India is facing an explosive issue. If our demographic balance is allowed to be disturbed by inept policies and political considerations, various demographic entities are bound to come in conflict, thus adversely affecting our security environment. The invasion of illegal immigrants from Bangladesh has led to an alarming growth in a section of the population in our North-East, Assam, West Bengal, and parts of Bihar and Delhi. In certain areas, a section of the population has grown by almost 100 per cent.

Towards a Revitalised Rural Economy

Our country has an abundance of natural resources — fertile lands, flowing rivers, rich mineral deposits and verdant forests. More than anything else, we have a large army of farmers that shoulders the onerous task of feeding our people. But the wrong priorities of the last 50 years of Congress misrule and the lopsided model of development pursued by policy-makers have impoverished vast sections of our farmers, rendering agriculture economically non-viable. Worse, bulk of the monies earmarked for infrastructural development, health, education and civic amenities has been canalised to the urban areas despite the fact that the majority of the population lives in villages.

Less than a quarter of the country's population, 23.31 per cent, lives in urban areas, compared to the overwhelming 76.69 per cent which lives in villages. As many as 71.4 per cent of our people are economically dependent on agriculture: This sector of our economy, therefore, generates the highest employment as well as provides the biggest market. Yet, this sector continues to be neglected by Congress policy-makers.

The Bharatiya Janata Party believes that India cannot emerge as a powerful nation until the lot of our farmers is improved, adequate attention paid to the agricultural sector, an all-out war launched against poverty, and investments are made in agro-industry as well as small-scale and cottage industry catering to the requirements of our villages. Our country's progress is linked to the well-being of our villages, our farmers and our poor.

Congress' Policy: Not to have a Policy on Agriculture

In the absence of any well thought out agricultural policy focussing on rural development and reconstruction, agriculture is fast becoming a losing proposition for our farmers. While fixing agricultural prices, successive Congress Governments have not taken into account the expenses incurred by our farmers on seeds, fertiliser, power, water, pesticides, machinery and labour. No effort has ever been made to bring about parity in the prices of industrial and agricultural produce.

As a result, our farmers are forced to sell the fruit of their labour at low prices even while they have to pay ever-increasing prices for the necessary inputs. Not surprisingly, this has contributed to the impoverishment and indebtedness of our farmers, pushing vast sections of them dangerously close to or even below the poverty line. According to the Planning Commission's own estimates, almost 42 per cent of our rural population lives below the poverty line.

No less alarming is the fact that the number of our villagers dependent on per acre of land has been steadily increasing, compared to other countries where this dependency has dramatically decreased with governments investing in agro-industry which offers alternative sources of employment. No effort has been made to set up an adequate number of small scale and cottage industries in our rural areas to absorb idle hands. This has also contributed in no small measure to the impoverishment of our farmers. In 1950-51, the ratio of the disparity between the per capita income in rural and urban areas was 1:2; in 1995-96 it stood at 1:4. Similarly, while per family income has risen by 52 per cent in urban areas since 1952, it has increased by a mere 7.8 per cent in rural areas.

Ironically, these neglected villages form a vast market—and from this market, as much as Rs 48,000 crores flow to our urban areas every year. By killing our villages, we will be destroying this market. Conversely, by developing our villages, we will be strengthening this market, which in turn will benefit our urban areas. In other words, urban India cannot survive without rural India.

But this simple truth has been ignored for the last 50 years. Today, three out of every four Indians live in villages, condemned to a life of exploitation and increasing social, political and economic marginalisation.

BJP's Agenda for our Farmers, our Poor

We pledge to reverse this trend of social, political and economic marginalisation of our rural population and empower our farmers. We are committed to restoring agriculture to its rightful place and thus steering our people into an era of prosperity and social equality by the opening decade of the new century.

No country can be great if its people remain poor. The first task for us will be to wipe out the dark curse of poverty. We will allocate greater resources for effective poverty alleviation programmes; we will invest in agriculture and small-scale industry; we will build from the bottom up, for that is the only way we can build an enduring edifice of development.

Literacy and Health for All

The Bharatiya Janata Party is committed to the creation of a Bharat whose citizens will not suffer from the dual affliction of illiteracy and malnutrition. We believe that the state should invest in developing every citizen's potential to contribute to the regeneration of our country. To achieve that, we will stress on health and education, both of which are challenges that have to be met by the first decade of the 21st century. India has to emerge as a powerful, self-reliant and proud nation. True development will be possible only when we draw sustenance from our citizens; they are our true wealth.

Education

The past five years have witnessed this core area of human resource development being increasingly deprived of state support. As a result, quality education is fast becoming the preserve of the social and economic elite of the country. The vast multitudes, who have been victims of inequity, continue to be denied the cherished ideal of literacy. The BJP will stress on providing opportunity of education, literacy and information. Towards this end, we will:

1. Increase state spending on education progressively to at least six per cent of our Gross National Product;
2. Spend more on primary education and enrol the help of non-government organisations in this area;
3. Provide free education in order to universalise access to primary education;
4. Offer incentives in the form of free text books, nutrition programmes and stipends to check dropout rate so that at least 80 per cent children, both boys and girls, who enrol complete primary school education.

Nari Shakti: Towards Empowerment

We hold that 'Nari Shakti' is not merely a phrase, it is the enunciation of our approach. Towards this end, the BJP will empower women, ensure that their dignity and rights are not trampled upon and help develop their full potential. We are also committed to protecting the rights of the girl child.

Towards a Sustainable and Balanced Growth

Our people are our primary concern—their basic needs of health, education and employment must precede everything else. To ensure an equitable disbursement of resources so that the largest number of our people benefit from development policies, we must arrest the country's runaway population growth. An increasing population can only mean a decreasing share of the fruits of development. Successive Congress Governments have ignored this crucial area of development planning, often for petty political motives. This has resulted in a steep rise in population and severe demographic imbalances. The Bharatiya Janata Party believes that children are born — and have the right—to be happy, and not merely for existence. We will, therefore, put population-related issues, especially family planning, firmly back on the national agenda, and launch a people's movement against the impending population explosion through persuasive policies.

Only One Earth

The BJP holds as a firm conviction that our "only one Earth" is the endower of all our wealth and natural resources. This, however, is not for endless exploitation. Our environment has to be protected, not only to prevent the sanctity of Mother Earth from being profaned but also because our forests, our rivers and our skies sustain a multitude of lives. No less important is the crucial role that environment plays in our nation's security. Environment must be protected by subscribing to the concept of 'sustainable development', a philosophical tenet that is integral to our civilisational and cultural consciousness.

Harmony and Equality Through Integral Humanism

The Bharatiya Janata Party's social philosophy, which is the bedrock of its social agenda, is rooted in integral humanism. It rules out contradictions between society and its various components, as also between society and the individual, or, for that matter, between the family, the basic building brick of our social structure, and the individual. From this stems the BJP's commitment to the eradication of social and economic disparities that have prevented India from emerging as a modern, dynamic nation; to the creation of a socially integrated Bharatiya society which can proudly enter the new century. The BJP will help all socially and economically weak and backward sections of society, through special welfare and other schemes, to reach their full potential. For us, it is a historic task which we are resolved to fulfil.

Enabling Our Disabled

As many as five crore of our people have been socially, politically and economically marginalised because of their physical and other disabilities. Successive Congress Governments have not only abdicated their responsibility towards these less fortunate of our citizens, but also resisted their empowerment and, therefore, their inclusion in the national mainstream. The level of official apathy can be gauged from the fact that during the last year of its tenure, the Rao Government allocated Rs 42 crore for the welfare of the disabled, which works out to Rs 8 per person.

The BJP believes that those who have been excluded from playing a participatory role in the nation-building process by being stigmatised as "disabled", should be empowered so that they become productive, proud citizens of our country.

Our Minorities

Wherever and whenever the Bharatiya Janata Party has been in power, it has ensured peace and security for all sections of society, irrespective of their religious identity. The BJP is committed to further strengthen this achievement. This is in stark contrast to the insecurity faced by minority communities under Congress rule. We have been steadfastly opposed to appeasement as state policy since it benefits only those sections which profess regressive and retrograde social norms in the guise of protecting their religious beliefs. The BJP will be guided by its policy of "justice for all, appeasement of none". A resurgent India will enter the 21st century with the resolve of one nation, one people and one culture.

Human Rights

The BJP subscribes to the view that human dignity, justice for all and protection of the individual from the tyranny of the state are among the basic tenets of *Hindutva.* We are committed to upholding the human, democratic and civil rights of every individual, irrespective of the person's caste, creed, religion or gender. But we will not allow this commitment to be used as a shield by those who commit inhuman atrocities and thus forsake their claim to human rights. The BJP believes that the state should be fair to all citizens, but firm while dealing with those who militate against civil society. The BJP will not allow any foreign interference in our country's internal affairs on the pretext of monitoring human rights violations.

Displaced Communities: Protecting Their Rights

Separatist violence and Islamic fundamentalism and terrorism in Jammu and Kashmir has forced more than 3,00,000 people, including 2,50,000 Kashmiri Pandits and Punjabi and Dogra Hindus, apart from thousands of Sikhs and even some Muslims, to flee their homes and hearths. Most of the displaced Pandits are living in abysmal conditions in refugee camps in Jammu and some other places. Together, they perhaps form the largest internally-displaced community in the world, forced to live as refugees in their own motherland, condemned to the mercy of an uncaring and callous Congress Government at the Centre and its puppet administration in Jammu and Kashmir. The Bharatiya Janata Party has mobilised its own resources, men and material to provide succour to these unfortunate victims of Government apathy and terrorist violence. But a lot more needs to be done.

Similarly, thousands of Buddhist Chakmas have fled the Chittagong Hill Tracts in Bangladesh in the face of persecution by Muslim settlers from the plains and the men from Bangladesh Rifles. Most of them are at present living in camps in Tripura. Regardless of the grim future that awaits them back home, the Government of India has shown unnecessary haste in trying to repatriate them—an action that is largely motivated by the petty politics of the Congress. The BJP is opposed to such forced repatriation in the absence of foolproof security guarantees from the Government of Bangladesh.

The escalating conflict in Sri Lanka between Sinhalese and Tamils is posing a demographic threat to South India with a large number of Tamil refugees beginning to pour into this region. Such a movement is bound to increase the influence of the LTTE which may in turn promote separatist tendencies.

We must also address ourselves to the concerns of non-resident Indians, especially those who had settled in Hong Kong and now find the future uncertain with Britain handing over this territory to China in 1997.

Our Identity, Our Culture

The Cornerstone of Bharatiyata

The Bharatiya Janata Party believes that modernisation does not mean the mechanical imitation of a particular way of life. It will redefine the concept of development to accommodate the Bharatiya way of living, belief system and values to reach the ultimate goal of Bharatiyata. We hold that it is necessary to emphasise the linkage of development elements to cultural elements, including local relevance, relevance to geographical and environmental factors, historical traditions, traditional knowledge and skills. We believe that cultural factors play an important role in energising a nation.

Media and Publishing

The BJP believes that a free Press is a *sine qua non* for a democracy. At the same time, we also hold that this freedom should not be misused to defame or malign any individual, organisation or institution.

Cinema

Popular cinema has played an important role in promoting social harmony and nationalism, apart from providing inexpensive entertainment to the masses. But in recent years, popular cinema, increasingly funded by the underworld, has had a negative impact on society, especially impressionable young minds. Sex and violence on the silver screen are beginning to gnaw at the moorings of our cultural ethos.

In the Vanguard of Change

Our youth form the backbone of our vibrant nation and they alone can shape the destiny of this country. The BJP has a tryst with the youth of India and will harness their creative energy for bringing about social, cultural and political change. We will aim at transforming Yuva Sankalpa into Yuva Shakti, which, in turn, will be the catalyst for reinvigorating India.

We will inculcate in the country's youth a sense of pride in our ancient traditions and heritage. We will instill in them a sense of self-confidence so that they can take their rightful place in the vanguard of change.

Our Achievements

Peace, Progress and Prosperity

Wherever and whenever the Bharatiya Janata Party has formed a State Government, it has provided the people with a caring, fair, clean and strong administration. The emphasis of our State Governments, be it in Rajasthan, Gujarat, Delhi or Maharashtra (where it shares power with the Shiv Sena), or earlier in Uttar Pradesh, Himachal Pradesh and Madhya Pradesh, has been on ensuring peace, progress and prosperity.

The distinctive feature of our State Governments is their singular achievement in curbing communal and caste conflict. This is in stark contrast to the situation that prevails in States ruled by the Congress or the Janata Dal where the law and order machinery has virtually collapsed. A shining example of our achievement on this front is the communal peace that prevails in Maharashtra which till recently was racked by riots and social conflict. Similarly, the BJP Government in Gujarat has ensured peace.

This had been achieved by cracking down on anti-social and anti-national activity. The underworld mafia, which flourished under Congress rule, has been brought to book.

The criminal-politician nexus has been broken. Black-marketeers, and other criminals, who survived because of Congress patronage, have been put behind bars or are facing prosecution.

The emphasis on enforcing law and order is not without reason. For, unless there is peace, there cannot be progress and prosperity.

In the field of development, our State Governments have focussed their attention on the rural sector, because, the bulk of our people live in villages. Not only have effective steps been taken to solve the problems of our farmers, but innovative schemes have been introduced to generate employment and fight the scourge of poverty.

For instance, the BJP Government in Rajasthan has earmarked more than 60 per cent of Plan allocation for rural areas. As many as 12.86 lakh farmers and artisans have benefited from the State Government's decision to write off loans amounting to more than Rs 300 crore. The State Government has also written off irrigation loans amounting to Rs 124 crore and introduced more effective means of irrigation. Tax relief on seeds, a wide range of agricultural produce and equipment has further helped the farmers. Similarly, the State Government has reduced sales tax on fertilizers and made a five-fold increase in agricultural loans.

On the social front, the Government has introduced innovative schemes like Gopal Gram Yojana and Saraswati Yojana. The first scheme not only aims at improving the quality of livestock but also providing people with a sustained income. Similarly, Saraswati Yojana has a two-fold purpose: Universalising primary education and providing employment to the educated youth of the villages. Schemes like Shiksha Karmi Project and Guru-Mitra Yojana have also contributed immensely to increasing literacy levels. Vikalp, a specially designed family planning programme based on incentives and which protects the girl child, has been immensely successful.

The Rajasthan Government has also introduced a new industrial policy to attract both Indian and foreign investors. The policy has already begun to pay rich dividends. The Government has signed MOUs for the setting up of new power plants. Soon, the State shall have the largest solar power plant.

In Gujarat, the BJP Governments has maintained communal harmony in the trouble-prone areas. Latif, a notorious criminal involved in bootlegging and anti-social activities, has been put behind bars. His underworld activities in the border areas of Kutch and Saurashtra have come to a grinding halt. Those involved in adulteration of petrol with solvents, which had become an extremely profitable crime during Congress rule, are facing prosecution.

With law and order restored, the State Government has turned its attention on development activity. Work on the Sardar Sarovar Project is progressing at a remarkable speed. Bonds worth Rs 300 crore were issued and the amount obtained in seven days from the cooperative sector. Simultaneously, those displaced because of the project have been rehabilitated.

On the industrial front, the State Government has adopted an investor-friendly policy which has evoked a tremendous response. An increasing number of non-resident Indians have begun to show keen interest in investing in Gujarat. At the same time, the interests of the agricultural sector are not being ignored. For instance, 42 per cent of the power generated in the State is channelised for agricultural use, compared to 34 percent for industry. New power plants are being commissioned to meet future requirements. In the last three years of Congress rule, not a single MW was added to the installed capacity.

On the social front, the State Government has reduced bus fares by 20 per cent, a move which has brought tremendous relief to millions of people. Poor families are being provided with wheat at Rs 2 per kg. More than 40 lakh families have already been covered by this poverty alleviation scheme.

The biggest success of the Gujarat Government has been the Gokul Gram Yojana, a scheme to develop the villages and provide a better quality of life to villagers. The aim is to make the 18,090 villages of the State self-reliant and provide them with basic facilities ranging from roads to drinking water to schools and proper sanitation. Since this is a participatory model of development, the Government has sought the people's participation. The response has been tremendous: Even NRIs have come forward to contribute to the scheme.

To empower women, the State Government has introduced schemes like Kuvarbai-nu-Mameru and Ghar Divda. Daughters of poor families receive financial support at the time of their marriage. Tribal girls have been provided with bicycles so that they can attend school. The Daridra Narayan Yojana has encouraged children from poor families to attend school. Under this scheme, children get free uniforms and books in addition to monetary incentives.

On the agricultural front, farmers are now allowed to buy land in any part of the State. New insurance policies have been introduced to provide extensive cover. The quality of seeds, pesticides and fertilizers has been improved and there has been a three-fold increase in the allocation for drip irrigation. Farmers today get adequate power supply.

In Maharashtra, the Shiv Sena-BJP Government has spared no effort to break the vicious grip which the mafia had established over the administration. The law and order machinery has been strengthened and the police made accountable.

In Maharashtra, too, the emphasis has been on restoring law and order and implementing schemes aimed at providing a better quality of life for the people. This is most obvious in the rural areas where even small farmer today are provided with power for their pumps and insurance cover for their crops. The Government has undertaken a massive programme to provide drinking water to every village.

To Protect the poor from inflation, the State Government has frozen the prices of five essential commodities. The poorest of the poor are covered by the jhunka-bhakar scheme: For a rupee, a person can have a meal. Those who cannot afford to pay for health care, have been provided with free health services. Meritorious students from poor families are being provided with all incentives to ensure that they do not drop out of schools. A programme has been adopted to provide free housing to 40 lakh slum-dwellers in Mumbai.

The State Government has initiated steps to ensure that those who perpetrate crimes against women are punished immediately. Kamdhenu Yojana provides women with sustained employment. For the girl child, a special scheme has been introduced to ensure that her education and health care needs are taken care of. The Maharashtra Government has taken the first bold step to dismantle the practice of polygamy.

Most important, the State Government has restored probity in public life: They have provided the people with a clean and transparent administration. The Enron deal was scrapped because the cost was inflated. A committee of experts renegotiated the deal with Enron and the new agreement has resulted in savings worth Rs 25,000 crore. The cost per unit of power has also been brought down by 54 paise. The biggest gain is that by bringing down the project cost, the Maharashtra Government has set new parameters for power projects elsewhere in the country.

The BJP Government in Delhi has achieved the unique distinction of fulfilling 94 of the 100 promises which the party had made with two years. This despite the fact that the State Government is hamstrung by restrictions imposed by the Union Government. The focus has been on improving the quality of life of the common man.

The BJP had promised that if voted to power, it would pursue the prosecution of those involved in the November 1984 anti-Sikh riots. We are proud of the fact that our Government has successfully reopened the investigations which were suppressed by the Congress. Some of the guilty people have been brought to book. The other will also be brought to justice.

The BJP Government has provided Delhi with a corruption-free administration. Several steps have been taken to end 'inspector raj' and simplify rules and regulations. Schemes have been introduced for employment generation and to encourage entrepreneurs. Those living in slums have been provided with basic amenities.

These are only some of our achievements, the highlights of our government's performance. Much more remains to be done and we are committed to completing the task we have set for ourselves.

Let's Commence a New Chapter

This then is the blue printwhich the Bharatiya Janata Party will implement on coming to power. The task will be undertaken by the party's inspiring team of leaders, each one of whom has an umblemished record of selfless service to the nation. It is through this blueprint that the BJP will bring about radical change in the country's polity, society and economy. It is this blueprint which will be the bedrock of a new India where every citizen shall be free from fear, hunger and discrimination. This blueprint will pave the way to the next century and the new millennium.

But to implement our commitments we need your support. The sweeping change that has become so necessary to save the nation can be brought about only with your help. To begin with, you have to change the leadership at the helm of the country's affairs and vote out the Congress. The time has arrived for a nationalist Government which will lead India from the dark curse of poverty to prosperity; which will free the administration from the clutches of criminals and restore probity in public life; which will reinvest the state with authority and strengthen our security forces; and, which will secure our country's frontiers so that we do not have to suffer once again the humiliations of this millennium. Such a Government can be provided only by the BJP.

The past five decades have been a tragic story of missed opportunities and self-serving opportunist politics. The Congress has abused power and authority for the benefit of few and to the detriment of millions of Indians. The leaders of the Janata Dal have demonstrated their inability to think beyond themselves. The Left parties, orphaned by the passing away of Communism all over the world, are struggling to come to terms with an ideological vacuum. None of these parties can boast of ideological commitment, moral courage and political conviction. On the other hand, the BJP has emerged as the only national alternative, a party that stands apart for its ideology, commitment and courage.

We are standing at an important crossroads of our nation's history. The BJP appeals to all patriotic Indians to join the noble mission of national reconstruction, the task of creating a strong and prosperous India. Let us be partners in a new era of equality, peace and progress.

Vande Mataram!

6. The BJP is committed to Article 44 of the Constitution. It will adopt a uniform Civil Code applicable to every community and foster a common *Bharatiya* identity, apart from ensuring gender equality. Regressive personal laws will cease to have legal validity.
7. The manner of appointment of Constitutional functionaries will be reviewed by the Party if voted to power.
8. BJP will maintain a national register of citizens and introduce a multi-purpose identity card.

ELECTORAL REFORMS

For free, fair and fearless elections BJP stands committed. This is important for upholding real Democracy, it thinks. The BJP has conviction that among the many causes responsible for the present plight of the polity of States, a major factor is faulty electoral practices. So the Party will:

1. Update and adopt the Goswami Committee report,
2. grant statutory status to the Code of Conduct drawn up by the Election Commission and will give it teeth,
3. introduce a scheme of state-funding of candidates to all legislatures,
4. provide suitable incentives for open, official corporate funding to all recognised political parties,
5. undertake fresh delimitation of Lok Sabha and Assembly constituencies on the basis of the 1991 Census,
6. make it mandatory for the political parties to submit audited accounts for public scrutiny annually,
7. examine the feasibility of introducing the list system,
8. expedite the process of issuing identity cards to all voters and make it mandatory requirement for voting,
9. scrutinize all voters' lists to ensure that no legitimate voter is excluded,

Manifesto: Bharatiya Janata Party

CONSTITUTIONAL REFORMS

BJP believe that Centre-State relations have been on the downslide for last 50 years, and hence needs to be improved.

1. It wants a strong Union and equal rights for all citizens. For that purpose it will effect reforms by implementing main recommendations of the Sarkaria Commission, such as:
   a) Restoring balance of resources in favour of the States;

   b) Ending misuse of Article 356 to dismiss State Governments and dissolve State assemblies. BJP will explore possibilities of making it mandatory for the Union Government seek Parliament's approval by two-thirds majority for dismissal of State Governments; and,

   c) Consulting the respective State Government before appointing the Governor for it.
2. BJP promises to carve out Uttaranchal, Vananchal, Vidarbha and Chhattisgarh and give them full statehood. We will further consider setting up a Commission to examine formation of smaller states. Delhi will naturally be given the full statehood.
3. BJP will institute regional development councils for Jammu, Kashmir and Ladakh in the State of Jammu & Kashmir.
4. The Party will abrogate Article 370 of the Constitution, which puts the State of Jammu & Kashmir on a separate and separatist pedestal, for full and final integration of the State with the Union of India.
5. The Party will set up an inter-State Council under Article 263 of the Constitution to settle all interstate and Centre-State disputes to avoid ad hoc responses to issues like that of Cauvery waters.

10. take steps to curb expenditure on elections by imposing ban on advertisements, cutouts etc,
11. introduce electronic voting machines to hasten the process of counting,
12. examine the possibility of simultaneous elections to Parliament, Assemblies and Panchayats,
13. ensure speedy and exemplary punishment for those who indulge in booth-capturing,
14. officials found guilty of involvement in poll-rigging will be given exemplary punishment,
15. amend the anti-defection law whereby a member of any Legislature who changes parties will lose his or her membership of the House, and
16. prevent the misuse of Doordarshan and All-India Radio by the ruling party.

Combined Reforms (Covering Elected representative of the people, members of the Executive, Police and also, Judiciary):

1. BJP will make it obligatory on every Elected Representative to make public his entire income and wealth within 90 days of the election.
2. It will introduce extensive regulations and requirements upon those who hold public office so that no conflict of interest is over permitted to influence proper discharge of their duties.
3. It will appoint a Lok Pal to entertain complaints of corruption against anybody holding public office, including the Prime Minister.
4. The Party will take measures to modify and reform the methodology of Government approval for contracts, schemes and large money value agreements so as to make them more transparent. The powers of patronage, the rights to say 'Yes' or 'No' to simple daily requirements of the citizens will be reduced drastically. BJP

believes that the government which intrudes the least, governs the best. It will endeavour to combine this with open and transparent governance.

5. Expeditiously the BJP deal with cases of corruption unresolved and in which no action has been taken in the past 10 years.
6. The Party will take steps to ensure that investigative and intelligence agencies like RAW, IB and CBI are not used to subserve the political designs of the ruling party.

JUDICIAL REFORMS

BJP will take positive steps for speedy, fair and inexpensive justice. It will, therefore,

1. appoint special judges to clear huge arrears at all levels of the judiciary,
2. fill the vacancies in High Courts and the Supreme Court without any further delay,
3. legislate to the effect that courts do not give unending adjournments and complete cases within one year,
4. constantly review the salary and pension benefits of all judges so as to attract the best legal talent to the Judiciary,
5. expand and strengthen the existing legal aid facilities for economically weaker section of the society and
6. set up National Judicial Commission which will be responsible for making judicial appointments in High Courts and the Supreme Court.

ADMINISTRATIVE REFORMS

For caring, just and accountable administration and to provide high quality services, value to citizenship and to usher in novel paradigm in public administration, BJP will take following steps:

1. It will make the district administration accountable for

any outbreak of violence, institute a time-bound enquiry, publish the findings, punish the guilty, and compensate the victims.

2. It will update and implement the National Police Commission report in time-bound manner.
3. It will ask each ministry and department to set clear performance standards, including cost consciousness, in quantifiable terms and monitor the adherence to these standards.
4. It will introduce a scheme of fixed minimum tenure for some identified posts at higher ranks, as for example, Chief Secretaries, Secretaries to Government, DGPs and the like.
5. It will disfavour extension to bureaucrats and police officers.
6. It will institute an annual Sardar Patel Award for the best three district officers, as a beginning.
7. It will ensure uniform housing and other related facilities for officers in the same grade and in the same station. The system allotment of houses will be made transparent.
8. It will introduce a system of allowing lateral entry of personnel from the private sector, NGOs, educational/ research institutes into Government.
9. It will identify areas from which Government must withdraw so that departments can be wound up in a phased manner.
10. It will strengthen the department of administrative reforms at the Centre and in the States.
11. Lastly, on this count, it will give citizens what is their due. A huge divide today separates the citizens, the society and the States. This is principally on account of the State not treating the rights of the citizens as sacrosanct; not fulfilling its obligations towards citizens sincerely; and not to the citizens the services that are its bounden duty. The BJP will, therefore, identify such

areas as warrant immediate correction, as they affect the daily life of the ordinary citizens, and implement reforms in them within a given time-Frame.

ECONOMIC REFORMS

BJP recognises two immediate priorities. First, it wants to provide the physical and economic infrastructure appropriate for stipulated growth in the Gross Domestic Product. Secondly, it wants to provide required social infrastructure for a minimum sustainable quality of life. While attempting at these, it would like to ensure fiscal deficit well contained. For the purpose, it feels a different approach is required to be taken. Therefore, BJP would work out measures to prune non-developmental expenditure, minimise the commercial activities of the government, severely cut back on bureaucracy, would shed the structure of controls and regulation and re-equip itself for providing a framework for free market operations which will accentuate growth, poverty eradication and build-up social infrastructure.

FISCAL REFORMS

1. It will, therefore, not seek to increase revenue by taxation alone. It will, on the contrary, endeavour in high order of investment and appropriate level of domestic savings.
2. It will structure nation's fiscal reforms so that savings and contracted savings are augmented to levels that will take care of a higher order investment necessary for faster growth.
3. In taxation the Party will ensure that not only levels and rates of taxation are such that growth is not constrained, but that burden-sharing of taxes is equally distributed among all affluent sections of the society. It will mitigate the undue rigours of indirect taxes, which today is 71% of the tax revenue, so that productivity and growth are not hampered.

4. It will devise a suitably structured value added tax (VAT) so as to ensure better burden-sharing among goods and services that contribute to value addition.
5. In tariffs it will ensure that the domestic sector gets a level-playing field, and doesnot become uncom-petitive.
6. It will also strive to lighten debt burden on the nation which in turn will contribute to stabilise the interest rate.
7. On items for mass consumption, the Party will not like the Excise Duties.
8. The Party will examine the aspect of sales tax reforms and equalisation.
9. The Party will ensure operational autonomy of the Reserve Bank of India.
10. It will adopt firm measures to prevent the generation of black money.
11. It will rationalise and simplify the present tax structure and raise the income tax exemption limit to Rs 60,000 per annum.
12. It will provide weighted deductions taking number of dependents on earning member.
13. The Party will exempt all investments in approved organisations in public or private sectors from levy of Wealth Tax.
14. It will give tax reliefs to employment-oriented industries in non-municipal areas.
15. It will ensure minimum contribution to Government exchequer by all profit-earning business units. The concept of "zero business units" will be done away with.
16. It will give special tax concessions to writer, artists, academics and others engaged in intellectual and cultural pursuits.

17. It will control the price level through maximisation of production and a minimisation of costs of production. This it will achieve through technology upgradation, economics of scale (that means, acquiring proportionate savings by utilizing larger units), and free competition. Towards this end, the BJP will ensure efficient, low-cost, corruption-free Public Distribution System (PDS).
18. Thereby, it will activate a pressure and ensure regular, assured, timely and adequate supply of commodities to consumers in rural, tribal, remote and backward areas of the country.
19. It will supply better quality foodgrains through PDS by enhancing the norms for quality standards rather than easing them as is done by the present regime.
20. It will make pulses, cooking oil and soap also available through PDS along with foodgrains, sugar and kerosene.
21. It will improvise upon the Consumer Protection Act of 1986, and ensure its application.
22. It will encourage consumer movement.

REFORMS IN SOCIAL ECONOMY

1. BJP will encourage capital creation through funds from such parallel economy, retaining the right of Government to tax the revenue flows from such created capital.
2. It will open up sectors such as social forestry, wasteland development and housing for rural and urban poor.
3. It will also review rationale of the Urban/Land Ceiling Act in this context.
4. BJP would invite foreign capital in the area of creation of INFRASTRUCTURE, and also would propose for founding a strong bond market within the country. This will, it believes, enable India meet its minimum re-

quirement of annual addition of 10,000 megawatt Power for 15 years. Also, capital accumulated thereby would help us build up necessary Railway network, which has been only 16% of the necessary network over the five decades, and also the National Waterways network inadequacy of which has become real constraints in our world trade development.

5. It will initiate a framework which will facilitate quick redressal of acute infrastructure crisis and would seek international cooperation and partnership.
6. For this purpose it will confine the role of the state to the level of facilitators, withdrawing in favour of suitably structured independent regulatory authorities.

Foreign Trade and Capital

To avoid the present status of foreign trade policy as palliative BJP shall do everything to strengthen the interface between industry and trade. It will therefore:

(1) Select core industries and a system of destinations,

(2) initiate integrated production for export planning with selective intervention to build up dynamism in this sector,

(3) it will enter alliance with trading blocs that will give impetus to export,

(4) it will, if necessary, take membership of regional trading blocs for the purpose,

(5) strive to minimise our dependence on foreign savings, through it will welcome foreign investments for acquiring knowledge, technology upgradation and sharpening quality for competitive edge in the world markets,

(6) patronise foreign investments in areas that will in turn promote India's export scopes, and would become conservative of foreign investments in sectors which will cater solely to our domestic market,

(7) utilize the foreign investment objective of dessemination of world-class technology by offering preference to overseas investors who have domestic partners,

(8) welcome foreign investment in infrastructure, high technology and Research and Development within India,

(9) would discourage as non-priority the multinational companies in areas of non-durable consumer product manufacturing.

(10) BJP doesnot consider that globalisation has to be ushered in our economy at the cost of domestic economic interest. It believes our national economic interests need to be preserved as components of our external economic relations considering the ensuing global competition.

REFORMS IN INDUSTRIAL POLICY/PUBLIC SECTOR, MODERNISATION AND DECENTRALISATION CONCEPTS

BJP believes in confining the public sector only to sensitive areas where nation's security is involved and to areas public sector is necessary for providing moderating or counter-poising role to ill effects, if any, of unchecked private sector.

It will therefore:

(1) continue the presence of public sector in areas furthering social objectives,

(2) see the public sector industries be managed with the least interference by the government,

(3) will constitute a Disinvestment Commission for taking care of disinvestment from ailing, non-profitable or sick public sector undertaking,

(4) of course see that while disinvesting, workers' interest are not harmed,

(5) realign National Renewal Fund to take care of the constant requirements of retraining and redeployment of workers that may be necessary in a fast growing economy,

(6) utilize the sale proceeds from Public Sector Undertakings' Disinvestment only on capital expenditure,

(7) stand for a modern and progressive India, open to new ideas, new technology and fresh capital,

(8) decentralise economic power of the government, ensure that role of the government become supportive and encouraging and not restrictive,

(9) encourage research and Development and Regulations Act by Industrial Development Act,

10) replace Industrial Development as part of industrial growth process and over-all modernisation,

(11) small-scale sector will be given all importance and encouragement, through egencies established for the purpose in matters of purchases, marketing and sales of their products,

(12) permit hazardous industries only in specified areas setting up separate industrial satellites for the purpose and

(13) ensure a healthy capital market.

REFORMS WITH REGARD TO EMPLOYMENT GENERATION AND LABOUR'S ROLE IN THE SOCIETY

The growth in economy, BJP feels, will naturally effect newer employment generation. This apart, BJP is duty bound to introduce scheme of Voluntary National Service to undertake task of national reconstruction. This service will aim at reclaiming waste land for commercial use, which in consequence develop gainful profession of horticulture, social forestry.

(1) Similar national service scheme will be launched for river management schemes.

(2) BJP will increase employment opportunities in all sectors of organized economy.

(3) It will introduce policies and programmes to develop agriculture, particularly in regions which are at present less developed and backward.

(4) It will promote agro-industry with special emphasis.

(5) It will undertake large-scale housing activity that will generate both jobs and additional shelter in both rural and urban areas.

(6) It will provide transport facilities with special emphasis in improving availability of transport in rural areas.

(7) It will additionally generate employment opportunities by launching schemes (as they did in Gujarat and Rajasthan) like Antyodaya, Gokul Gram, Gopal Gram, Saraswati Jojanas.

(8) It will provide improved infrastructure specially in rural areas, such as roads, small dams and water conservation projects.

(9) It will also promote vocational training for the youth and the able-bodied.

(10) BJP believes in healthy trade unionism, therefore, will rationalise and simplify labour laws.

(11) It will recognize unions on basis of secret ballot, and would permit provisions of comprehensive bargaining .

(12) It will encourage workers' participation from shop floor to the board room in all public sector projects, public limited companies and foreign companies operating in India.

(13) It will protect workers from inflation in the economy.

(14) It will evolve an effective mechanism to implement protective laws for labour from occupational health hazards in such industries as asbestos, mica, cement,

slate, chemicals, textiles and the like. Workers will be adequately informed of the possible hazards they could be exposed to on the shop floor.

(15) It will not allow exit policy without fulfilling corresponding obligations towards the labour .

(16) BJP will set up permanent Employees Welfare Board with a view to resolving the long-standing problems related to:

a) time scale promotions;

b) revision of pay scale and award of bonus;

c) implementation of awards;

d) housing etc.;

e) social welfare measures and travels concession for retired personnel.

REFORMS IN FOREIGN POLICY

(1) BJP will reject any kind of political or economic hegemonism, and therefore, will establish sovereign equality amongst nations.

(2) It will promote Asian solidarity, develop South Asian Regional Cooperation improving relations with our neighbours. It donot accept outside interference in this region as being beneficial for it.

(3) Pakistan continues to follow a policy of fomenting insurgency with a view to create instability and unrest in India. BJP stands committed to thwart all those attempts. In this context, BJP affirms unequivocally:

a) Inida's sovereignty over the entire of Jammu & Kashmir including Pakistan-occupied Kashmir.

b) That it will not accept any interference in our country's internal affairs.

(5) BJP will ascertain that Inida's relation with the USA will be based on mutual repect and congruence of interests. It will bring reforms to India's current USA policy which suffers from lack of vision disregarding India's political

and security interests.

(6) India and Russia have a long tradition of good relations and have much to gain from compatibility of mutual geo-politcal interests in Asia. The BJP will endeavour to further explore avenues of bilateral cooperation in this direction.

(7) BJP will try to avail itself of the opportunity, if voted to power, to improve India's present good relations with People's Republic of China, putting them on firm footing of friendship and cooperation. For this goal it is necessary the border disput existing between the two countries be resolved in fair and equitable manner, which BJP will strive to do. However, there is deterrence, like China's persistent support of Pakistan militarily and otherwise.

(8) BJP sincerely regrets continuing bloodshed in Sri Lanka, though India througout its history enjoyed fraternal ties with all sections of people in that country. It, therefore, will pursue its conviction that aspirations of Tamil people can best be realised in a untied Sri Lanka.

(9) BJP welcomes restoration of democracy in Nepal, the neighbour with whom India is united both religiously, culturally and historically. It is BJP's determination to foster our relation with Nepal economically and socially weeding out all irritants over outstanding issues.

(10) BJP will extend its support to reconciliation and reconstruction in neighbouring Myanmar with whom India has a long border and ageold religious, cultural and historical ties.

(11) BJP will try to consolidate further the existing close and friendly relations with Bhutan and India.

(12) BJP holds illegal immigration into India from Bangladesh is a major irritant. This issue has cast its shadow on the bilateral ties between the two countries. This problem needs to be solved immediately.

(13) Non-Resident Indians settled overseas are assets of the

country. Their deepemotional attachment to their motherland must find a proper expression. BJP will examine afresh the issue of dual citizenship for them, and schemes will be drawn up to attract substantial investments. They will also be welcomed to set up industrial units and industrial parks and invest in the infrastructure.

(14) BJP will launch vigorous campaign for a permanent membership for India in the UN Security Council.

(15) BJP is committed to peace among all nations, prosperity for all people of the world, and for India an international role that befits this great nation with ancient heritage.

COMMITMENT TO NATIONAL SECURITY

BJP will correct damaging imbalances caused by present Congress government under Mr Narasimha Rao and will appoint a permanent Defence minister, do everything to update and improve combat effectiveness of our security forces and will accord due importance to all security related issues—according to emerging global realities and regional complexities.

Internal Security:

(1) BJP will restore national commitment to its rightful place by establishing harmonious relations between state and the society, so that citizens' allegiance to the nation be restored and firm. BJP will make its government sensitive to their problems and caring for them.

(2) It will defuse tension in long-festering trouble spots.

(3) It will ensure its government do everything for protection of life and property from insurgents and foreign mercenaries.

(4) It will provided our security apparatus with free hand to deal with terrorism.

(5) It will revitalise and reinforce law and order machinery.

(6) It will institute the police reforms and upgrade the capability of the force, and

(7) It will legislate tough deterrent laws against terrorist and disruptive activities while safeguarding democratic rights.

Jammu & Kashmir

(1) BJP realises the magnitude of the challenge from the situation arising from the strategic border state of Jammu & Kashmir and dedicates itself to the task of not only solving the internal problems of the state but also reclaiming the portion of Indian territory illegally held by Pakistan for nearly five years.

(2) It will immediately strengthen the civil administration by inducting capable and honest administrators.

(3) It will provide free hand to the security forces to deal with menace of terrorism, induction of men and arms from Pakistan and also ensure that democratic rights of the genuine citizens are not violated.

(4) It will cleanse the local police and administration of the malcontents who have aligned themselves with the terrorists and are pro-Pakistani.

(5) It will declare Doda as a Disturbed Area and invoke the Armed Forces (Special Powers) Act to prevent this district from becoming a haven for mercenaries and terrorists.

(6) It will launch massive welfare programme for all regions of the state, and ensure that there be no seepage.

(7) It will rehabilitate all persons displaced from terrorism-afflicted areas of Jammu & Kashmir.

(8) It will set up regional councils for Kashmir, Jammu and Ladakh.

North-East:

(1) BJP will address itself to the problems of north-eastern States and institute a grievance redressal cell monitored

from New Delhi.

(2) Check inflow of foreign arms and terrorist from training camps across the border.

(3) Strengthen the security apparatus and intelligence network.

(4) Provide the citizens with identity cards on priority basis.

(5) It will check the narcotics trade and attendant ills in the region.

(6) It will plan and execute an integral and accelerated economic development programme.

Himalayas:

(1) BJP will strive to regain our lost initiative in this strategic Himalayan bastion.

(2) BJP will evolve a security policy for the Himalayas so that India's national interests are fully safeguarded.

External Security:

(1) BJP will evolve pro-active defence diplomacy, a policy that would enable India adequately prepare against foreign aggression.

(2) For that purpose a National Security Council will be set up.

(3) BJP will re-evaluate the country's nuclear policy and exercise the option to induct nuclear weapons.

(4) BJP is committed to nuclear-free world, and cannot accept a world of nuclear apartheid. Therefore:

a) BJP will not agree to Comprehensive Test Ban Treaty (CTBT) unless there is simultaneous agreement for a time-bound global elimination of nuclear weapons in their entirety.

b) The BJP will not agree to the Fissile Material Technology Control Regime (FMCR).

c) The BJP will not agree to the Missile Technology

Control Regime, (MTCR), too.

(4) It will expedite the serial production of Prithvi missile and make Agni-I operational for the deployment of these missile. In addition to that BJP will hasten the development of Agni-II also.

(5) It will immediately upgrade conventional weapons systems of the armed forces.

(6) Strengthen the intelligence gathering system, inclusive of all intelligence agencies, initiate a Centre-State initiatives on intelligence gathering and sharing, step up air surveillance of our country and acquire the state of the art electronic equipment.

(7) Strengthen the Air Force fleet with new generation aircraft.

(8) BJP will make qualitative and quantitative improvement in our naval capabilities.

(9) It will invest in R&D in areas of defence and missile technology so that we become increasingly self-reliant.

(10) BJP will peg defence-related expenditure to real requirements.

(11) BJP will re-examine the role, structure and composition of the numerous para-military forces and reorganise and reform them.

JAI JAWAN

For our valiant soldiers engaged in defence of our nation, BJP has prospective programmes.

(1) BJP will improve the terms of service, including pay and allowance, housing education for children and pension, of all ranks which eventually attract the persons of high calibre. BJP does not want that present shortage of men and officers have to be met by lowering standards of entry.

(2) It will give higher benefits to widows and dependents of Jawans who die in action and higher compensation.

(3) It will levellised pension disparities and anomalies sorted out expeditiously.

(4) BJP will set up hospitals for veterans throughout the country, so that no ex-service persons irrespective of his/her rank is denied medical care.

(5) Ex-servicemen's welfare will be included in the concurrent list.

(6) BJP thinks that services of ex-servicemen will be used to the maximum extent possible, especially in insurgency-affected areas. Wherever there is a stipulated percentage for employing ex-servicemen, it will be fulfilled.

(7) It will make necessary changes in agricultural and urban tenancy laws to secure the proprietary rights of servicemen.

(8) BJP will strengthen the district Sainik Boards.

DEMOGRAPHIC INVASION - THREAT TO SECURITY

BJP is worried by the demographic invasion of the country form illegal immigrants, mostly from Bangladesh. It believes that has direct impact on India's security, transforming the geography, sociology, economy and indeed on the politics of the nation. It will, if voted to power:

(1) complete the barbed wire fencing along the Indo-Bangladesh border starting from the plains so that infiltration can be prevented;

(2) detect the illegal immigrants, delete their names from the voters' lists and deport them without any further delay;

(3) declare all property deals between Indians and the illegal immigrants as null and void;

(4) amend the immigration rules and other laws to impose stringent checks on illegal entry into India; and,

(5) expedite issuance of identity cards to all citizens of India.

POLICIES TOWARDS VILLAGES, FARMERS AND THE POOR

BJP has great agenda for the farmers and the poor populace of the country, which might dawn a new phase of understanding among people away from erstwhile policies of the government during the last five decades. BJP promises to allocate greater resources for effective poverty alleviation programmes. It will invest, as already emphasized in its economic programmes, more in agriculture and small-scale industries, build up from the bottom up which, it thinks, is the only way how it can build an enduring edifice of development. Its programmes, if voted to power, will be as under:

(1) It will allocate 60 per cent of fund from Plans for agriculture and rural development.

(2) It will treat villages as the basic unit of development and provide each village with basic facilities like roads, irrigation, drinking water, education, health and sanitation.

(3) It will provide shelters for the homeless in rural areas.

(4) It will develop agriculture, enhance production and improve living standards in our villages by:

   a) fixing agricultural prices after taking into amount all expenses incurred by farmers;
   b) reducing per acre cost of production;
   c) increasing average per acre production;
   d) reducing overall dependence on agriculture;
   e) providing alternative employment to displaced farmers.

(5) BJP will gives agriculture the same benefits as industry.

(6) It will set up an Agricultural Costs and Prices Commission in which farmers and agricultural specialists will together comprise two-third of the members. The Commission will be autonomous and its recommendations

will be binding.

(7) BJP will announce total cost of inputs, the total expenditure incurred by farmers, and thereafter announce the support prices.

(8) It will link support prices to the price index.

(9) It will ensure a parity between agriculture and industrial products in respect of pricing.

(10) It will conduct extensive research to evolve methods of dryland farming.

(11) It will give priorities to farmers interests while determining the eximp policy for agricultural produce.

(12) BJP will enforce prompt payment for the agricultural produce. There will be automatic interest addition to payments delayed more than two weeks.

(13) It will extend crop and animal insurance to all agricultural produce. The insurance schemes will be organised to cover the natural calamities.

(14) It will establish a chain of warehouses with facilities for grant of advance payment of upto 80 per cent of the agricultural produce deposited.

(15) Encouragement will be given by the party, if it comes to wield power, to use fruit juice in the production of all beverages.

(16) It will allow free movements of food grains throughout the country.

(17) BJP will free the sugar industry from the system of licensing, and also remove all restrictions for production of molasses. At the same time it will ensure that farmers receive the adequate share of total prices.

(18) BJP will maintain the subsidy to the farmers.

(19) It will establish the farmers' service centres.

(20) BJP will improve the Public Distribution System.

(21) It will give comprehensive documents to the farmers that would cover land records, ownership and all other

relevant papers.

(22) It will reform the land acquisition laws and ensure that agricultural land receives prompt and full compensation at market rates.

(23) BJP will free bonded labour and rehabilitate them.

(24) It will launch employment guarantee schemes in rural areas of the country that will cover the largest possible number of people.

To revive village industry:

(25) BJP will establish an extensive chain of tiny and small-scale industrial units.

(26) BJP will sharpen the agricultural edge of agro-based rural industries and food-processing.

(27) It will provide all facilities, including easy access to credit and marketing to rural artisans and craftsmen.

(28) It will set up national Artisan Development Bank.

(29) It will set up special institute for skill upgradation.

(30) It will give thrust to wasteland development, social forestry and horticulture.

To Provide Facilities on Irrigation:

(1) BJP will launch time-bound irrigation project and complete the ongoing ones.

(2) It will give priority to the small and minor irrigation projects.

(3) It will remove disparities between districts with States.

(4) BJP will encourage the use of alternative sources of irrigation through incentives and better water management.

(5) BJP will ensure that farmers are made to pay only the water they consume.

(6) It will draw up a master plan for food control and harnessing for food waters for irrigation. It will offer

prompt compensation for crops lost in floods.

To Provide Power for Agriculture:

(1) BJP will encourage rapid electrification of our villages so that no village is left without power by the turn of the century.

(2) It will ensure adequate supply of power for agricultural activity.

(3) It will set up power stations and sub-stations in rural areas for supplying power exclusively to villages.

(4) BJP will make the electric board to make compensation if they fail to supply assured quantity of power. At the same time BJP will insist that farmers pay the electricity bill in time.

To Strengthen the Cooperative Movement:

(1) It will free cooperatives from political interference.

(2) Prevent intrusion of the vested interest.

(3) BJP will simplify the rules and regulations governing the function of the cooperative societies.

(4) It will make entry in passbooks mandatory for all money deposits, which is not a regular practice today.

(5) It will see that only those exclusively dependent on agriculture be members of farmers' cooperative societies.

(6) BJP will ensure free and timely elections to cooperative bodies.

To Implement Land Reforms:

(1) BJP will enforce implementation of Land Ceiling Laws in all States.

(2) It will set up designated courts to speed up expeditiously all the land ceiling disputes and monitor enforcement of verdicts.

(3) It will expedite distribution of ceiling surplus lands among the landless farmers.

(4) It will monitor the distribute lands and prevent its alienation from beneficiaries.

(5) Reclaiming cultivable land lying fallow is BJP's firm determination.

(6) It will ensure time-bound registration of all lands.

7) It will decide ownership rights at all level of Gram Panchayats without any delay.

To alleviate Poverty:

(1) It will enhance public outlays for poverty alleviation and social infrastructure.

(2) It will restructure the Public Distribution System, as is already declared above, confining it only to the poor and the needy. It is noted that despite burgeoning foodstock availability, the offtake has been vastly reduced and the per capita consumption of cereals has been further declined. This is not the sign of inflation indices, the talk of which is rather misleading. On the contrary, it is the sign of poverty. BJP will suitably adjust PDS prices, and regulate the intervals of the offtake so that the scheme become meaningful for the needy. At the same time, BJP will make the PDS dovetailed to provide 'Food for Work' in employment programmes linked with poverty eradication.

(3) BJP will identify poverty through indexation reflecting not only the level of consumption of the calories but also the minimal social infrastructure status as literacy, housing, drinking water, health and sanitation.

(4) BJP will introduce "Antyodaya" schemes throughout the country because it believes sustainable employment is at the core of poverty eradication. The "Antyodaya" will be targeted at the poorest of the poor. Five crore families will be selected for immediate relief.

(5) BJP will allocate more resources for 'Food for Work' programmes that they can be implemented round the year, as well as, monitor their implementation.

(6) It will introduce Langar Yojana and Annadan Yojana to ensure that no man, woman or child goes hungry in India.

POLICIES ON TALENTS IN SCIENCE AND TECHNOLOGY

BJP will use the science for benefit of the poor and encourage to develop technologies which have humane face. Towards this end, it will:

1) foster scientific temperament among people;
2) use science and technology for increasing productivity and generating employment;
3) implement vigorous programme of science education and research for improving quality of life;
4) establish a network of centres for application of science and technology to rural areas, implement "Lab to Land" programmes and develop low-cost agro-industrial base;
5) put new life into National Laboratories making them centres of excellence in applied research;
6) direct these laboratories to evolve appropriate technologies for Indian need;
7) accelerate production of scientific literatures in regional languages and evolve national terminology for science and technology;
8) create right working condition for our best brains to remain in India to serve the nation and not migrate to other lands;
9) make organised efforts bringing national laboratories and industry together to set up "Technology Parks" that would be patronised by the Industries sector. This would harness both resources and talents.
10) Encourage research and development by safeguarding national interests and intellectual property rights;
11) BJP will organise researches in the fields of drugs, microbiology, bio-technology, bio-fertilisers and others;

12) BJP will at the same time give impetus to researches in indigenous systems of medicine.

POLICY TOWARDS POPULATION CONTROL

BJP is seriously worried about present population problems in the country. An increasing population means decreasing share of fruits of development—a reality the successive Congress governments ignored repeatedly just to foster petty political advantage and, gains thereby, in successive elections.

(1) BJP proposes to act upon the National Development Council reports and the Swaminathan Committee to formulate a National Population Policy which will stabilise the population growth by the first decade of the oncoming century.

(2) It will enact laws that will debar the candidature, for an elected office, of the person who will have more than two children. For that the cut-off year will be 1996.

(3) The economically weaker people who would opt for two-children norm will be given special facilities for health, education, nutrition and employment opportunities.

(4) At the same time the BJP will introduce disincentives like limiting subsidised ration and maternity benefits to two children with 1996 as cut-off year.

(5) These disincentives will apply to people of all sections of the society irrespective of social, economic or religious status, with a purpose to discourage large, unsustainable families.

(6) BJP will ensure access to family planning information and quality facilities by involving non-government organisations. It will promote awareness among people especially women through counselling and educational programmes.

(7) BJP will introduce family planning methods and facilities that will allow women greater freedom of choice without

imperilling their health.

(8) BJP will launch a special campaign to educate local communities about negative practice and encourage women to seek reproductive health services.

(9) BJP will offer a special incentive of a fixed deposit that will mature in 21 years for the couple who has only one girl child or such couple who would adopt one girl child under "Dattak Putri Yojana".

(10) BJP will make the family planning programmes the nation's integral part of development and would ensure widest applicability of these incentives and disincentives.

POLICY TOWARDS HEALTH AND WEALTH

To creat a productive workforce by the beginning of the new century, BJP will endeavour a programme 'health for all'.

(1) It will do everything to end scourge of malnutrition.

(2) It would spend more on pre-natal and post-natal health care programmes and thereby check infant mortality and under-five mortality.

(3) It will immunize every child against killer diseases.

(4) BJP will provide every panchayat with a free primary health care centre each with facilities for mother and child care, also access to these centres.

(5) BJP will canalise substantial portion of health care allocation on preventive rather than curative aspects.

(6) It will promote awareness on cleanliness and disease prevention.

(7) Re-evaluate existing programmes on sexually transmitted diseases, and specially AIDS. It will make screening of blood at blood banks mandatory, violation of which would invite severe punishment.

(8) It will hold doctors, para-medical and non-medical staff at government hospitals, health centres accountable; and

also institute mechanism for quick disposal of complaints.

(9) Revising the pay scale and emoluments of the staff in all these hospitals and centres will be BJP's regular endeavour to attract the best of the talents.

(10) Alternative medical services will be promoted, especially one like Ayurveda and Unani medicines.

(11) It will endeavour to protect traditional medicinal herbs and plants.

(12) BJP will prevent drug prices escalate to a point where they become unaffordable for the masses.

(13) It will introduce health insurance schemes at a minimal cost to the subscriber.

(14) It will also institute a mechanism to monitor and collate health-related information.

POLICY ON EDUCATION

(1) BJP will make education spread to the grassroots level, providing equal opportunity of education, literacy and information.

(2) It will increase state spending on education progressively to six per cent at least of the GNP (Gross National Product).

(3) It will provide free education in order to universalise access to education.

(4) It will offer incentives like free text books, nutrition programmes and stipends to check dropout rates so as to get at least 80 per cent of enrolled children complete primary education.

(5) It will reduce learning period and introduce self-employment oriented vocational training programmes at high school level.

(6) It will introduce anti-cheating law throughout the country and devise preventive methods of its abuse.

(7) It will launch community-level adult education at func-

tional Level to cover 90 per cent of illiterate adults in villages and cities.

8) It will set up special monitoring authority to scrutinize quality of education and remove gender disparity

9) It will ensure autonomy to universities, encourage them mobilize resources for research and higher education and provide, academic freedom to scholars, especially in social sciences.

10) It will improve pay and emoluments of teachers at all levels and remove anomalies in college/university promotion rules.

11) It will enrol industry's help to set up more technical and agro-industrial institutions that will provide affordable education.

12) BJP will abolish system of capitation fees and monitor institutes' functioning, especially that of medical and engineering colleges.

13) BJP will launch low-interest bank loan scheme for meritorious students desirous of higher education.

14) It will thwart attempts by foreign universities, colleges and institutes of dubious reputation to open branches in India and thus would prevent foreign exchange outflow on studies abroad, unless the course is relevant to Indian needs.

BJP's SOCIAL PHILOSOPHY: SC, ST, OBCs, MINORITIES, HUMAN RIGHTS, HUMANITY SEEKING POLITICAL ASYLUM

(1) BJP will uphold principles and goals of equity and equality as enshrined in our country's Constitution, and would abide by the ideals.

(2) It will promote a casteless society on socio-economic order which will effectively provide access to equal opportunities to all citizens irrespective of caste, creed, religion and gender.

(3) The BJP will ensure that the place of an individual in society will not be determined on the basis of his birth.

(4) The BJP will dismantle practices, customs, beliefs, usages and institutions which are divisive and discriminatory, and which in any manner hurt the dignity of the individual.

(5) It condemns the practice of untouchability which is not only against the law of the land but runs counter to the very concept of integral humanity.

(6) The BJP will endeavour to create an ethos of equality in social and inter-personal relationships.

(7) It will make the existing provisions in the Constitution for the safeguards of the Scheduled Castes and the Scheduled Tribes more effectively operational.

(8) BJP will continue with the existing policies of special facilities and special opportunities, like reservation policy, enshrined in the Constitution till social and economic equity is achieved. Reservation policy will be backed up with a statute.

(9) It will stringently enforce the law against untouchability.

(10) It will inquire all cases of atrocities, publish the findings, punish the guilty and rehabilitate the victims as expeditiously as possible.

(11) It will lay stress on education, vocational training and skill upgradation.

(12) Take prompt action to fill up the backlog of jobs reserved for Scheduled Castes and Scheduled Tribes.

(13) BJP will set up a financial agency on the lines of NABARD to cater to the individual and institutional credit needs of the Scheduled Castes and the Scheduled Tribes.

(14) It will provide more facilities so that members of the SC, ST can participate increasingly greater in number in areas of small-scale and cottage industries, rural in-

dustries and also in trade and commerce.

(15) BJP will end the pernicious practice of carrying the night soil and accelerate the rehabilitation of the scavengers.

(16) It will eradicate the evil of bonded and child labour and rehabilitate the victims.

(17) It will launch the massive housing programmes for the homeless in villages.

(18) It will allot pattas for land, home site and homes in the name of the wives or widow or daughters.

(19) It will take necessary steps to protect the tribals from exploitation, especially by contractors, and indebtedness.

(20) It will amend the existing forest policy to restore to the *Vanbasis* their rightful share of forest wealth and produce and provide viable marketing facilities.

(21) It will expedite the processing of claims of *Vanvasis* and *Girijans* for pattas in forest and hill areas.

(22) It will strictly disallow diversion of money from the Plan and Tribal sub-Plan funds which are meant for the development of *Vanvasis* and the *Girijans*.

(23) It will prevent land alienation through conversation of tribal lands for industrial and other purposes.

(24) It will formulate and implement a National Policy for the rehabilitation of families displaced by development projects. BJP has envisioned this rehabilitation policy in multi-dimensional perspectives and not merely to provide financial compensation or means of livelihood. BJP looks at it with a principle of "total rehabilitation" which would include social, economic, educational, environmental, occupational and cultural aspects.

(25) BJP will encourage setting up of inter-State regional coordination councils to implement a common welfare programmes for the tribals living in contiguous area of neighbouring States.

(26) The Party will also erect befitting Memorial of Maharshi

Valmiki and Babasaheb Ambedkar in the National Capital.

POLICY FOR SOCIALLY AND ECONOMICALLY BACKWARD CLASSES (OBCS)

(1) BJP would continue social and economic justice through instruments like Reservations. However, it does not believe that path of progress can be brought by social divisions through such casteist policies, but through progress by social harmony. It will therefore continue the Reservations until they are socially and educationally integrated with the rest of the society.

(2) It will naturally institute a uniform criteria for determination of the "creamy layer".

(3) It will ensure the flow of reservation on the basis of ascending order so that the most backward sections of the OBCs get them first.

(4) It will institute 10 per cent reservation to all the economically weaker sections of the society, apart from the Scheduled Castes and Scheduled Tribes and the OBCs.

(5) It will ensure special programmes to provide education and vocational training as well as awareness campaigns.

(6) BJP also believes those who have been excluded from playing a participatory role in the nation-building process owing to being "disabled", should be empowered so that they become productive and proud citizens of the country.

(7) It will order a special survey to find our exact numbers of such people, nature of their disability.

(8) It will use this data to formulated policies aimed at empowerment rather than merely welfare.

(9) It will actively campaign to remove social prejudices.

(10) It will sensitise the bureaucrats to the needs and aspira-

tions of the disabled.

(11) It will provide employment in all suitable categories of Government service through the policy of equal opportunity.

(12) BJP will give incentives to private sector to provide disabled people with job opportunities.

(13) BJP will offer medical, counselling and rehabilitation facilities at the health centres and will increase budgetary allocation for the purpose. It would also encourage the State Government to make matching contribution.

(14) It will also ensure that the disabled get access to public utilities and services.

Policy Towards the Minorities:

BJP is steadfastly opposed to the appeasement policy of the State since it benefits only those section of the people who profess regressive and retrograde, social norms in the guise of protecting their religious beliefs. BJP will be guided by the policy of justice for all, appeasement to none". A resurgent India will enter the 21st century with the resolve of one nation, one people and one culture.

(1) BJP will guarantee all minority community equal opportunities for economic development.

(2) It will lay stress on education and vocational training.

(3) It will provide incentives to those who are self- employment especially artisans, and those who want to set up their own business enterprise.

(4) BJP will launch community programmes to create awareness among women members of the minority communities.

(5) It will ensure quality for all, will discriminate against none, on grounds of religion or in matters of education, by Amending Article 30.

(6) Disband the Minority Commission and entrust its responsibilities to National Human Rights Commission.

(7) BJP will set up special courts to speedy trial of those accused of participating in communal riots.

(8) It will protect the Wakf property from being misused and usurped by unscrupulous individuals and organisations and help Wakf boards to become self-sustaining bodies so that they do not have to depend on Government doles.

(9) It will set up trust along the line of Tirupati Temple Trust with official nominees for managing the affairs of the dargah.

(10) It will ensure that no religious property is misused or usurped.

(11) BJP will ban all foreign funds irrespective of the organisation which is recepient.

(12) BJP will declare fraudulent conversation a punishable offence. Even those conversions made on the promise of economic and social benefits, will be held punishable offence. BJP will introduce a system of registering all conversions.

(13) BJP will ban all publication of job advertisements that mention religious identity as a criterion.

(14) BJP will set up a Commission of Inquiry (similar to the Neogi Commission) which will enquire into the activities of the foreign missionaries and other organisations that have been receiving foreign funds.

POLICIES TOWARDS HUMAN RIGHTS

The BJP subscribes to the view that human dignity, justice and protection for all from the tyranny of the State is the basic tenets of the *Hindutva*. BJP is committed to upholding human, democratic and civil rights of every individual, irrespective of the person's caste, creed and religion or gender. But it will not allow this commitment to be used as a shield by those who commit inhuman atrocities and thus forsake their claim for the human rights. The BJP believes that State should be fair to all citizens, but firm while dealing with those who militate against the civil society. At the same time BJP will not allow any foreign interference in our country's internal affairs on the pretext of monitoring human rights violations.

(1) BJP will strengthen the existing National Human Rights Commission with more powers. It will also provide the commission additional resources and better infrastructure.

(2) It will disband the Minorities Commission which has so far only succeeded in feeding separatist sentiments and giving rise to imagined grievances, and entrust its responsibilities to the National Human Rights Commission.

(3) It will take swift action on the basis of the Commission's findings and punish the guilty.

(4) It will include the study of the human, democratic and civil rights in school curricula.

Displaced Communities: Protecting their Rights

Keeping in view the separatist violence and Islamic fundamentalism and terrorism in Jammu and Kashmir that has displaced more than 3,00,000 people (of whom 2,50,000 are Kashmiri Pandits alone and the others comprise Punjabi and Dorgri Hindus and a few Muslim families), BJP has resolved decisive policies. If examined properly, these people indeed form the largest internally displaced community world over. Who are rendered homeless within their own State. BJP has mobilised its own men and material to provide succour to these unfortunate victims. They are also victims of the Government apathy and incorrect policies, the Party feels.

Similar problems are with the Chakma refugees from Chittagong Hill Tracts of Bangladesh who had to flee their country under persecution of Muslim settlers in their areas from the plains, and who eventually took shelter in Tripura. Despite their grim future at home, Government of India has shown unnecessary haste in trying to repatriate them. BJP opposes this hasty repatriation.

Demographic imbalance has also caused in South India as a large number of Tamil refugees has started entering India due to escalating conflict between LTTE and the Sri Lankan military. Problems of Indians settled abroad is further exposed with the bleak future of such Indians in Hong Kong, after Britain hands that territory over to China in 1997. BJP, therefore, proposes following programmes :

For Kashmiri Pandits

(1) BJP would designate the Pandits who have been forced out of the Valley as internally displaced community.
(2) It will provide adequate financial relief, proper health care, housing, education and employment facilities on priority basis to all displaced families.
(3) It will take adequate steps to protect their assets and properties in Kashmir Valley till such time they are able to return home.
(4) Elections in the Valley should be held only after the displaced people return to their homes, it believes.
(5) It will ensure proper documentation of the displaced Pandits, and their assets.

For Chakmas

(1) It will resettle the Chakma refugees in different camps in other contiguous States, as their conglomeration in one State is giving heavy economic pressure on the State.
(2) Provision of financial help to the respective State governments should be given, and BJP will do that if it comes to power.
(3) BJP will provide full citizenship to those Chakmas who donot want to return there, and whose children are born

in India.

(4) BJP will negotiate with Bangladesh for phased repatriation of those Chakmas who want to return, provided Dhaka guarantees their safety and well-being.

(5) It will ensure full security for the Chakmas who live in refugee camps so that they are not harassed or threatened.

(6) It will maintain an official register of Chakma refugees and their whereabouts.

For Sri Lankan Tamil Refugees

(1) BJP will house them in refugee camps and monitor their movements.

(2) It will prevent their association with the local organisations or opening local chapters of Sri Lankan organisations.

(3) It will screen the antecedents of the Tamil refugees and disallow asylum to those who have or had links with Tamil terrorists.

(4) It will maintain a register of all such refugees.

(5) It will repatriate Tamil refugees as soon as the situation is conducive for their safe-being.

For Non-Resident Indians

(1) BJP will provide citizenship to those Hong Kong based Indians who would like to return to their motherland.

(2) It will help rehabilitate the returning Hong Kong Indians.

(3) It will examine afresh difficulties in granting dual citizenship to non-resident Indians all over the world.

POLICY ON ENVIRONMENT

ENVIRONMENT, according to Bharatiya Janata Party, is the protector of nation's security, as much as it sustains a multitude of lives through our rivers, forests and skies. BJP is duty-bound to protect the environmental sanctity, and upholds the concept of "sustainable development", which indeed is the philosophical tenets that is integral to our civilizational and cultural consciousness. Hence, BJP will:

(1) Introduce a National Environment Policy incorporating a healthy balance between development needs and preservation of natural resources. The interests of and consultations with the respective States will be fully ensured.

(2) To implement the policy BJP will recast the ministry of Environment and Forests as the Ministry for Ecological Security.

(3) It will control land, air and water pollution by industry and urban centres. Municipal sewage treatment plants will be made obligatory.

(4) It will formulate a programme for developing sustainable cities, with special emphasis to waste management and use of natural resources like water.

(5) BJP will make environment studies a part of the school, college and university curriculum and make environment issues an integral part of the visual media so that our children develop a caring and protective attitude towards ecological system that sustains life.

(6) It will protect traditional and other rights of the *Vanvasis* and *Girijans* over forest resources and produce.

(7) It will involve local self-governments at all levels, both in village and cities, in implementing the national policy.

(8) It will provide easy access to information on conservation and sustainable use of natural resources.

(9) It will ban import of hazardous chemical wastes for recycling by any industry or for dumping.

(10) Minimise the use of non-biodegradable material for packaging by the consumer non-durable product industry.

(11) It will restrain the conversion of forests or grazing areas for other purposes.

(12) It will adopt afforestation policies to be fulfilled within a given time-frame and prevent the degradation of forests by natural or man-made causes. The cornerstone of the BJP's forest policy will be a part of the total framework of land management, adoption of a dynamic programme of productivity forestry from total State management of forests. A programme will also be drawn up for conversion of degraded forests, waste land and marginal land into quality forests.

(13) It will deny offshore exploitation offshore resources, especially marine life, by big trawlers.

(14) It will promote R&D in environment related studies and eco-technology for application in agriculture, industry and services sectors.

(15) BJP will provide incentives to manufacturers of eco-friendly products.

(16) It will not sanction tourism related projects that disturb the environment and cause degradation.

POLICY TOWARDS WOMEN ISSUES

BJP believes "Nari Shakti" is just not a rhetoric to appease a vote bank. It has objective policy towards women issues, and for the sustenance of rights of the girl child. The BJP, therefore, will happily endeavour to do the following:

(1) It will encourage gender sensitivity and end every discrimination against women. Hence, all its national policies will be subjected to gender analysis.

(2) It will reserve 33 per cent seats in all elected bodies, including State Assemblies and Parliament. It wants to groom up the women participants in a resurgent India of the 21 century.

(3) It will actively promote the legal and economic rights of women which must be equal to those of men and not subject to the debilitating clauses of personal laws.

(4) BJP will introduce a Uniform Civil Code that will:

i) Give women property rights;

ii) ensure women's rights to adopt;

iii) guarantee women equal guardianship rights;

iv) remove discriminatory clauses in divorce laws;

v) put an end to polygamy.

(5) It will create conditions in society and work place to ensure equal opportunities in employment and promotion, and end sexual harassment.

(6) It will enforce the principle of equal wages for equal work whether in the organised or unorganised sector.

(7) It will evolve a scheme for part-time job for the women.

(8) It will promote a health care system that will focus on the non-reproductive health needs of women, especially in rural areas.

(9) It will provide state supports for single and working mothers through grants and subsidy, and formulate a forward looking housing policy to help women.

(10) It will make women partners in the management of community assets and properties.

(11) It will set up micro-credit system with the help of a national corpus to which both the Union and State governments, apart from banks, will contribute.

(12) It will encourage setting up of cooperative societies in rural areas to be managed by women and to benefit women entrepreneures.

(13) It will introduce skill-based training programmes and employment schemes which are area-specific.

(14) It will enrol the help of the local governments to set up latrines for women in the rural areas.

(15) It will design special programmes for women of functional literacy.

(16) It will amend laws dealing with molestation, rape and dowry to provide for in-camera trial, swift justice and

tough deterrent punishment as well as rehabilitation of the victims of these crimes.

(17) BJP will amend the Prevention of Immoral Traffic Act to make the client as culpable as commercial sex workers.

(18) The party will rehabilitate the commercial sex workers and set up a special fund to provide health care and education to their children.

(19) It will enact laws that will make registration of marriages with foreigners mandatory.

(20) BJP will make it compulsory that mother's name also be mentioned in all Government and non-Government records, starting from a child's birth certificate to a parent's death certificate.

(21) It will set up designated courts in every district for expeditious trial of civil and criminal complaints relating to women.

(22) BJP will rapidly induct more women in police force and appoint them in senior positions as well as set up a "Crime Against Women Cell" in every police station.

(23) It will set up a special law to deal with crimes of domestic violence to women.

(24) BJP will promote a social agenda designed to discourage negative influences and end discrimination against the girl child in any form.

(25) It will ruthlessly punish them who will indulge in unethical practices with regard to child-birth, like pre-natal sex determination test, or female foeticide or infanticide.

(26) BJP will invest in girl child's health, nutrition and education from infancy to through adolescence.

(27) It will universalise primary and secondary education to narrow the gender gap and offer incentives for the girl child's education in the form of free uniforms and books.

(28) BJP will strictly enforce age of consent laws and end

child prostitution.

(29) BJP will have a fresh look at the UN Convention for elimination of Discrimination Against Women (CEDAW) to determine whether the reservations expressed by the Government of India are justified.

TOWARDS INDIAN IDENTITY

BJP will redefine concept of development and modernization after accommodating the Bharatiya way of life, belief system and values to reach ultimate goal of *Bharatiyata.* It believes cultural factors play an important role in energising a nation. For resurgent India, therefore, whose people can flaunt proudly their *Bharatiyata* BJP will:

(1) strengthen and revitalise India's cultural traditions and values;

(2) revive and rejuvenate our positive cultural relations and values;

(3) establish a Bharatiya Sanskriti Kendra in each district;

(4) include Indian cultural studies and "Naitik Shiksha" as part of school curriculum;

(5) declare all places of pilgrimage as national heritage centre;

(6) encourage study of Sanskrit and strictly enforce three language formula in schools;

(7) promote Bharatiya classical music and performing arts through state support;

(8) discourage indecent representation of women in advertisements and publications.

POLICY TOWARDS MEDIA AND PUBLISHING

BJP believes that Press in sine qua non in Democracy, yet it is necessary for proper face of democracy that this freedom do not get misused to defame or malign any individual, organisation or institution. For free, fair and fearless Press, BJP will:

(1) expedite the recommendations and implementation of wage board set up for journalists and non-journalists as well as evolve a mechanism for the automatic institution of a wage board for journalists every five years;

(2) free All India Radio and Doordarshan from Government control and implement Prasar Bharati Act;

(3) ensure that no book or publication is banned without proper scrutiny;

(4) disallow foreign print media to launch Indian editions;

(5) evolve a comprehensive visual media policy for uplinking facilities and transmission via our satellite transponders;

(6) review the practice of contracted jobs in newspaper;

(7) strengthen the Press Council for speedy and fair disposal of complaints;

(8) review the practice of contracted jobs in newspapers?

(9) consider the legislation of a "Right to Reply" law which will enable any person who has been unfairly vilified to publish his or her version.

POLICY TOWARDS CINEMA

BJP is worried to find that sex and violence on the screen are beginning to gnaw at the moorings of our cultural ethos. To check this abuse of popular cinema, the BJP will:

(1) provide film-making the status of industry so that production can be made accountable for their resources and expenses;

(2) enable film-makers, through suitable provisions in law, raise resources from financial institutions to curb the influence of underworld financiers and mafia don;

(3) analogues to the concept of the Customs' "green channel" provide automatic certification for films which do not

contain explicit scenes and dialogues of violence and sex—producers and exhibitors of such films will not have to queue in for Censor Board clearance. Deterrent punishment will be meted out to any producer who abuses the facility; theatre owners who screen such films will also be penalised;

(4) exempt quality films, which will be certified as 'Q' from entertainment tax;

(5) encourage viewers to form local Darshak Sanghs — on the lines of consumer organizations — to monitor the quality of films being screened in their area;

(6) set up special theatres at district headquarters and metropolitan cities for screening art and quality films;

(7) appoint 50 per cent women on the Censor Board and Censor Panels;

(8) create a special fund for promoting regional cinema;

(9) introduce legislation to ensure minimum wages and retirement benefits for film extras and crew members.

POLICY ABOUT YOUTH

BJP aims at transforming Yuva Sankalpa into Yuva Shakti, which in turn will be the catalyst for reinvigorating India. Towards this end BJP will:

(1) inculcate in youth the sense of indebtedness to the society and, therefore, involving them in the nationa-building process through development programmes in social cultural and economic activities; which is how they can repay their debt;

(2) initiate schemes both at governmental and non-governmental levels to achieve overall development of young talent;

(3) mobilise the youth to fight regressive and retrograde social practices and customs by making community service a compulsory integral component of college and university curricula;

(4) set up a National Youth Commission and a Youth Development Bank to design and implement comprehensive employment oriented education policies as well channelise youth power for the purpose of nation-building;

(5) encourage the youth form "Yuva Sena" and "Dharti Raksha Vahini" for voluntary community service with the ultimate aim of generating employment;

(6) launch massive self-employment programmes to provide employment opportunities to the educated unemployment;

(7) allocate adequate time for youth programmes on Doordarshan;

(8) promote sports through enhanced expenditure on training and rehabilitation of sportspersons after they retire;

(9) establish network of youth hostels throughout the country and provide travel concession;

(10) encourage the study of yoga and promote our cultural heritage by incorporating them in educational curricula.

POLICY ABOUT RAM MANDIR

BJP is committed to the concept of one nation, one people, one culture — this is not just what is defined by its geographical and political identity, it rightly believes, it is well-explained by ancient cultural heritage. From this belief is generated the concept of Cultural Nationalism which is the genesis of *Hindutva.* That is the identity of our ancient nation *Bharatvarsha.*

Hindutva is the unifying principle which alone can preserve the unity and integrity of our nation. It is collective endeavour to protect and re-energise the soul of India, to take up into the next millennium as a strong and prosperous nation. *Hindutva* is also the anti-dote to the shameful efforts by a section of people to benefit at the expense of others.

BJP believes that only by recognizing the abundant strength of cultural nationalism, can the nation be moulded. When the BJP joined the movement for construction of Sri Ram Mandir, it was to strengthen just these foundations.

On coming to power the BJP government will facilitate the construction of a magnificent Shri Ram Mandir at Janmasthan in Ayodhya which will be a tribute to Bharat Mata. This dream moves millions of people in our land. The concept of Rama lies in the core of their consciousness.

3

Backgrounder: Indian National Congress

PREAMBLE

Election is the life-line of democracy.

An election presents a choice to the people. The choice to vote a party into government. The choice to vote a candidate to office.

What is the choice today?

The Congress presents an India with a bright future. The Opposition presents an India that will be thrown back to the past.

The Congress presents an India which is growing, creating wealth, generating jobs and providing more incomes. The Opposition presents an India which will be stagnant, inward-looking, poor and likely to become bankrupt.

The Congress presents an India which rejoices in its unity and celebrates its diversity. The Opposition presents an India that will be inflamed by caste and religious passions.

The Congress presents an India that has earned new respect among the countries of the world. The Opposition presents an India that will be ignored, ridiculed and forgotten.

The Congress presents an India with a stable Government and a vibrant economy. The Opposition presents an

India with a tottering government and collapsing economy.

Never before has the choice been so clear. Never before has the choice been so stark and simple.

I THE 1991 ELECTIONS

The nation went to the polls in 1991 to elect the Tenth Lok Sabha.

It was after a period of 16 months of darkness, drift and economic disaster.

The Indian National Congress promised the people that it will get on with the task of rebuilding India.

As the Tenth Lok Sabha convened, there was a pall of gloom. Shri Rajiv Gandhi had been snatched away cruelly. He fell victim to the most despicable act of terrorism. As in life so in his death, he upheld the causes of unity and sovereignty at home and peace and brotherhood in the world.

The Congress called upon Shri P V Narasimha Rao to shoulder the onerous responsibility of leading a Government which did not have a majority in the Lok Sabha. Shri P V Narasimha Rao, steeped in the Congress tradition of sacrifice and service, accepted the daunting task.

In his first major address to the nation, he pledged that the theme song of his government would be Continuity with Change.

Since 1991, the Congress has ushered in unprecedented change.

Never before in the history of India has so much change been wrought in so short a time. Never before in the history of the world has so much change been wrought with so little pain or suffering.

How did the Congress work this near-miracle?

II THE CONGRESS — A PARTY AND A MOVEMENT

Let us go back to that historic day when the Indian National Congress was born. The founding fathers of the Congress recognised that what the people of India needed was not a mere political party. Because no political party could unite within its fold the plurality and diversity of India.

The Indian National Congress was, therefore, cast in different mould, the mould of a national movement. Its purpose was to mobilise the Indian people into action and lead them to new frontiers.

During the freedom struggle, the goal was Independence.

During the early years of independent India, the goal was Unity and Sovereignty.

During the years of nation building, the goal was Growth with Social Justice.

After the wasted years of 1977 to 1979 and 1990 to 1991, the goal was restitution of a Government that Works.

During the period 1991 to 1995, the goal was to re-establish a Stable Government and resume the task of nation building.

It is Because of the Support of the People that

- a minority government could add to its strength and command a majority in the Tenth Lok Sabha;
- the nation could be pulled back from the brink of an economic catastrophe;
- economic reforms of an unprecedented magnitude could be unfolded;
- the pledge of ushering in Panchayati Raj could be redeemed and power given to the people;
- the world could be compelled to take note of India and her stable polity and resurgent economy.

III THE CONGRESS' RECORD

The Congress is a unique political party. It mirrors the basic ethos of a civilisation that is over 5000 years old.

It is the Congress that has created an India which is agriculturally prosperous, industrially advanced and scientifically developed. Above all, the Congress has maintained a commitment to democracy. Indeed, parliamentary democracy would not have taken roots in India and been nurtured, but for the Congress.

Many other political parties are one-issue parties. Some exploit caste. Some exploit religion. There are parties which encourage fanaticism. The Congress has always rejected these divisive issues.

The Congress reflects differing and divergent interests and reconciles them into a single harmonious national mosaic.

IV THE CONGRESS THEME : STABILITY, NATIONAL SECURITY, HARMONY AN DEVELOPMENT

The Congress Party belongs to you.

It belongs to you regardless of your caste or religion, colour or race. It belongs specially to the poor, the neglected and the disadvantaged.

It belongs to the worker and farmer. It belongs to the teacher. It belongs to the scientist.

It belongs to the soldier who defends the country.

It belongs to the millions of ordinary men and women who toil every day.

It belongs to the farmers and agricultural workers who produce record levels of paddy and wheat, pulses and oilseeds, cotton and sugarcane, tea, coffee and tobacco and a number of other crops.

That is why the Congress has remained true to certain unchanging values. These are :

- Unity and Integrity;
- Democracy based on the Parliamentary system;
- Secularism;
- An Independent Judiciary;
- Freedom of Speech and Expression and Freedom of the Press;
- Stability, Social Harmony and Development.

Neither victory nor defeat in an election has altered the Congress Party's allegiance to these values. Because these are the values inscribed in the soul of every Indian.

Because it is these values which can enfold the plurality and diversity of India.

It is not just unity in diversity; it is unity through diversity.

The Congress alone provides the link between all communities and sections of society. The Congress alone represents the composite nature of our ancient civilisation.

It is the Congress, and the Congress alone, which mirrors this India. The Congress pledges that it will remain true and faithful to these fundamental values of the country.

V CONGRESS PROMISES STABILITY

Stability is the plank on which rests good governance. It is the foundation on which rests civil society.

There were only two periods of political instability in India. They were from 1977 to 1979 and from 1990 to 1991.

These were the years in which the Congress was not in office in the Central Government.

In 1977, the first non-Congress Government had the numbers on its side. Yet it failed miserably. Ultimately it fell.

In 1989, the second non-Congress Government obtained outside support and thus claimed a majority in Parliament.

It was an opportunistic alliance. The bubble burst in 11 months. That Government also fell.

Neither their numbers nor their shifting affiliations could keep the non-Congress Governments going for a full period of five years.

Voted back to office in 1991, the Congress has redeemed its pledge of providing a Stable Government.

While the Congress remained united and strong, other political parties broke up. Several State Governments formed by other political parties crumbled.

Through this period, the Central Government has been remarkably stable.

It was not only stability of numbers. It was the stability of policies and continuity of programmes. Indeed of sometime it was stability in spite of the inadequacy of numbers.

The stability envisaged by the Congress is a comprehensive one.

It necessarily includes:

i) National Security.
ii) Strong secular character leading to social harmony and cohesion.
iii) All-round development and economic growth with social justice leading to general prosperity.

Each of the above three aspects is an important function of Stability.

The Congress pledges that it will provide a stable government for the full period of five years in the Eleventh Lok Sabha.

VI STABILITY—SPRINGBOARD FOR CHANGE

A Congress Government is a Government that believes in and constantly works for the people.

During the five-year period of every Congress Government since 1952, the Government has taken the country forward.

The Congress has always rejected the status quo.

The Congress has always advanced the aspirations of the people for a better life and a better tomorrow.

The Congress has used stability not as resting place but as a springboard to usher in change.

Stability brings change, positive and wholesome change.

We need not delve too far into the past. The period from 1991 to 1996 contains many examples.

The new economic policy is the product of a stable government.

Reservations for the Other Backward Classes is the product of a stable government.

Peace in Punjab is the product of a stable government.

Unprecedented increase in investments in rural and social development is the product of a stable government.

The employment boom since 1991 - three crore jobs in five years—is the product of a stable government.

These examples can be multiplied.

Your vote for Stability will be a vote for Change.

VII BOOM IN ECONOMY

When Shri PV Narasimha Rao's Government assumed office on 21st June 1991, little did the nation know about the impending economic catastrophe.

In point of fact, the nation was on the brink of default.

Foreign exchange reserves were at an all time low of Rs 2,100 crore. It was good for just two weeks' import.

Inflation was 13 per cent and threatened to increase, as it did, to 17 per cent.

Industry had come to a grinding halt.

The 8th Five-Year Plan had been abandoned by the two previous governments.

Government was living on borrowed money. When they could not borrow more, the government pledged India's gold and borrowed more money.

It was an hour of shame. It could have turned into an hour of grief.

At that crucial point, the Congress Government took over and took up the responsibility of rebuilding the Indian economy.

Five years of hard work have yielded rich dividends.

Foreign exchange reserves are now are over Rs 60,000 crore, enough for eight months' import.

Last year, our farmers produce 19.1 crore tonnes of foodgrains. States like UP, Bihar, Madhya Pradesh, West Bengal and Orissa are now witnessing the type of agricultural change that Punjab and Haryana saw in the 1970s and 1980s.

Farmers are getting more income in relation to what they spend. Agricultural wages have increased.

New and lucrative export opportunities have been opened up to our farmers. Today, India is among the top three exporters of rice and wheat.

Industry is booming. Last year, the industrial growth was 8.5 per cent. This year, it is expected to be 10 per cent. This has resulted in increased supply of goods like bicycles, scooters, tractors, watches, televisions, shoes, cars, textiles, paper, cement, steel, fertilisers and medicines. For the first time, shortages have disappeared. Indians have the choice to buy what they want.

More jobs are being created every year. In the last five years, over three crore jobs have been created.

India's GDP has been growing at a satisfactory rate. From just 1 per cent in 1990-91 to 6.2 per cent in 1994-95 is, by all accounts, a remarkable achievement. 1995-96 will again witness growth of more than 6 per cent.

India's exports have averaged over 20 per cent growth in the last three years.

Inflation is down to below 5 per cent, a record for 10 years.

We are today the sixth largest economy in the world. Soon we will be the 4th largest.

That is the real picture of our economy.

VIII GREATER SELF-RELIANCE

It is Congress which first put before the people the goal of self-reliance.

That goal has been corrupted by some self-styled protagonists of national interest.

What is true self-reliance?

True Self-reliance is Measured by:

- capacity of the country to save more and invest more;
- potential of the economy to create more jobs and generate more incomes;
- capacity of industry and agriculture to absorb more investment and better technology;
- capacity of the country to pay for the import of capital goods and raw materials;
- capacity of the Government to pay for the import of essential articles like fertilisers, edible oils and petroleum products to meet the needs of the people;
- capacity of the Government to repay the national debt and to pay interest charges.

The poor countries of the world are not self-reliant. It is the affluent countries which are self-reliant.

Our goal is to make India affluent. Our goal is to make

India truly self-reliant.

IX PEACE IN PUNJAB

As many as twenty seven candidates were killed by the terrorists when elections were ordered in Punjab during Shri Chandrashekar's regime as Prime Minister. Therefore, hours before the installation of the Congress Government, elections in Punjab were cancelled. Punjab was still torn and reeling under terrorism.

The Congress picked up the thread from where it had left it in November 1989.

Fencing on the border was resumed. The Punjab police was entrusted with the job of restoring law and order.

Within months, there was a gradual return to peace and law and order.

The Congress Government then took the courageous decision: to hold elections to the Punjab State Legislature and Lok Sabha.

Elections were held. The Congress was returned to power with an overwhelming majority.

That marked the beginning of a new era in Punjab. Elections to the Legislature were followed by elections to Nagarpalikas and Panchayats.

Today, the people of Punjab rule themselves through their elected representatives.

Today, there is peace in Punjab.

There has been a tremendous increase in economic activity.

Both industry and agriculture are thriving as never before. Indian and foreign companies are flocking to Punjab to make massive investments.

Punjab is a testimony to the statesmanship and wisdom shown by Prime Minister Shri PV Narasimha Rao, in handling an explosive situation.

X A NEW BEGINNING IN KASHMIR

The State of Jammu & Kashmir was relatively peaceful until November 1989.

The pitch was queered during the rule of Janata Dal. The Janata Dal was aided and abetted by the BJP.

Together they sacrificed the interests of the people of the State for political expediency. Together they destroyed the bond of trust and friendship between the people of Jammu and Kashmir and the rest of India.

The Congress has strained every nerve to rebuild this bond.

The Congress believed and continues to believe that the people of Jammu and Kashmir deserve a Government of their choice.

The Congress has, therefore, promised that Jammu and Kashmir can enjoy a large measure of autonomy within the framework of the Indian Constitution. Article 370 of the Constitution of India shall stand.

The Congress believes that elections—howsoever difficult— are the only way to break the gridlock in Jammu and Kashmir.

Elections have already been ordered for the Lok Sabha from J&K.

The Congress further pledges to hold elections to the State Legislature. The Congress pledges to restore democratic government in that State.

XI PANCHAYATI RAJ *RAJNITI* TO *LOKNITI*

Shri Rajiv Gandhi's last great legislative initiative was the introduction of Constitution Amendment Bills to provide for Panchayats and Nagarpalikas.

He dreamed of restoring power to the people.

He dreamed of a government close to the people.

He dreamed of a vibrant grassroots democracy with women, the Scheduled Castes and Scheduled Tribes sharing power and exercising authority.

But the Opposition Parties combined to defeat the Bills in Parliament in 1989.

Rajiv died in 1991, his dream unfulfilled.

Shri PV Narasimha Rao revived that dream.

The Constitution Amendment providing for Panchayats and Nagarpalikas came into force on 24th April 1993.

Seats at every level, including that of President or Chairman have been reserved for SCs/STs.

30 per cent of the seats are reserved for women.

Elections have been held in all but three states of India to Panchayats and Nagarpalikas.

A silent revolution has taken place in the towns and villages of India. Its full impact will be felt in the next few years.

There are only 4000 MPs and MLAs representing the people in our political system. In a population of 95 crore, that was not enough. 30 lakh representatives at the grassroots — one-third of whom are women — will now emerge as leaders of the people.

XII MANDAL REPORT IMPLEMENTED PEACEFULLY

Reservations for the Backward Classes was an idea of the Congress. Jawaharlal Nehru made this into a Constitutional Principle in 1952. Reservations became a part of the Congress Party's social justice programme.

Since then, Congress Governments have successfully implemented reservations for the Backward Classes in several Congress ruled States.

In 1990, due to its ham-handed and opportunistic approach the Janata Dal Government triggered a virtual caste war in several parts of India.

The election of a Congress Government in 1991 brought peace to a society that was threatened with disruption by caste strife.

Quietly, but firmly, Shri PV Narasimha Rao's Government implemented the recommendations of the Mandal Commission.

27 per cent of the jobs were reserved for the Other Backward Classes (OBCs) in the Central Government and in Public Sector Undertakings.

Today, even in the IAS and IPS, OBCs have been appointed, thanks to the implementation of Mandal Report by Congress Government.

A National Commission for Backward Classes has been established.

A National Backward Classes Finance and Development Corporation has been established with an authorised capital of Rs 200 crore. Its object is to promote economic and other developmental activities for the Backward Classes.

XIII ANTI-POVERTY PROGRAMMES

The abolition of poverty remains the foremost objective of the Congress Government.

Since the days of Shrimati Indira Gandhi, Congress has declared its faith in programmes which attack poverty at the grassroots.

The very poor in India do not have property. They do not have jobs. Often they do not have work.

Needless to say they do not have houses, or sanitary latrines. Till recently the village artisans did not have efficient tool kits for improving their production.

These are some of the reasons of poverty.

These issues have been addressed by Congress Governments through a number of anti-poverty programmes.

The PV Narasimha Rao Government has enlarged and expanded these programmes. It has also introduced new programmes.

The investment in rural development and poverty alleviation during the period 1991-1996 has been Rs 34,000 crore. This is thrice the amount spent in the previous five years. It is proposed to increase this outlay by three times more, to around Rs 90,000 crore, in the next five years during the Ninth Plan.

The record speaks for itself.

In the Four Year Period—July 1991 to July 1995:

- 115 lakh families were assisted under the Integrated Rural Development Programme (IRDP).
- 8.12 lakh wells were constructed under the million wells scheme.
- 28 lakh houses were constructed free of cost for Scheduled Castes/Scheduled Tribes, freed bonded labourers and other peoples below the Poverty Line under the Indira Awas Yojana.
- 2.60 lakh villages/habitations were covered under the rural drinking water supply scheme.
- 21 lakh sanitary latrines were constructed under the rural sanitation programme.
- 4.21 lakh took kits were distributed to 3,87,696 rural artisans all over the country.
- 1.2 lakh groups consisting of several lakh persons were benefitted under the Development of Women and Children in the Rural Areas Scheme (DWCRA).
- 13 lakh youth were trained under the scheme of Training of Rural Youth for Self-Employment (TRYSEM).
- 7,837 projects were approved and Rs 160.85 crore were released to 1,600 voluntary agencies for rural development.

The greatest success has been the creation of work — work which translates into incomes for the very poor and assets for the country.

Employment Assurance Scheme to provide wage employment for two persons in the household and agricultural labourers was introduced in 3198 Blocks in 391 Districts.

Wage employment under Jawahar Rozgar Yojana was intensified in works based upon local needs and priorities.

These Employment Schemes would be expanded to provide wage employment to all persons seeking and needing it. This is the way poverty is being attacked.

XIV NATIONAL SOCIAL ASSISTANCE PROGRAMME

The Congress Government launched a National Social Assistance Programme on the 15th of August, 1995. This programme has three components and allocation of funds in the last two years has been over Rs 1500 crore.

A National Old Age Pension Scheme provides Rs 75 per month to destitute persons of 65 years and above. This will benefit 54 lakh people.

A National Family Benefit Scheme provides a lump-sum benefit of Rs 5000 in case of natural death and Rs 10000 in case of accidental death of the primary bread earner of a family below the Poverty Line and aged between 18 and 64 years.

A National Maternity Benefit Scheme provides a lump sum assistance of Rs 300 to a pregnant woman above the age of 19 years below the poverty line. This is estimated to benefit 46 lakh women each year.

XV AGRICULTURE

Farmers are the backbone of our country and the economy. The Indian National Congress has always given the highest priority to them.

The Eighth Plan outlay for the Ministry of Agriculture was enhanced to Rs 10,000 crore as against a little less than Rs 3,500 crore in the Seventh Plan, an increase of over 180 per cent.

No Government ever gave farmers such high remunerative prices by way of Minimum Support Price as was done by the Congress during the last 5 years. Thus the Minimum Support Price of paddy which was Rs 230 per quintal in 1991-92 was increased to Rs 360 per quintal in 1995-96. Similarly the support price of wheat was increased from Rs 275 per quintal to Rs 380 per quintal over the same period.

As a result of policy initiatives and special programmes introduced, the agriculture sector has become more competitive and efficient. Indian agriculture has been freed from controls of domestic and international trade which have substantially enhanced the opportunities for our farmers to reap remunerative returns.

Our progressive policies have enabled farmers to reach new heights of production and productivity. Higher production and productivity has in turn led to higher wages, enhancing the purchasing power of the rural poor.

Foodgrain production has increased to record level of 19.1 crore tonnes in 1994-95. A major thrust was given to horticulture—the Eighth Plan outlay on horticulture is Rs 1000 crore against an expenditure of only Rs 24 crore in the Seventh Plan. India is now the largest producer of fruits and second largest producer of vegetables and coconuts in the world. The production of milk has increased substantially from 5.39 crore tonnes in 1990-91 to above 6.3 crore tonnes in 1994-95. Total agricultural exports have increased from about Rs 5,000 crore in 1990-91 to over Rs 10,000 crore in 1994-95. For the first time the export of marine products crossed US $ billion in 1994-95.

From a position where we used to import agricultural products, the agricultural sector today has become a dynamic outward looking sector, helping the economy by producing enough to meet the country's needs and also by earning valuable foreign exchanges.

Our agricultural production strategy has moved to encompass all soil and agro-climatic conditions specially in the rain-fed areas and drought-prone areas, in which the bulk of our rural poor reside. Watershed development projects for sustainable development of these areas have been launched under National Watershed Development Projects for Rain-fed Areas (NWDPRA), Drought-Prone Areas Programme (DPAP) and Integrated Wasteland Development Projects (IWDP).

DPAP has now been extended to 946 Blocks in the country and its outlay has been more than doubled between 1991-92 and 1995-96. Its guidelines now provide for greater people's participation through Panchayats, Watershed Associations and self-help groups.

Another important step which has been in active consideration and which will be implemented forthwith, is de-licensing of the Suger industry.

The time has come when in overall terms, Agriculture needs to be accorded the status of an Industry. This will be done now, since all the other steps required in this behalf have been completed.

To protect the interests of Traditional Fisherman in the Coastal areas and to ensure the growth of joint ventures to be established under the Deep Sea Fishing Policy, the recommendations of the Review Committee under the Chairmanship of Shri P Murari will be processed and implemented.

XVI ESSENTIAL COMMODITIES

Essential commodities such as rice, wheat, sugar, palmolein and kerosene are distributed through the Public Distribution System (PDS) at prices generally lower than the market price through fair price shops.

In 1992, the Congress Government launched a scheme to revamp the PDS in 1752 backward blocks falling in drought-prone areas, desert areas and hill and tribal areas. Additional commodities like tea, soap and pulses are also distributed through the Revamped PDS shops. Additional allocations of foodgrains have been earmarked and food grains are distributed at prices lower than even in the PDS. The most vulnerable sections of our population are served through the Revamped PDS.

The PDS subsidy bill in 1995-96 was Rs 5,500 crore. The objective is to benefit the very poor and bring them relief.

The Congress promises to extend the Revamped PDS to 694 more blocks.

XVII SCHEDULED CASTES

The National Commission for SCs and STs has been conferred Constitutional status and has recently been recons- tituted.

The National Commission for Safai Karmacharis has been constituted and has been in operation for the past two years. The Commission looks into the specific problems of Safai Karmacharis and recommends specific programmes for elimination of inequalities in status, facilities and opport- unities for them.

A National Scheme was launched in March 1992 for liberation and rehabilitation of Safai Karmacharis so as to eliminate the inhuman practice of carrying night soil and filth on head by the end of the Eighth Five-Year Plan.

A separate Finance and Development Corporation for extending concessional finance to Safai Karmacharis for starting self-employment projects is being set up with an authorised capital of Rs 200 crore.

Reservations for Scheduled Castes and Scheduled Tribes, now made through an executive order under Articles 15 and 16 of the Constitution, will be provided for under suitable Acts to be made by Parliament and the State Legislatures.

The Scheduled Castes and Scheduled Tribes (Prevention of Atrocities) Act and other applicable laws will be reviewed, amended and strengthened with the object of ensuring quick justice to the affected Scheduled Castes and Scheduled Tribes.

Rules under SC & ST (Prevention of Atrocities) Act, 1989 have been modified with effect from 31st March 1995 wherein payment of compensation to the victims has been increased manifold and the procedure for payment has also been simplified.

The Congress Government amended the Constitution in order to continue the reservations for SCs/STs in promotions.

In order to honour Dr Babasaheb Ambedkar and to disseminate his message of social justice and social emancipation, the Dr Ambedkar Foundation has been set up as a registered society to manage and administer the long term schemes and programmes identified during his centenary celebrations.

Dr Ambedkar University in Lucknow has been converted into a central university.

Dr Ambedkar Chairs have been instituted in 9 Universities in India.

Dr Ambedkar Overseas Scholarships are awarded to meritorious students for pursuing advanced studies.

Dr Ambedkar National Award has been instituted for promoting outstanding contribution in the field of social understanding and work done for weaker sections.

XVIII TRIBAL DEVELOPMENT

The Tribal Cooperative Marketing Development Federation (TRIFED) was established in 1987 with the primary aim of marketing Minor Forest Produce and surplus agricultural produce collected by the tribals so as to get them remunerative prices and to eliminate the middlemen who exploit the tribals.

The authorised share capital of TRIFED has been increased from Rs 50 crore to Rs 100 crore. The turnover of TRIFED has gone up 10 times from Rs 40 crore in 1990-91 to Rs 400 crore during 1995-96.

Tribal Commission under Article 339 (1) of the Constitution will be constituted soon to report on adminis tration of Scheduled Areas and welfare of Scheduled Tribes in States.

XIX BACKWARD CLASSES DEVELOPMENT

Congress Government took the historic decision to provide reservation of 27 per cent to socially and educationally backward classes in civil posts and services under Government of India on 8th September, 1993.

The OBC candidates were given age relaxation of three years and three additional attempts in Civil Service Examinations.

A permanent statutory Commission for Backward Classes has been set up to make recommendations to the Government for inclusions/exclusions of castes in the Central List of OBCs.

The National Backward Classes Finance and Development Corporations has been set up with an authorised share capital of Rs 200 crore for providing concessional finance to the poorer sections of backward classes for setting up self-employment ventures. During the last four years Rs 146.5 crore has been disbursed so far.

The Pre-examination Coaching Scheme has been introduced with effect from 1992-93 to prepare candidates from Other Backward Classes and Minorities for competitive examinations. The number of candidates coached under the scheme during the past three years has been around 6,630.

A new scheme for welfare of street children has been started under which NGOs are given financial assistance for care, protection and development of street children. 81 centres have been set up under this scheme covering 37 important cities.

A new scheme for setting up homes for the aged was launched in 1992-93. Under this scheme 209 old age homes, 239 Day Care Centres, and 29 Mobile Units have been functioning.

XX WOMEN

Women have been in the forefront of the Congress while championing the causes of the people and in the freedom struggle.

Apart from the legislative and other measurers taken from time to time, the Congress Government has set up the Rashtriya Mahila Kosh to develop a network of credit services for women working in the formal sector and to support self-employment ventures.

The Mahila Samriddhi Yojana has been launched for the welfare of women. A woman who deposits Rs 300 in the post office will get Rs 375 after one year. A sum of Rs 1,000 crore has been set aside for the scheme which will make our women self-confident, self-reliant and independent.

The Congress Government has established the National Commission on Women. Besides, there is a Commissioner for Women's Rights to promote the social well-being of women and check atrocities and violence directed at women.

The Congress Government has already provided reservations for women in Panchayats and Nagarpalikas. By a suitable amendment in the Constitution, Congress will provide reservations for women in State Legislature and Parliament.

XXI WELFARE OF MINORITIES

The Congress regards all Indian citizens as equal.

Yet we recognise Minorities of several kinds because we recognise the special disadvantages that they suffer and the special help that they need.

This is not appeasement. This is heeding the call of the Constitution of India.

Equal status to all people and protection of the Minorities are fundamental features of the Indian Constitution. They are also the fundamental features of any plural society.

The cornerstone of Secularism is the security of the Minorities. The cornerstone of a civil society is the security of all people. The Congress will leave no stone unturned to secure the life and liberty of all the people including the Minorities.

The Congress regards the 15-point Programme for the welfare of Minorities as a charter of duties. The programme will be reviewed from time to time, revised and updated.

For instance, and Rapid Action Force, consisting of young men of all communities, has been established. They are stationed at sensitive places. Although new, it has already shown its mettle and earned public confidence.

The Congress Government has established the National Minority Finance and Development Corporation with a capital of Rs 500 crore. The Corporation will support projects and schemes that will promote the well-being of Minorities.

The Minorities Commission has been given statutory status.

The Congress Government has enacted the Protection of Places of Worship Act, 1991. The status of all places of worship as it existed on the day of independence will be preserved. No one can now misuse any place of worship to divide Indian society.

After wide-ranging discussions and consultations with Muslim Members of Parliament, Members of Central Wakf Council and other leaders of the Muslim community, a comprehensive legislation to amend and consolidate the law relating to the administration of Wakfs has been enacted. The Wakf Act has come into force with effect from 1st January 1996.

The Maulana Azad Education Foundation has been set up as an independent entity with a Corpus Fund of Rs 30 crore with a view to promoting education amongst educationally backward Minorities in particular and the weaker sections in general.

XXII PERSONAL LAWS

The Congress has made its position very clear on the question of Personal Law. The Congress believes that there should be no imposition by Government of any change in the Personal Law of any community or any section of people. Such changes, against the wishes of the community concerned, would neither be favourable nor acceptable, if attempted in the name of uniformity.

XXIII WORKERS

The Congress is proud of the role played by the Indian workers in accelerating the pace of industrial development. The interest of workers has always been uppermost in the minds of successive Congress Governments.

It was Shri Rajiv Gandhi who set up a high level National Commission on Rural Labour when he was Prime Minister. The Government of Shri PV Narasimha Rao has taken important steps to implement the recommendations of the Commission and in extending social security and insurance schemes to various sections of unorganised labour.

The Congress Government has raised the eligibility limit for payment of bonus from Rs 2,500 to Rs 3,500 per month and the ceiling for calculation of bonus from Rs 1,600 to Rs 2,500 per month. Earlier it had increased the ceiling under the Payment of Gratuity Act to enable workers to get gratuity upto Rs 1 lakh.

XXIV EX-SERVICEMEN

The Congress Government issued order in March, 1992 sanctioning "one time increase" in pension with effect from 1st January, 1992 involving a recurring expenditure of about Rs 140 crore. About 8.3 lakh defence pensioners will benefit under this scheme. Till April, 1995 over 5 lakh pensioners have already been sanctioned one time increases under this scheme.

The Congress Government has also undertaken various steps for the welfare of ex-servicemen and their families. Amounts of financial assistance provided from Raksha Mantri's Discretionary Fund to ex-servicemen in penury for marriage of their daughters, repair of house, education of children and medical treatment have also been enhanced.

XXV WELFARE OF DISABLED PERSONS

In the last four years, a number of initiatives have been taken for promoting the welfare of disabled persons.

A comprehensive legislation for safeguarding the rights of persons with disabilities and enabling them to enjoy equal opportunities and participate in national life will be introduced shortly.

A National Finance Development Corporation with an authorised share capital of Rs 400 crore and a paid-up share capital of Rs 200 crore has been set up to extend concessional finance to the disabled for self-employment projects and promoting technical skills.

A National Trust for welfare of persons with mental retardation and cerebral palsy will be set up for which a Bill was introduced in the Lok Sabha last year.

The Indian Spinal Injury Centre has been set up in collaboration with the Italian government to provide treatment to persons suffering from spinal injury.

XXVI YOUTH

The Congress Government of Shri Rajiv Gandhi lowered the voting age from 21 to 18. Millions of young men and women have thus been given an opportunity to participate directly in the political process.

The population of India is getting younger. About 60% of the population is below the age of 40. That is 55 crore people. A Committee on National Youth Programmes has been set up under the Chairmanship of the Prime Minister.

XXVII EDUCATION

The Congress Government of Shri PV Narasimha Rao has made a public and firm commitment to spend 6 per cent of the country's GDP on education. This would mean a doubling of investment in education by the turn of the century.

The Congress Government launched a new mid-day meal programme to increase nutrition and improve school attendance of 11 crore children in classes I to IV in three years. In the very first year of the scheme, 3.4 crore children have been covered.

An innovative programme has been launched for overhauling primary education in 42 of the educationally backward districts of the country. This programme is focussed on the education of girls and disadvantaged groups such as girls, Scheduled Castes, Scheduled Tribes and children with disabilities. This programme, which is in operation in 42 educationally backward districts of the country would be extended to all districts soon.

In more than 300 districts of the country total literacy campaigns have been taken up. The National Literacy Mission has made big strides and its achievements have been acknowledged widely. These total literacy campaigns would be further strengthened with special emphasis upon marginalised groups like child workers, pavement dwellers, migrant labour, etc.

Despite tight fiscal constraints, the Central Plan budget allocation for education has gone up by over 90 per cent in the last three years. The Congress Government's commitment to education can be seen from the fact that Plan investment in elementary education has gone up by 130 per cent in the same period.

The Congress is committed to ensuring universal access to elementary education by the year 2001, laying particular emphasis on the Girl Child and imparting a strong vocational bias to secondary education.

Access to Technical education, Vocational education and Higher education would be expanded and improved through distance learning modes, open schools and open universities.

Emerging areas of technology and management would be encouraged, supported and nurtured through centres of excellence.

XXVIII POWER

Power is essential infrastructure of agriculture and industry. There is also growing demand for electrification of households. Development and prosperity means increased consumption of power. The improvement in the quality of our lives depends to a large extent on the reliable supply of power.

With the best of efforts, the country is able to add about 4500 MW every year through public investment. A full 20 per cent of the 8th Plan outlay has gone to the power sector alone. The demand for power is about 14,000 MWs per year for the next 10 years.

Hence the Congress Government took a decision to encourage the entry of private and Indian companies in the power sector. More private investment would release Government resources to be used in social sector programmes. A 1000 MW power station, if implemented in the private sector, would release Rs 3,000 crore which is the annual expenditure on the education sector. Thus investments in education could easily double.

The full effect of the Congress Government's policy of encouraging foreign and Indian private companies in the power sector will be felt in the years to come. The last four years have been a learning process for both the Government and companies involved.

In the last five years, between April 1991 and March 1996, power generation in the country has grown steadily despite considerable odds. While in 1990-91, 286.7 billion units (BU) of electricity was generated in the year 1995-96 the generation was 379.8 BU, i.e., an increase of 93.1 BU, which, in percentage terms, represents an increase of 32.5 per cent.

During this period the annual per capita consumption of electricity in the country grew by almost 24 per cent to approximately 330 units.

Even this level of growth is not adequate and efforts are being intensified to meet the growing demand for power which is annually increasing by about 8 per cent.

The plant load factor, denoting efficiency of available capacity, rose substantially from 55.8 percent to 63 percent.

The Central Public Sector Undertakings in the power sector have shown a superb performance and made record profits of about Rs 1800 crore in 1995-96 and are now paying dividends to the Government regularly.

Besides electrifying about 75,000 new villages, over 21 lakh agricultural pumpsets in the rural areas were energised in the last five years. To improve the general health of the electricity sector, special efforts are being made to reform and restructure the State Electricity Boards so that their functioning becomes more viable and responsive to consumer needs.

Overwhelming response has come from investors within India and abroad and nearly 140 projects aggregating to about 66,000 MW of new capacity and involving an investment of Rs 2,50,000 crore are at various stages of active processing. Given political stability, continued infusion of such massive investment into the power sector is sure to be achieved.

XXIX FERTILIZERS

The production of nitrogenous and phosphatic fertilizers has reached an all time record level of 104.3 lakh tonnes.

Fertilizers are also imported liberally. Thus, the availability of fertilizers has been ensured to fully meet demand at all times. In fact, at times there has been a glut.

Seven expansion projects in the public and cooperative sectors involving an investment of Rs 4200 crore are under implementation.

The price of Urea continues to be heavily subsidised. On every tonne of Urea sold to farmers, the Government of India bears a subsidy of Rs 2500. The sale price of urea in India is the lowest among our neighbouring countries.

To ensure that there is no shortage in the supply of fertilizers to our farmers, the Congress Government has taken steps to initiate joint ventures abroad. Projects in Iran, Oman and Tanzania are being finalised.

Fertilizer factories owned and operated by organizations of farmers' cooperatives like KRIBHCO and IFFCO have turned in excellent performances. They have major plans to set up new fertilizer plants in the country.

XXX TELECOMMUNICATIONS AND POSTS

The Congress Government has ushered in a revolution in telecommunications.

The National Telecom Policy of 1994 is a landmark development. The Opposition parties criticized this policy, but the Government's stand was vindicated by the judgement of the Supreme Court in January, 1996.

In the last four years, 1.38 lakh villages have been provided with telephone facilities. Out of 2,43,555 Gram Panchayats, 1,55,410 have been provided with telephone facilities. By 1997 all villages and gram panchayats will be on the National Telecom network.

STD Public Call Offices have doubled in the last four years, providing gainful employment to nearly 10 lakh unemployed educated people in the country. All the 500 District headquarters, 90 per cent of Sub-division headquarters and 85 per cent of Tehsil headquarters have been provided with STD facilities. In this way telecommunications is being used to bring the country closer together.

To ensure that more and more Indians have access to the latest telecommunication technology at affordable prices, the Congress Government has taken far reaching steps along with private sector participation. The private sector will mobilise resources and obtain the most cost-effective equipment. The Department of Telecommunications will continue to be a major provider of telephone services.

The postal system continues to play a vital role in our country. In order to speed up transmission of money orders, a Satellite Money Order service has been launched covering 75 locations. This will enable instantaneous transfer of money benefitting lakhs of users in villages and towns.

XXXI SMALL SCALE INDUSTRY

The Congress is deeply conscious of the critical role that small scale industry plays in our economy. One of the very first steps taken by the PV Narasimha Rao Government was to announce a package of policy measures in July 1991 to strengthen the small scale industry.

A full-fledged Small Industry Development Bank of India (SIDBI) has started functioning. New legislation has been introduced to ensure timely payments to small scale entrepreneurs. Bank facilities have been strengthened in about 100 centres in the country where there is a cluster of small scale units.

The Khadi and Village Industries Commission has been revived. A Rs 1000 crore investment programme is under implementation to modernise these industries. This will creat lakhs of jobs and open new markets for rural and small scale production enterprises.

All the steps taken by the Congress Government in the field of industrial and trade policy will create a new environment for small scale businesses. Improved technology is already flowing into the small scale sectors and new markets both in India and abroad are being opened up.

XXXII THE PUBLIC SECTOR

The Public Sector belongs to the people.

The savings of the people, tapped as borrowings and taxes, have gone into the Public Sector.

Our experience with Public Sector enterprises has been mixed.

Some enterprises have always done well. Some have been turned around recently. Others are chronically sick.

Some enterprises were put in the Public Sector because of security and strategic considerations. They will remain in the Public Sector.

Over Rs 1,50,000 crore of the people's money has been invested in the Public Sector. The annual return is less than Rs 3,000 crore. This is grossly inadequate.

The restructuring of the Public Sector is therefore of the highest priority.

The Congress Government has set up a National Renewal Fund to fully protect the interests of labour and to provide adequate funds for retraining and skill development. Almost Rs 2,000 crore has been allocated to this Fund in the last two years.

The goal is to make these enterprises productive, efficient and profitable. The Congress is committed to achieve this goal.

XXXIII SCIENCE AND TECHNOLOGY

Successive Congress Governments have been deeply committed to the development of Indian Science and Technology. It is because of this sustained support given by Pandit Jawaharlal Nehru, Shrimati Indira Gandhi, Shri Rajiv Gandhi and, since 1991, by Shri PV Narasimha Rao, that India has emerged as a leading nation in the development and application of Science and Technology.

Only five countries in the world have designed, built and launched satellites into space. India is one of them.

The INSAT satellite series are being used extensively for telecommunications, TV broadcasting, weather forecasting to our farmers and in giving early warning on disasters like floods.

The Council of Scientific and Industrial Research has developed many processes for several vital and essential drugs. This will help in timely production of these drugs. And at a cost which is one-third to one-fifth the price of the imported drugs. These include drugs for the treatment of Malaria, Gastro-enteritis, Cancer, T.B. and AIDS.

New technology programmes have been launched to modernise tanneries, improve recovery of sugar and improve productivity of fish farms.

The country's atomic energy programme has been consolidated in the last five years. About 700 MWs of additional Power capacity has been added. Nuclear technology is being used in preservation and storage of food, introduction and extensive use of high yielding and insect and drought resistant varieties of ground-nut, moong and urad, high yielding varieties of bananas, cleaning of sewage, etc.

Impressive progress has also been made in fields like computers, robotics and lasers.

For the first time oral polio vaccine will be manufactured in the country. This will benefit 20 million children who are born every year.

Bio-technology applications to develop new varieties of cotton and rice and to improve the yield of our livestock population are now undergoing extensive transfer from laboratory to the field.

XXXIV ACCOUNTABILITY

The people elect their representatives. Election carries the obligation of accountability.

The Congress Government is committed to providing an open, accountable and responsive administration at all levels.

The Congress Government is committed to the principle that all executive action—administrative or quasi judicial — shall be according to law.

The accountability of all to Parliament will remain supreme.

The Congress is committed to an independent judiciary. The accountability of all to the law and to the judiciary shall also remain supreme.

The revolutionary Panchayati Raj and Nagarapalika initiative will place power in the hands of people where it truly belongs. The strengthening of local governments will make the administration more accountable to the people.

The Congress will take steps to set up a Lok Pal. It will ensure that all those Congressmen and Congresswomen elected to public office will make a public declaration of their assets.

All elected representatives belonging to the Congress will declare their assets on the day they enter upon their offices. They shall also make a declaration of their assets on the day they vacate their offices.

XXXV STRONGER DEFENCE

The Congress Governments have a proud record in securing the defence of India.

Every Congress Government has added to the strength of India's defence.

The period from 1991-1996 has been another period of strengthening India's defence forces.

The Important Achievements of this Period are:

- The commissioning of the main battle tank 'Arjun'.
- The successful launch of Prithvi, Nag and Akash missiles and the successful completion of the Agni project.
- The development of the light combat aircraft (LCA).
- Commissioning of INS Shankul and India joining the select club of countries possessing frontline technology for submarine construction.

By the turn of the century, India's defence forces will have the most versatile main battle tank and the most modern military aircraft of its kind.

The Indian defence forces have always been soldiers of peace.

Following the great traditions of the past, Indian defence personnel were deployed abroad in several countries including Kampuchia, Somalia and Rwanda as part of the UN peace keeping missions to these countries.

XXXVI FOREIGN AFFAIRS

The world has changed dramatically in the last five years. Indian foreign policy has had to face new challenges arising out of fast moving global political and economic developments. The Congress Government under Shri PV Narasimha Rao has adopted a pragmatic and flexible approach to meet these challenges and has reoriented foreign policy to make it an effective instrument for furthering India's economic and political objectives.

India's prestige in the world has been restored by the Congress Government. The country is now respected and sought after. The Association of South East Asian Nations (ASEAN) has made India a full dialogue partner — an honour that India now shares with the US, the European Union, Japan, Canada, Australia and New Zealand. By becoming a full dialogue partner India becomes a major player in the economic and security policy consultations involving some of world's most dynamic and fast growing countries.

A large number of developed and developing countries have supported the inclusion of India as a permanent member of the UN Security Council.

Prime Minister Shri PV Narasimha Rao's visit to China in 1993 resulted in the conclusion of the historic agreement on the maintenance of peace and tranquillity along the line of actual control. It is an important step towards cordial relations and harmony between the two giant countries. Bilateral trade with China has registered a rapid expansion and Consulates have been opened in Shanghai and Mumbai.

With Shri PV Narasimha Rao's highly successful visit to the United States in 1994, the relationship between the two countries is growing closer by the day and the United States continues to be India's largest trading partner and the single largest investor country.

A large number of bilateral agreements have been signed with Russia covering the entire spectrum of political, economic, technological and defence relations with Russia.

India's ties with countries like Japan, UK and Germany have greatly expanded following Shri Narasimha Rao's visits. These countries are taking greater interest in India's economic and social development.

India has always had close ties with developing countries. Traditional friendly relations with countries in the Gulf region, Iran and the Central Asian Republics have been further cemented and upgraded and given a tangible economic dimension.

New and close relationships have been forged with emerging economic powers like Israel, South Korea and South Africa.

A path-breaking development in India's foreign policy has been the launching of regional economic cooperation initiative around the only ocean that takes its name from a country — the Indian Ocean. The Indian Ocean Rim initiative launched in March 1995 will cover all areas of cooperation.

The SAARC nations took a significant step forward and launched the SAARC Preferential Trading Arrangement (SAPTA) with effect from 7th December, 1995. They have resolved to usher in a Free Trade Area (SAFTA) by the year 2005 and preferably by the year 2000. India's pioneering role in promoting SAPTA and SAFTA has been recognised in the South Asian region and elsewhere in the world.

The long-standing problem between India and Bangladesh relating to the Tin Bigha corridor was finally resolved by the Congress Government of Shri P V Narasimha Rao.

The voluntary return of Sri Lankan refugees to their homes commenced in January, 1992.

A landmark agreement for the development of the Mahakali river was finalised with Nepal. A large number of India-funded project were commissioned in Nepal and Maldives.

An important border trade agreement was finalised with Myanmar thereby promoting trade, including border trade, for the benefit of the local people on both sides.

The Congress Government has taken every step to establish cordial and good relations with Pakistan. It proposed a serious of confidence building measures that were, unfortunately, rejected by Pakistan. Shri P V Narasimha Rao has repeatedly said that India is ready to discuss bilateral issues with Pakistan without any preconditions and to resolve all outstanding differences peacefully.

The Congress favours a nuclear weapons free world and will continue efforts for total and complete disarmament, particularly nuclear disarmament. Our nuclear policy is geared for peaceful purposes.

We are deeply concerned that Pakistan is developing nuclear weapons unabated. They have already inflicted four wars upon India. In case Pakistan persists in the development and deployment of nuclear weapons, India will be constrained to review her policy to meet the threat.

Manifesto: Indian National Congress

CONGRESS (I) sincerely believes election presents a choice to the people, choice to vote a party into Government, choice to vote a candidate into office.

The Congress (I) presents an idea with a bright future. The Opposition presents an idea that will be thrown back to the past.

The Congress (I) presents an India that is growing, creating wealth, generating jobs and providing more incomes. The Opposition presents an India which will be stagnant, inward-looking, poor and likely to become bankrupt.

The Congress (I) presents an India which rejoices in its unity, and celebrates its diversity. The Opposition presents an India that will be inflamed by caste and religious passions.

The Congress (I) presents an India that had new respect among the countries of the world. The Opposition presents an India that will be ignored, ridiculed and forgotten.

The Congress (I) presents an India with a stable government and a vibrant economy. The Opposition presents an India with a tottering government and a collapsing economy.

A Pledge

The Congress Government at the Centre has fulfilled almost all the promises made in the manifesto of 1991. It has amply demonstrated that the Congress is a doer and not a talker. Its main concern has always been and will always be for the emancipation of the poor and their early entry into the middle and higher classes of the society.

In the foregoing pages the Indian National Congress has revealed a vital and important agenda that will provide the national with the strength and stability and take us forward.

Internal peace and harmony, national security and political stability are the sine qua non of a strong India. An India that can hold its head high in the world. The Indian National Congress, as in the past, pledges to strive for these goals vigorously without any compromise or let up.

Within the framework of a large agenda the Congress presents the following concrete programme which will be implemented straightaway upon securing the mandate of the people. The programme is necessarily composed of ::

a) consolidation of past achievement, and

b) a great advance in the future.

Our vision for the next five years, containing the main items for better life, is as follows ::

Better Life

- Houses for houseless poor
- Jobs for jobless; near full employment by 2002 AD
- Cheaper rice and wheat for the poor
- Drinking water of all habitations
- Mid-day meal for all primary school children
- Improved health and educational facilities for all children
- Complete implementation of Operation Black Board all over the country by the end of the IX Plan
- Broadguage Railway all over the country
- Rail and Road linkages to all villages
- Empowerment of women, including by Reservation in Legislative bodies
- Age of superannuation of 37 lakh Central Government employees to be raised as, may be recommended by, the Pay Commission
- Remunerative prices for farmers
- Detailed comments on these and other important items of the programmes are given hereunder.

ECONOMIC AND INSTITUTIONAL REFORMS:

(1) To carry forward the momentum of economic reform and restructuring of economic policies, to achieve a higher trajectory of economic growth, efficiency and competitiveness in all production sectors and achieve 8 to 9 per cent growth in GDP per annum.

(2) To initiate rural structural transformations, which is consistent with and supportive of national reform. The main objective is to transform rural areas and backward regions to prosperity, with a diversified economic base, rural industrialization and reduced rural urban gap in transport, communication and services.

(3) To extend and enhanced support to our scientists and technologists and foster rapid utilization of science and technology in all our national tasks, specially defence.

(4) Re–orient agricultural science and technology, extension and other support systems towards rain-fed and draught-prone areas and extended watershed Development Projects.

(5) Intensify promotion of agro-processing, tiny and household enterprises, ventures and activities through arrangements for infrastructure and credit facilities and freeing them from bureaucratic and procedural formalities.

(6) Continue and strengthen the policy reforms, price incentives and input subsidies which have improved the relative profitability of agriculture and have enabled our farmers to reach new heights of production and productivity.

(7) Time-bound implementation of the recommendations of Committee on Revitalization of Land Reform Administration and Computerization of Land Records (P S Appu Committee), in consultation with the states.

(8) Usher in a new policy on cooperatives to restore their democratic structure and autonomy management.

(9) Formulate the Ninth Five-Year Plan in time with wide ranging consultations especially with the State governments.

(10) Enhance the functional and financial domain of the self-governments, institutions established under Constitution (3rd and 4th Amendments) Acts and support measures for training and decentralized planning at the micro-level.

(11) Ensure that District Planning Boards as envisaged under Article 243 ZD of the Constitution, are established in every state at the district level to initiate, integrate and consolidate participatory local level plans.

(12) Implement the recommendations of the Committee of Members of Parliament and experts on the law concerning extension of constitutional provisions relating to Panchayats and Nagarpalikas to scheduled arears.

Reforms for Removal of Poverty and Unemployment:

(1) To extend the employment assurance schemes (EAS) to all 4997 blocks in the country and intensify the Jawahar Rojgar Yojana (JRY), to provide wage employment to all adults seeking and needing such employment.

(2) To extend the revamped Public Distribution System (RPDS) to all the 3198 backward blocks in the country and to families residing in urban slums. Reduce the issue price of rice and wheat distributed in RPDS blocks by Rs 2.00 a kg.

(3) Extend integrated Child Development Scheme (ICDS) to all 4997 block in the country and ensure arrangements for nutritional support equivalent to 150 gms of foodgrains per day to all the eligible pre-school children, expectant and nursing mothers.

(4) Extend National Mid-day Meal Programme:

To cover all elementary schools in the country and enhance the quantum of foodgrains supplied per child from 3 kg per month to 5 kg per month, with the condition of 20 days' attendance of the child per month in the academic year.

(5) Provide skill development and self-employed opportunities to all literate youth belonging to poor households through intensification of integrated rural Development Programme (IRDP) and the Prime Minister's Rojgar Yojana (PMRY).

The Congress promises near-full employment by the 2002 AD on the following basis:

Estimates of additional employment in the first three years of Eighth Five-Year Plan have been made on the basis of Provisional Estimates of the GDP for 1992-93.

Quick estimates of GDP for 1993-94 and Advanced Estimate of GDP for 1994-95 released by the Central Statistical Organisation and estimates of employment elasticities made in the Planning Commission.

According to these, additional employment opportunities of the order of 187.8 lakh are estimated to have been generated during the first three years of the Eighth Five Year Plan, implying an average rate of employment growth of the 2.03 per cent per annum.

During 1995-96 and 1996-97 employment is likely to grow by 150 lakh, making a total of 337.8 lakh during Eighth Plan.

If these are stepped up through intensive implementation of Special Employment Programmes as mentioned in Chapter XIII and growth of 7 to 8 per cent is achieved during Ninth Plan period, achievement of 100 to 110 lakh jobs in a year during 1997 — 2000 is feasible. This would give near-fulfilment of the objective of employment for all by 2002 AD.

(6) Enhance the quantum of benefits to persons from poor households under the National Social Assistance Pro-

gramme (NSAP) being implemented with the active participation of Panchayats and Municipalities to:

(a) Rs 100 per month for old persons above 65 years of age; and

(b) Rs 500 for maternity assistance.

(7) EXTEND Mahila Samriddhi Yojana to group savings and activities to rural women and provide facilities at their doorsteps for opening of accounts and receipt of interest income. Bring about a five-gold increase in the number of accounts opened.

(8) Take measures for substantial reduction of Child Labour and total abolition of Child Labour from hazardous industries.

Pledge on Basic Needs and Human Development:

(1) Ensure that 6 per cent of the country's DGP is spent on education and intensify all related activities for promotion of capabilities and involvement of teachers and provision of school buildings and educational aids on a mission mode to achieve universalistation of elementary education and foster excellence in higher education.

(2) Launch a national sanitation programme to intensify public health and immunization activities, to secure a disease-free atmosphere in the country, with involvement of the Panchayats, Nagarpalikas and NGOs. Implement innovative school health programme to provide health education as well as health services to all the school children through the help of primary school teachers and primary health care providers.

(3) A comprehensive survey on the status of drinking water in rural habitations conducted during 1991-93 has revealed that even after almost completing all the main villages, there are still a large number of habitations without adequate source of drinking water or chemical contamination of drinking water through excess of flu-

oride iron, arsenic and salinity. All these habitations would be provided with drinking water sources through infestation of outlays and implementation of Accelerated Rural Water Súpply Programme by the Rajiv Gandhi National Drinking Water Mission.

(4) The 1991 Census has revealed the total rural housing shortage comprising houseless rural families or those living in unserviceable rural kuchha houses as 1.3 crores. The Indira Awas Yojana will be expanded to provide a pukka house to all those households.

(5) Launch a massive housing programme to provide savings-linked housing assistance at subsidized rate of interest with the insurance cover to benefit all economically weaker section households in rural and urban areas. This scheme will be administered through HUDCO and other housing corporations, boards, development authorities, cooperative societies and NGOs and with direct credit from LIC, GIC etc. The programme will be designed to benefit one crore households.

(6) Strengthen the post-harvest activities, cold-storage, pre-cooling, refrigerated marketing and transport facilities in the country, thereby minimizing the post-harvest losses and enhancing incomes of the cultivators in these districts.

(7) Protect our biological and environmental heritage through strict vigilance over pollution, denudation and displacement and promotion of sustainable development through participatory mechanisms such as Joint Forest Management Groups.

(8) Introduce a system of "proximity benefits" in favour of a specified number of villages adjacent to a large industry to be funded out of the fund of the industry upto about one per cent of its outlay. Details will be worked out at an early date after the new Congress Government takes over.

Reforms for the Excluded Sections of Our Society:

(1) Formulation and implementation of a national strategy to promote full participation and equality, of persons with disability in all programmes of rural development and other social sectors under the newly enacted legislations for the disabled persons.

(2) Enhance the allocation of funds and installations of activities of the Commissions and Corporations established for the welfare of the Scheduled Castes, Scheduled Tribes and Backward Classes, Minorities Women and Disabled persons, to pull up their socio-economic development and to deal with gaps and missing links in their development process.

(3) Extend reservations for certain excluded categories in deserving cases, such as Dalit Christians and Women for Vidhan Sabhas and Lok Sabhas.

(4) Appoint a Commission on Tribal Areas under Article 339 (1) of the Constitution to report on good administration of Scheduled Areas and welfare of Scheduled Tribes in States and implement its recommendations within one year.

National Security and Integration:

(1) Relentless fight against terrorism and all other anti-national activities with special developmental efforts in states and regions which continue to disturbed.

(2) Strengthen the steps taken by the Centre, with State co-operation, to protect our borders on land and sea in dealing with infiltration of foreigners, smuggling and narco-trafficking.

(3) Elimination of criminal nexus with influential segments and control of organised crimes, that has come to vitiate our social, political and administrative structures.

(4) Central support for modernisation and training of police service, aimed at improving their response, quality of

investigations and accountability to crime and treatment of offenders.

(5) Simplification of procedures and strengthening of judiciary for disposal of all pending cases in three years.

(6) The National Security Council formed in 1990 proved to be unwieldy. The Congress Government after it came to power in 1991, had made a thorough reapprisal of the aspects of the national security and a new blue print, suited to the Parliamentary system of government, has been evolved. At the apex is the Cabinet Committee on National Security (CCNA) with three sub-cabinet Committees on Internal Security Defence and Foreign Policy. A strategic policy group will contribute to CCNS, assisted by Joint Intelligence Committee and strategic technology sub-group. Experts from outside the government could be associated with these groups, giving a wide scope for fresh ideas and papers to be produced for the decision of the CCNS. The new body will be set up as soon as the new Congress Government takes over at the Centre.

Reforms on Vigilance and Corruption:

(1) Appoint a high-powered Commission consisting of eminent jurists, parliamentarians and administrators to recommend legal, administrative and enforcement measures to control and contain corruption and implement these measures within 6 months.

(2) Establish LOK PAL with jurisdiction over all political offices, including that of the Prime Minister and the Chief Ministers.

(3) Reduce the amount of the discretion obtaining in administrative decision-making, including at minister's level so as to render than public, transparent and accountable.

(4) All members of Parliament, Legislatures and local bodies to declare their assets, when assuming and leaving office.

(5) Review the work of the enforcement agencies at the Centre and the states with a view to accord adequate autonomy and insulations from interferences in discharging their duties.

(6) Involvement of the public in vigilance and control of corruption through public hearings, access to information and promotion of voluntary organisations in the area.

(7) Strengthening internal vigilance and anti-corruption mechanisms for preventive and punitive vigilance in all governments, quasi-Government and public agencies and organizations.

4

Backgrounder : Janata Dal

The Challenge

The National Front Government, which lasted only for eleven months, will for ever be remembered for the glorious manner in which it sacrificed itself at the altar of it's twin and interwined ideals of promotion of social equity and protection of secular polity. It's historic decision to order reservation in Central Government services for the Other Backward Classes (OBCs) on the basis of Mandal Commission recommendations and Janata Dal Manifesto led to a quantum jump in the democratic aspirations of the masses in all spheres of life, but provoked the BJP to rake up the diversionary issue of Ayodhya, and to overthrow the National Front Government in collusion with the Congress(I).

The political tides have since been encountering both radical currents and reactionary cross-currents. The massive social forces, which have been submerged for millennia, have been unleashed through a quiet democratic process overturning entrenched governments, splitting established parties, and marginalising ruling classes. The vested interests, threatened by this democratic destabilisation, have dropped their secular defences and abandoned their progressive pretences. They are now torn between the neo-capitalist attraction of Congress (I) and the naked communal appeal of BJP. As the social bases of Congress and BJP have thus converged at a swift pace, the political space of Congress has come to be easily usurped by the BJP in varying degrees in UP, Bihar, Gujarat and Maharashtra etc. The Congress, fossilised by the family rule and profligacy of power, has not had either dynamic leadership or sense of direction to retrieve its lost ground. In fact, it's endless equivocation on such incandescent issues as social justice and secular order compounded by it's elitist craze for economic liberalisation has only led to further erosion of its base. The Congress, which has been declining steadily and speedily since 1989, is now historically heading towards final disintegration. The splits and revolts, which have recently afflicted it in continual instalments, are unmistakable indications of this process.

Even while the Congress has kept contracting rapidly in terms of political and social ground, it's governance during the last five years has been pockmarked by numerous scams such as the securities scandal, fraudulent disinvestment of the PSU's shares, sugar import muddle, deals in railways, power, oil, mines and telecom sectors. The manner in which the Hawala racket was suppressed and side-tracked by the Government for over four years is scandal in itself. It is now known that the stable Government, which the Congress proudly claims to have given to the country, was literally purchased as is evident from the bulging bank-accounts of some MPs. During its so-called stable regime, the fabric of communal harmony of the country has been torn asunder not only through the wanton demolition of Babri Masjid, but through a sense of profound insecurity spread among religious minorities. During the same period, the foreign exchange crisis in mid-1991, which was caused by the fiscal profligacy of Congress rule during the late 1980s, was utilised to topsyturvy the national policy of self-reliance in the name of liberalisation under the pressure of World Bank of IMF.

The New Economic Policy of Congress was enthusiatically endorsed by BJP, which has of late donned swadeshi mantle as a tactical ploy. Even while the Hindu chauvinism and upper caste bias of BJP has become absolutely naked, its carefully constructed image as a disciplined party by the open infighting within it, particularly in Gujarat, Madhya Pradesh and Delhi has been exploded. The involvement of innumerable BJP leaders in Hawala racket has conclusively demonstrated that BJP and Congress are two pieces of the same cloth not only in respect of its ideological proclivities such as *Hindutva* and pro-rich approach, but in respect of moral frailties such as corruption and indiscipline.

In this background of the collapse of Congress and desperate attempt of BJP to fill the void caused by the retreating Congress, the historical task of replacing the Congress and keeping BJP at bay, devolves squarely on Janata Dal, its National Front allies and Left Parties. The challenge is nothing less that accomplishing a political transition to the post-Congress India, while steering clear of communal and reactionary elements. Janata Dal is determined to convert this momentous challenge into an historic opportunity in close cooperation with its National Front and Left allies.

Out Parties, inspired by the bold vision of self-reliant and pluralist India, are far stronger now in the vast tracts of the country than ever before to rise to the pregnant occasion and usher in a new era of economic prosperity, distributive equity, sectarian amity and cleansed polity. Janata Dal, as the leading constituent of this progressive combine, pledges itself to the task of playing its befitting role in bringing about the national regeneration.

State of Economy

India's economy has been damaged by Congress Government's pursuit of policies of so-called liberalisation, faulty privatisation and improper manner of globalisation. The so-called achievements of Congress Government on this front are purely chimerical. One of the overarching objectives of its economic reforms was to reduce fiscal deficit. But, this deficit remains almost as high now as in 1991-92. Revenue deficit has now risen to about 4 per cent of the GDP from 2.5 per cent in 1991-92.

Towards Foreign Debt Trap

When the Congress Government assumed power in 1991, it made much of the foreign exchange crisis which was facing the country. It however failed to admit that the depletion of our foreign exchange reserves had been brought about in the 1980s when our foreign debt increased from Rs 20,000 crore in 1979-80 to Rs 9,000 crore in 1989. In particular, the government led by Shri Rajiv Gandhi incurred huge debts by way of short term loans at commercial rates of interest even for balancing its budget.

Our exchange reserves stood at $21 billion only a few months back—time close to hustings. Hot money accounts for much of this reduced level of reserves which can fly away easily, thereby exposing the country to the vulnerability of Mexican type crisis.

We are also finding ourselves in a foreign debt trap. The debt-service ratio is one of the highest in the developing world, accounting for over a third of India's export earnings.

Another result of these policies was that India's industrial sector, including small scale sector, has been exposed to the competition of multinational companies without proper preparation. Industries, big and small, have been affected by industrial sickness and closures. Yet another reason contributing to this phenomenon was indiscriminate import liberalisation.

Speculative activities for short-term gains were encouraged while investment in green field projects was not up.

Shrinking Employment

Unemployment rate had grown. Although Government invested Rs 1300 crore in Central public sector units, 75000 workers were thrown out through voluntary retirement schemes. In 53 loss making CPSUs, jobs of three and a-half lakh workers were under threat from closures and privatisation. At present, there are 2,50,000 sick private industrial units. A conservative estimate of employment thus affected was 2.5 million jobs.

While public and private investment had not picked up much during these years Congress rule, savings declined from 23.7 per cent of GDP in 1990-91 to 20.2 per cent in 1994-95.

Rising Prices

Consumer Prices Index had continued to go up. The real value of rupee had declined by 67 per cent between 1982 and 1995; so its value is only 33 paise. It gives a lie to the government's claim that rate of inflation has gone down and eased the price situation.

Public investments in agriculture and infrastructure have fallen. Consequently, private investment has fallen too. Contrary to the Government's claim, 40 per cent of India's population is still living below poverty line.

The sale of the equities of even the profitable PSUs were resorted to. But this money was spent not on modernising the PSUs or building the core industrial sector, but to meet Central Government's current expenditure. Moreover, the sales were made at throwaway prices, inflicting a loss of over 5000 crores on the public exchequer.

Manifesto: Janata Dal

ECONOMIC REFORMS

Janata Dal would reorganise the entire economic perspective and would adopt an economic development policy which it will term as Alternate Economic Strategy.

1. It would give accent on the labour intensive technology. It will pursue a policy to maximise employment generation through intensification of agriculture and allied occupation and development of agro-based and forest based industry.
2. Janata Dal will deploy the industrial infrastructure for production of mass consumption goods.
3. Dal will also bestow high priority on improving physical infrastructure in both urban and rural sectors so that minimum needs of poor people regarding their employment, shelter, education, health and food are taken care off. Modernisation can be speeded up only by increasing the purchasing power of the masses by these means.
4. For a close integration of modern industry, small scale industry and agriculture will be grown up. Eco-friendly technology hence will be preferred to avoid pollution and degradation of environment, as far as realistically practicable.
5. The Janata Dal sees the necessities to harmonise the roles of modern and traditional growth processes. It agrees the demands of competitive world order that requires the country adopt the latest technology in different fields. On the other hand, it finds the imperative that our traditional growth processes continue to play the important role, ever since upheld. It is the people themselves who are the producers as well as the consumers.

   Janata Dal therefore will adopt only such model of economic development that can solve their problems. The model should be able to utilise the productive powers of the common people who are neither functionally educated nor possessed of the skills relevant to the modern development process.

6. Janata Dal would expand Public Distribution System (PDS) as to make available all essential commodities, such as rice, wheat, sugar, edible oils, and cheap cloth to all poor people in urban and rural areas at highly subsidised rates. Towards this end, Janata Dal favours considerable increase in the subsidy to be made available in the budget.
7. It believes that stability of the nation's development is vitally linked to stability of our water systems, Primary importance will be given to ensuring long term water stability through (a) harvesting rain waters in catchment areas, thereby effectively controlling floods and restoring the perennial character of Indian rivers and augmenting ground water recharge: (b) through conserving water use in both agriculture and industry, and (c) through strict protection of water system from pollution by industries and civic bodies.
8. Wasteful use of water in elite areas will be contained.
9. The irrigation policies of the Janata Dal are based on a rational water-management approached of mini-watershed development and development of the sub-basin, fulfilling the need of the local population and also ensuring the riparian rights of the downstream farmers.
10. Formation of a national grid to optimise utilization of water resources will be pursued. The potential of river Brahmaputra will be harnessed through long term measures to combat floods and generate power.
11. Expeditious solutions to inter-state water disputes will be found in a fair and equitable manner on the basis of uniform criterion.

STEPS FOR AGRICULTURAL AND RURAL DEVELOPMENT

1. Janata Dal carries forward its earlier approach to address problems of cultivators, landless workers and artisans.

During the term of the National Front government in the late seventies, loans to the farmers upto Rs 10,000 had been waived and prices of several agricultural commodities such as wheat, rice, sugarcane and cotton were raised to comfortable relief of the farming community. The Dal, if voted to power, would devote 50% of all developmental expenditure to agriculture and rural development.

2. The Dal will pronounce a national Agricultural Policy embodying the principle of minimum support price for agricultural produce with a guarantee of purchasing the same.
3. It will also offer remunerative prices on the basis of equitable balance between agricultural and industrial produce.
4. Its earlier promice of allotting 15 per cent of credit to this sector from financial institutions shall be fulfilled. It will rather increase it to the rune of 20 per cent.
5. On prompt repayment of agricultural loans, interest rebate will be provided as incentive.
6. For the development of agriculture and rural areas, 60 per cent of all planned budget resources will be allocated for this sector.
7. The cultivators will be protected by insurance of crops and cattle against natural and unforeseen calamities.
8. Godown facilities will be greatly expanded.
9. All restrictions of movement of agricultural produce will be removed. Processing of agricultural produce will be deregulated.
10. Dal will encourage dryland farming substantially.
11. It will also restore the cuts in agricultural subsidies. At the same time, the Dal will also issue subsidies to other agricultural inputs.
12. Dal will arrange for export and import of agricultural commodities through marketing cooperatives of societies of farmers.

ZEALOUS INDUSTRIAL POLICY

1. Janata Dal will give high priority to small scale, cottage and agro-based industries. Certain items like handlooms will be exclusively reserved for them. Interests of Indian entrepreneurs engaged in these industries will be zealously safeguarded and their exploitation by selling their products under the brand names of other companies will not be permitted. Therefore, entry of multinational companies in areas which affect interests of the people, economy and environment will be avoided.
2. Dal will undertake modernisation programmes with a view to step up efficiency and improve the product quality, but will never allow large scale of displacement of labour.
3. On the issue of privation of Public Sector Units Dal will see that 40 per cent of its equity be invested in newly created National Social Security Fund (NSSF), 10 percent be sold to the employees and the rest be sold to the public.
4. While ensuring the industrialisation, Janata Dal will ensure that malpractices regarding they change of land use from agriculture of industry be prevented.
5. To mobilise necessary resources, the Janata Dal will enforce strict fiscal discipline, curtail administrative expenditure, unearth black money, change the direct and indirect tax ratio so as to give the greater relief to the lower and fixed income groups and encourages austerity to public life.
6. The Janata Dal considers that their utmost duty is to secure for our economy a measure of delinking from imposition on Indians of unequal and exploitative order on the terms of conglomerates of multinational corporations and governments of developed countries, to which in the name of NEW ECONOMIC POLICY the Congress Government by the large have collaborated.

   To that end, Janata Dal has the priority to isolate the sensitive areas of financial services like insurance and capital markets etc., from the influence of international financial cartels.

7. Janata Dal wants that the concept of liberalisation be clear and wants to make liberalisation complete success by removing negative practices, which are squandering opportunities created by liberalisation. It believes the goal of liberalisation is to create a competitive environment that should actually improve supplies and manage shortages. Some business groups, it feels, have indulged themselves in speculative practices and manipulation of stock markets, which have negative impact upon the concept of liberalisation, which needs to be checked.
8. Janata Dal wants that agriculture an small industries also should be liberalised.
9. It would work for never to wind up the public sector, but improve its functioning by inputs of professionalism in management and providing the real autonomy.
10. Janata Dal favours to adopt a policy of preparing list of 'Yes' and 'No' for entry of multinationals.
11. Janata Dal wants state must resume leading role in development of infrastructure and believes that infrastructure cannot be left to the private sector or MNCs alone. For, it thinks infrastructure sector have been sadly neglected during the last five years.
12. It would deregulate the domestic economy so as to give full scope to entrepreneurial skills to people and to minimise the scope for corruption.
13. It would safeguard the Indian patent regime to protect interests of farmers in respect of fertilisers and seeds, drugs and textiles sectors.
14. It would take solid step to create a level-playing field before opening up the economy. It must also adopt measures to protect established companies from hostile takeovers. However, it would of course welcome globalisation of our economy and thereby welcome competitions from MNCs.

15. It would also explore avenues of forging closer economic and trade links with the developed countries. That will give solidarity to us and would greatly help us in countering the encroachment on our economic sovereignty.

LAND REFORMS

1. Janata Dal will review and revise existing land reform laws to plug the loopholes and to ensure their stringent implementation.
2. Apart from organising distribution of surplus land, special credit facilities must be made available to the assignees of surplus land.
3. It would constantly be vigilant in guarding against direct and indirect dilution of land ceiling laws.

ELECTORAL REFORMS

1. Legislative initiatives will be taken to organise wide-ranging reforms based on Dinesh Goswamy Committee Report prepared during National Front's regime. Janata Dal favours State funding of elections and legitimate activity of recognised political parties.
2. Janata Dal strongly opposes the weakening of secularism which is part of India's cultural ethos and had been one the basic values behind our freedom struggle, for it would tear apart the fabric of nation's unity and impede nations's progress.
3. Dal feels it necessary to screen the text books to remove the references intended to distort attitudes with a view to discriminate people on the basis of sex, caste, religion.
4. Dal also feels it necessary to do progressive modulations of attitudes related to such discrimination on sex, caste, and religion, some of which find sections through scriptures, history books, for extending frontiers of social and cultural justice.

5. The Dal will carry out strong, vibrant and people-based reform movement inspired by teachings of saints, sufis, and social reformers to promote religious tolerance.
6. It will not over- emphasise the intellectual dissent.

SOCIAL REFORMS

1. Dal will inculcate the concept of social justice through economic empowerment as a must. For, it believes, in promoting social justice, democratisation of the power structure is crucial, because only that will empower the sections which have been historically denied all privileges and opportunities.
2. The Dal, therefore, will adopt strategies to broaden social justice and economic empowerment of the dispossessed groups. At the same time it will integrate policies of full employment, land reforms, full literacy and removal of economic disparities.
3. The quantum of reservations for the scheduled castes and the scheduled tribes must be so revised as to conform to the increase in their population.
4. Janata Dal will consider to extend the affirmative benefits to Dalit Christians too, and if necessary through Constitutional amendments.
5. It will extend the reservations to the OBCs to the judiciary also.
6. Janata Dal will ensure that the States which have not yet provided for reservation in elective positions in Panchayati Raj bodies for OBCs, must do so in line with other States which have so reserved the elective positions for OBCs.
7. The Dal will ensure reservation in promotions for Other Backward Classes also, in line with that for SC and ST members.
8. Moreover, in acceptance by Parliament of the situation in Tamil Nadu where the quota of reservations is far above the ceiling of 50 per cent imposed by the Supreme

Court, it is well-highlighted that the need to extend similar benefits to other States where the need to exceed the ceiling is felt. Constitutional measures to increase this limit must be taken expeditiously.

9. The Dal also recommends that the independent commission be constituted to examine in depth, the actual quantum of each State to settle the issues relating to the needs for further social categorisation among the socially and educationally backward classes.
10. The Dal feels the need to set up independent commission to determine quantum of reservation to be provided for certain religious minorities without disturbing the reservation already given to backward sections among these religious minorities.
11. At the same time the Dal is opposed to the idea of removal of so-called creamy layer until the reserved quota is fully provided.
12. Janata Dal favours a Constitution amendment to provide reservation for the economically backward among the forward castes.
13. Janata Dal feels it necessary to stress upon the injustice done to socially and educationally backward classes by removing reservation through privatisation of public sector units.
14. It will, therefore, see that the reservation policy also covers the public sector units, as well. For the time being in all the decisions relating to privatisation, a provision to continue the reservation of jobs in the concerned units must be inserted.
15. It will see that reservation policy is applied to distribution of licences and quotas concerning economic activities under Government control.
16. A commission will be constituted to recommend measures by which the SCs, STs and OBCs can acquires adequate participation in private sector employment.

SOCIAL REFORMS FOR SCHEDULED CASTES AND SCHEDULED TRIBES

1. Steps will be taken to fight all vestiges of untouchability and other social disabilities. Propagation of untouchability shall be severely dealt with.
2. Implementation of reservation policy will be made effective by resorting to special recruitment drives so as to fulfil the quotas of SCs and STs in the shortest possible of time.
3. The Plan allocation for welfare of SCs and STs shall correspond to their share in population and shall exclusively be utilised on priority basis for specific schemes of direct relevance to them. A separate agency for intensive economic development of SCs / STs shall be created.
4. Cooperatives of producers from among the SCs and STs engaged in crafts, cottage industries and collection of minor forest produce, will be encouraged in order to eliminate middlemen.
5. Within next two years scavenging will be eliminated and alternative employment will be provided in place of that.
6. Wherever Safai majdoors are not permanent in their jobs, they will be made so.
7. Payments of their salaries will be the first charge of the municipal bodies.
8. Janata Dal recognises inalienable right of the rural poor in general, and the tribal communities in particular, over land, water and forest resources being utilised by them traditionally. It further recognises that such communities depend on these natural resources even to meet their subsistence needs (food, fuel, fodder, building materials, etc.) and to sustain their cultural life. In view of this, the Janata Dal commits itself to the following :

   (a) All relevant laws and policies shall be reviewed and amended to gurantee customary rights of the rural communities, particularly of the adivasis, over land water and forest resources.

(b) The tribal people will be removed from their habitat only in cases of compelling public interest and, that too, not until their consent is obtained.

(c) As and when such displacement becomes unavoidable, full compensation, adequate rehabilitation (including socio-cultural) and alternative employment shall be guaranteed to them.

(d) The affected communities shall be fully involved in preparation and implementation of the rehabilitation plans. The government shall create a special fund for the purpose.

(e) A policy package shall be worked out and executed to restore and regenerate country's natural resource base which has been fast denuded in recent decades. The affected communities would be fully involved in planning and implementation of such programmes locally.

9. Alienation of Tribals lands shall be stopped.
10. There will be a joint forest management which will monitor development and maintence of forests. This will be done according to Forest Policy resolution, 1988.
11. In developing tribal areas and creating employment for them strategies sensitive to their habitat and community life shall be followed. Besides, strategies will be taken so that would promote their self-management of local resources and self-governance corresponding to their cultures.
12. In this respect recommendations of Bhuria Committee will be implemented.

SOCIAL REFORMS

Protection of Minority Rights

1. Communal riots shall be put down strongly by effective prohibition of incitement to communal passion and by pursuing appropriate recruitment policies in the police services. The National Front can claim legitimate pride

in having curbed communal violence and provided security to the minorities. It may be noted, says the Janata Dal, that communal clashes erupted mainly in Congress (I)-ruled States and in States ruled by BJP or Janata Dal (S).

2. A special anti-riot force will be created so as to ensure totally impartial conduct from them.
3. Full compensation will be provided to victims of communal and caste riots.
4. Action will be taken against officers who fail to contain communal riots.
5. Religious minorities will enjoy the full protection and opportunity to pursue their modes of worship, their religious beliefs and practices and develop their institutions whether religious, cultural, educational or welfare-oriented. Complete non-interference will be observed.
6. Wakf properties shall be brought under Public Premises (Eviction) Act. Properties belonging to Wakf and other religious endowments shall be exempted from Rent Control Act as means to augment their income to fulfil their commitments.
7. Minority Commission will be give statutory status. The Janata Dal in Bihar government has already conferred legal status on its Minorities Commission by an ordinance and a Bill is to be adopted soon.
8. The economic backwardness and unemployment among the minorities shall be reduced by setting up Minorities Financial Corporations, thereby assuring representation for minorities on various recruitment committees and boards, giving encouragement for establishment of technical and polytechnic institutions by minorities. Concrete steps will be taken to ensure adequate employment opportunities and jobs for minorities.
9. Minority character of the institutions guranteed by the Constitution shall be respected.
10. Janata Dal ensures that all retrogradesteps — like (a) recent actions and pronouncements of Shiv Sena-BJP State

government in Maharashtra, (b) attempts to impose a common civil code on all communities without their willingness, (c) changing names of cities and towns, (d) closing down the Urdu Academy, winding up of the Minority Commission, (e) dissolution of Srikrishna Commission inquiring into the riots of 1993, and (f) harassment to which a large number of Bengali-speaking people are being subjected in the name of illegal Bangladeshi immigrants in various States—are reversed.

11. It will fully respect the Act adopted by Parliament in respect of religious shrines. All disputes related to religious shrines including the Ayodhya dispute, will be referred to the Supreme Court for settlement by it under Article 138 (2).

Women Causes

1. Janata Dal feels social equity cannot be made meaningful without vigorous steps to remove gender inequality. The Constitution may have to be amended to include sections on women to be given preferential reservation in public employment.
2. Janata Dal thinks one-third of all the jobs reserved for socially and educationally backward classes need to be reserved for women of respective sections. This principle should apply non-reserved jobs also.
3. The Dal would secure, through proper legislation and actual implementation, women's rights in ancestral and matrimonial property. They must also get the right to shelter and the community property.
4. The Dal would also see that in allotment of houses, flats, or pattas of land, joint ownership of husband and wife is ensured.
5. It will introduce National Education Insurance or some guranteed incentive schemes to ensure that children particularly the female children of even the poorest families get education and to eliminate the phenomenon of drop-outs attractive schemes must also be introduced. The

physical and social vulnerability of women has to be assured by sensitisation of the entire police and by extensive recruitment of women in judiciary and police force. Also women-policing will be introduced in more sensitive areas.

6. The Dal feels the present structural adjustment policies by the Congress Government would further create adverse effects on social status of women, and would degrade their condition too, particularly in rural India. It will, therefore, introduce self-employment schemes, necessary training programmes, extend minimum needs programmes that will solve their problems regarding nutrition, drinking water, fuel and fodder and toilets for women exclusively. At the same time it will encourage temperance amongst the males.
7. It will extend to the Union and State legislature level the policy of reservation of 30 per cent of elective posts in local bodies for women.
8. It would expeditiously constitute the state level commissions on women and would make it effective.
9. All kinds of discrimination will be treated as violation of human rights.
10. The Dal will vigorously implement the resolutions of International Convention on elimination of all forms of discrimination, which is now ratified by the government.

Children

1. Janata Dal as a partner of the National Front would reverse all kinds of socio-physical injustice done to children through a number of interrelated approaches.
2. It will recognise and restore the human rights of children by ratifying, implementing and monitoring the Convention on the Rights of the Child.
3. It will meet the development needs of the children. It is a central concern of national planning, by implementing

a time-bound programme of action towards basic inter-linked goals in nutrition, health and education in a holistic approach to the mother-child life-cycle.

4. It will break the nexus of people responsible for female illiteracy, children ill-health and early marriage.

Youth Programmes

1. Janata Dal will evolve a national youth policy on the basis that employment and elementary education are made fundamental rights.
2. Its will stop the dualities of education whereby wealth and other elitist privileges will be ended.
3. Its representative youth councils at national, State and district levels will look after cultural, social, and economic welfare of the youth.
4. These councils will also become vehicles of their participation in decision-making in respect of issues vitally affecting them.
5. These councils will play the key role in evolving youth policies and monitoring their implementations.
6. Janata Dal will expand the self-employment schemes for youth and strengthen it by providing liberal credit facilities and necessary entrepreneurial skills.

Right to Work

1. Janatal Dal believes that every body has the right to work, productive and gainful, and live meaningfully with dignity. Social and economic policies of the Janata Dal will, therefore, be geared to realisation of the "Right to Work" as fundamental right of the citizens of India.
2. It will find productive work for the people at wages that are commensurate with human need and dignity.
3. It will convert the "Right to Work" into a reality by implementing Employment Guarantee Schemes all over the country.

4. To realise conditions of full employment an alternative strategy of social and economic development will be followed which would accord primacy to deveopment of agriculture and allied occupations. Emphasis will be given to building up infrastructure of essential physical and social services in villages and towns.
5. It will reserve the basic consumer goods for the cottage and smalll scale industries.
6. With a view a achieve the objective the former National Front Government's Planning Commission had drawn up a plan to increase the growth of employment generation to such magnitude that would provide gainful employment for all.
7. In addition to all this, several special employment schemes were to be launched for self-employment of the poor.

Corruption

1. Janata Dal will institute Lok Pal Bill to enquire into complaints of corruption against Union ministers including Chief Minister and the Prime Minister and others holding high public offices.
2. The Lok Pal will be multi-member, and appointed by the President in consultation with the Chief Justice of India, Speaker of Lok Sabha, Chairman of the Rajya Sabha, leaders of the Government and the Opposition in the two Houses of Parliament.
3. An independent commission will be set up that will scrutinise the statutory provision that all those holding public offices and offices of political parties declare their assets annually.
4. Official Secrets Act will be drastically revised. Right of Information will be included in the Fundamental Right of the Constitution.
5. The CBI will be made autonomous and freed from the control of Department of Personnel.

6. Janata Dal will set up a separate autonomous organisation on the line of CBI to investigate the white collar offences.
7. It will make the public auditing of accounts of political parties a statutory requirement.
8. Transperancy in all business dealings of the government will be introduced, especially foreigners.

Transparency will be introduced also to contracts of sale and purchase and granting of credits by financial public institutions.

Urban Development

1. Janata Dal will build up new towns through imaginatively conceived policies which will encourage diffusion of industries and also would develop nodal centres. This would help in quickening rural development. These nodal centres and new towns would absorb large number of migrant population from villages seeking jobs in metropolices.
2. The Planning Commission of the first National Front government had calculated that all over the country, 4000 new towns would have to be set up to function as nodal centres of rural development. Janata Dal feels that the plan needs to be pursued.
3. It also feels that for developing such nodal centres, huge house construction endeavours have to be taken, for which joint partnership of public and private enterprises have to be invited.
4. At the same time slum improvement and clearance bids will have to be taken up with utmost intensity.
5. Janata Dal will amend the Urban Land Ceiling Act to remove the legal impediment to private endeavours.
6. It feels that the State has the obligation to provide subsidised shelters to the poorer sections in urban as well as rural areas. This will be met. TDP's government in 1985-89 and Janata Dal's governments in Karanataka and

Bihar in 1993-96 have taken laudable initiatives in this direction.

7. It will provided in urban areas infrastructural facilities like transports and roads, basic amenities like healthcare, education, sewage, drinking water and pollution-free atmosphere.
8. It will promote the programme of "sustainable cities" through municipal bodies which will provide the above infrastructural and basic amenities and also include in the list the facilities of waste management, sanitation and pollution control.

Food Security

1. Janata Dal has a unique programme—a programme of offering to the citizen the food security, that strengthen livelihood security of all members within a household and ensure physical as well as economic access to balanced diet.
2. The Dal will, therefore, encourage active participation of the local neighbourhood communities in conservation of natural resources base, as for example, conservation of land, water, forests, biodiversity, oceans, and the atmosphere.
3. It will promote eco-friendly technologies to enhance productivity, profitability and sustainability of agriculture.
4. It will introduce public policies to ensure physical and economic access to food and nutrition including expansion of Public Distribution System.
5. It will clear rules in respect of conversion of food-growing land into non-food growing crops or commercial lands with a view to unexceptional cases.
6. It will experiment projects of free kitchens in poorer districts during off-seasons. These kitchens will be run by PRIs out of funds made available from State governments to Centre.

INDUSTRIAL POLICY AND LABOUR WELFARE

1. Due to New Economic Policy, there has been pressure for 'Exit Policy' to facilitate industrial restructuring whereby Hire & Fire trends and industrial closures can be allowed freely arbitrarily. Janata Dal opposes this.
2. It will re-orient Indian Industrial Relations laws, for healthy industrial relations.
3. It will re-orient registration formalities and recognition of trade unions.
4. It will institute an independent machinery that will oversee trade unions and other industrial relations matters to ensure speedy resolution of industrial and individual disputes.
5. It will revamp the implementation machinery of Labour Laws and give right of prosecution to the union.
6. It will consolidate various labour laws into one comprehensive Industrial Relations Law which will provide for basic obligations, rights and standards under an employer-employee relationship.
7. It will form a system of industrial relations which will rely less on governmental intervention, depend more upon bipartite nogotiations and will have an authority for independent arbitration or adjudication.
8. Social security of the workers will be guaranteed and further expanded by undertaking sympathetic review of existing laws.
9. It will index the social security benefits for workers commensurating cost of living.
10. Payment of social security (under different laws and provisions) will be dealt with under a single window scheme.
11. Social security will be given to daily wage earners. At present, it has been seen, the daily wage earners are exploited lots even in government organisations.

12. At present, there appears to be no social security measures for employees against occupational hazards. Even the Employees' State Insurance Scheme has ignored the occupational health work.
13. Janata Dal feels Employees' State Insurance Scheme should be taken away from the State governments and handled entirely by the ESI Corporation, with workers' representatives at each appropriate level.
14. In view of industrial restructuring and loss of jobs, there is urgent need to set up Industrial Workers' Rehabilitation Fund, and Janata Dal will go for that.
15. Pension Scheme for the members of Provident Fund will be reviewed and substantial improvement will be made in it in consultation with trade unions.
16. Janata Dal shall promote interests of the workers of unorganised sectors of the economy by enacting appropriate legislation. Such legislation will guarantee security from eviction payment of minimum wages, compensation of accident and security in old age.
17. Old age pension, grant of home stead land, creches and free medical aid shall also be provided, under such legislation.
18. Construction Workers' Ordinance will be revised susbtantially to remove anti-worker biases. It will also revise the Workers' Pension Scheme introduced by the government.
19. It will make effective the provision of workers' participation in management and decision-making at the highest levels.
20. The future of mofussil journalists will be safeguarded by suitable amendments to Working Journalists Act.
21. Constructions Workers' Ordinance will be replaced by one on the line of recommendations of Petitions Committee of Lok Sabha.

POLICY ON FEDERALISM AND RELATED ISSUES

1. Janata Dal believes that centralisation of policies on political and economic powers in the Union government, gross abuse of Article 356 of the Constitution to dismiss State governments and to dissolve legislative assemblies, misuse of offices of the Governor and refusal to restructure economic and fiscal arrangements in order to make States economically viable have bred fissiparous tendencies in our polity.
2. National Front Government will go on, as it did in the past, examining and implementing the Sarkaria Commission's recommendations on Centre-State relations.
3. The Inter-State Council set up by National Front government will undertake comprehensive review of Union-State relations based on the report of the Commission on Centre-State relations (Sarkaria Commission) and other reports on the subject.
4. The Inter-State and National Development Councils will be activated to ensure cooperation and coordination between the States and the Centre and to make India truly a federal republic.
5. True federalism alone can broaden and deepen bonds of our unity and integrity of our great nation. The Janata Dal believes that strengthening of States need not be at the expense of the Union. It believes that strong States would, in fact, enable the Union to discharge its responsibilities more effectively.
6. It will ensure states get truly enjoy genuine autonomy—political, legislative, economic, fiscal and administrative powers within the federal framework.
7. Adequate financial resources and administrative powers will be develped on the States to enable them discharge their responsibilities to people without submitting themselves to the indignity of becoming supplicants before the Centre.

8. Janata Dal will review the functions and powers of Governors to ensure their Constitutional accountability. They must be prevented from being used as agents of the party in power in the Center, Janata Dal holds.
9. It will review the much-abused Article 356 of Constitution.
10. Janata Dal has recorded demands for several decades for creation of smaller States. It has also rightly observed economic backwardness of certain regions in the respective States, noticed the popular aspirations for regional identity and large size of the States that causes difficulties to people in dealing State-level administration.

    The Dal will appoint a commission to go into these demands and make appropriate recommendations.
11. Inspite of specified provision in the Constitution, certain State governments have, on one plea or another, refused to hold elections to the Panchayati Raj Institutions (PRIs) as per schedules. A way will be found so that it does not recur.
12. The Constitution will be amended to redefine the functions of PRIs with precision. The discretionary powers that the States enjoy in this respect will be curbed.
13. Reservations for OBC members in elections to the PRI seats will be made a statutory provision in all States.
14. PRIs will be given funds according to their developmental functions as is provided in the Constitution and through the respective State governments.

EDUCATION, SCIENCE, TECHNOLOGY AND RELATED ISSUES

1. Janata Dal will implement Pandit Nehru's assurance regarding language policy and all efforts will be made to promote Indian languages.
2. Use of regional languages in administrative and education at all levels will be promoted.

3. Gujral committee's recommendations for promoting Urdu will be implemented.
4. The Eighth Schedule of the Constitution will be extended to respond to urges of other linguistic groups.
5. Janata Dal believes that education as an activity must contribute to the social justice, promote knowledge and excellence in society with equality and accelerate economic growth.
6. It will therefore see that education becomes an effective instrument for securing equality and justice for women, the Scheduled Castes and Tribes, other socially, educationally and economc backward classes, and monitorities.
7. It will implement recommendations by the Kothari Commission to raise the investment in education upto six per cent of the Gross National Product.
8. It will also invest at least 50 per cent of the allotment to education in elementary education.
9. Half of all the funds allocated to education will be invested for promotion of education to women and girls.
10. Janata Dal commits itself to fulfill the goal of universal elementary education. For this, it will devise package of suitable incentives with a special emphasis on mid-day meal scheme.
11. It will introduce the Neighbourhood School concept and universalise it gradually by stages in order to correct elitist aberrations in education. Special programmes will be started to develop excellence and talent without discrimination on grounds of caste, creed, gender or economic status.
12. The Janata Dal considers that education to the minorities of both religious and linguistic origin a national responsibility. It will take vigorous steps to see that constraints on their educational progress are removed as speedily as possible through planned and concerned action.

13. It will consider and take up for early implementation of the Acharya Ramamurty Committee Report (1990) on the review of the 1996 National Policy on Education.

14. The Janata Dal recognises the necessity of reordering the priorities in science and technology with a view to promote self-reliance. It aims at reducing India's dependence upon foreign technolgy.

15. The Dal, therefore, will work out a policy framework to expand the role of industry both in private and public sectors on Research and Development.

16. It wil motivate Indian Industries to work toward the goal of integrating R&D within the production sectors so that indigenous technology can be rapidly developed and foreign technology approximately absorbed.

17. Janata Dal is committed along with the National Front to evolve a new Science and Technology Policy in order to orient science and technology for the benefit of the poor and disadvantaged sections of the society, particularly the tribals, agricultural labours, small farmers, artisans, and women.

18. As this would necessitate re-orientation of the entire scientific community, including engineers and doctors, Janata Dal would give fresh emphasis to development of appropriate and sustainable technology that would include labour-intensive technology, organic farming, rain-fed agriculture, renewable energy sources, biological control of pests and durable houses with local materials.

19. Steps, therefore, will be taken to integrate science and technology policy with agricultural, industrial, health, education, fiscal and import policies of the country.

20. Janata Dal will take urgent steps to promote and nuture the multi-disciplinary fields which are emerging these days quite fast. These fields are informatics, telematics, biotechnology and its application in agriculture, health, medicine, environment and industry, development of novel materials, and non-conventional energy sources.

21. Janata Dal will particularly ensure that all innovative spirit and excellence are nurtured in scienctific community. It will ensure that all possible support is given to the young and creative mind.

ENVIRONMENT POLICY

1. Janata Dal recognises need to review and amend all laws which thwart customary rights of the rural poor over the environmental resources. All programmes of environment protection and development shall be built upon this basic understanding.
2. Its planning process would therefore ensure long-term security for ecology, livelihood and community life for all sections of the society.
3. In its State policy, the Dal will enlist regeneration of nation's resources base as the priority concern. This would be achieved by restructuring developmental priorities.
4. Janata Dal shall take all necessary steps for immediate protection to conserve fragile and critical eco-system.
5. It will also ensure that environmental criteria are part of each planning in each of the developmental sectors.
6. Environmental appraisal of all developmental projects will be ensured from the earliest stage of the Planning.
7. Janata Dal is committed to amend all existing laws and policies and formulate wherever necessary fresh laws on environment protection.
8. It will stop hazardous human interference with environment through industrial operations.
9. It will regulate siting, production and storage of pesticides and toxic chemicals.
10. It will ensure control on air and water pollution.
11. Janata Dal shall formulate laws that would give prior right to the community-level groups to scrutinize new

industry or projects in their neighbourhood and obtain relevant information.

12. It will empower employees obtain similar right to learn in advance about industrial processes and products involved in their work.

MEDIA POLICY

1. The Janata Dal will ensure adopt the Prasar Bharati Act, which the National Front Government had got the Parliament accept. It would stop misuse of the Act which the Congress Party blatantly did while projecting entirely false image of the Prime Minister.
2. Janata Dal believes that self-respect of the nation the demoratic polity of the country militate against such tendencies as exemplified by the Congress Government.
3. The Dal will see that broadcasting observe greater degree of responsibility and sensitivity to Indian cultural ethos. It should achieve an Indian Personality in telecasting and broadcasting.
4. It believes that there should be a regulatory body to oversee both broadcasting and telecasting.
5. This regulatory body would ensure strict adherence to programmes and advertisement codes and other stipulations.
6. The regulatory body would ensure an effective mechanism for public grievances redressal and also would be able to implement its recommendations.
7. It will not allow foreign equity participation in companies directly or indirectly entering the field of private broadcasting.
8. It will set up the apex regulatory body. This body will be an independent autonomous public authority that would represent all sections of and interests in the society. It would control and regulate use of air waves in the interest of people and would prevent invasion of

their rights.

9. It will bring the foreign satellite channels into the ambit of the said regulatory body in order to made them amenable to the Indian laws.
10. Janata Dal will allow the small and medium newspapers grow. It would recommend that suitable environ be created for the section of the Press by helping them modernise.
11. The Dal believes the government's advertising policy and rate structure to the newspapers be uniform and rational, though the financial viability of a paper depends upon its ability to attract ads. It would eliminate the possibility of using advertisements as a lever to influence the press and thereby affecting its freedom.
12. Janata Dal appreciates that there should be a nodal agency to import newsprint on behalf of small and medium newspapers as they donot have necessary infrastructure and the bargaining power for such imports. This extra arragement is needed despite the fact that import of newsprint has been put under the Open General Licence.

ADMINISTRATIVE POLICY

1. Janata Dal believes that present administrative system is in-built with colonial hang-over, therefore, needs radical overhaul.
2. It will hence build up a novel administrative structure with new systems, procedures, tools and would promote new work culture.
3. It will make the administration responsive to the need of the common people.
4. It would make the administration convert into an effective instrument to achieve radical socio- economic transformation.

5. The Dal, thereby, would end alienation between the ruled and the rulers and would give new orientation to the role of the civil servants.
6. It will protect honest civil servants at all levels from harassments and highhandedness.
7. It will seriously undertake to eliminate red-tape botherations, and would instead simplify procedures.
8. Rules of business governing administrative work will be reviewed and role of people's representatives at all levels will be strengthened in relation to administrative processes.

FOREIGN POLICY AND SECURITY APPROACH AND RELATED ISSUES

1. Janata Dal will pursue the foreign policy primarily as a means of advancing national interests.
2. Beyond the national interests, our goal will be realising broader objectives of peace, disarmament and just fair equitable world order.
3. The Dal will be accorded high priority to improving relations with neighbours.
4. These relations will be marked by active partnership in all areas of cooperation and continuing dialogue at all levels.
5. Bilateral issues with neighbours will not be allowed to festered, and active efforts will be there to resolve them.
6. The current tensions in relations with Pakistan will not be be allowed to block people to people contacts. Long-term objectives will be pursued to foster close and friendly relations with Pakistan.
7. Our stand with regard to our relations with neighbours will be India has a vested interest in stability of its neighbouring countries.
8. Janata Dal will take initiatives to revitalise SAARC particularly for moving quickly towards a free trade area

in the region with adequate monetary and financial underpinnings.

9. The Janata Dal will make efforts to forge close links with the United States in diverse fields. However, while doing so it will compromise with India's sovereignty issues.
10. Janata Dal will take corrective measures while dealing with development policy with a view to avoid dependence on other nations, which can effectively close India's options and inhibit its pursuit of independent foreign and security policy.
11. It will resist any effort by the United States or any other major power to play overbearing role in South Asia in the name of balance of power or so-called humanitarian reasons.
12. Janata Dal will impart further momentum to the process of improvement of relations with China.
13. It will make particular efforts to revitalise relations with Russia, which are of crucial importance.
14. It will take steps to safeguard security of the country against threats from any source: internal or external, military or non- military, nuclear or conventional.
15. Its principal plank of disarmament policy will be to seek complete elimination of nuclear weapons worldwide within an agreed time scheduale.
16. It is within the framework of the pursuit of total nuclear disarmament that measures such as freeze on the production of feasible materials, a comprehensive test ban treaty, and non-proliferation of nuclear weapons, have their value.
17. Janata Dal, however, will continue to oppose NPT and its adjunct CTBT.
18. We will work, it says, for the prevention of the qualitative arms race and of the development of any defensive weapon system.

19. It will work for universal arrangements for controlling arms proliferation; and instead would promote commercial and technological cooperation.
20. It will oppose adhoc discriminatory regimes controlled by handful of developed countries.
21. It will formally give a pledge of first non-use of nuclear capability against Pakistan.
22. Janata Dal will work to arrest the erosion of the role of United Nations in the economic fields and its residual role in the security field.
23. It will work to restore the UNO to its holistic functions under the Charter and ensure its financial viability and independence.
24. Apart from UNO, the Dal will use NAM, G-77 and G-15 groups as chosen instruments for conduct of India's multi-lateral diplomacy. It believes that these institutions retain there relevance in the backdrop of vestiges of cold war and the hegemony of new alliance.
25. It will establish a national security council as a top priority. The highest level of expertise from all available sources in the country will be associated with the functioning of the Council. All the necessary institutional arrangements will be made and adequate resources will be provided for effective functioning of the Council.
26. This National Security Council will formulate and disseminate widely a national security policy that would remove any ambiguity in people's mind about safeguard of security.

POLICY TOWARDS TROUBLED STATES

Jammu & Kashmir

1. Janata Dal will end practice of dismissing the elected State governments in the Jammu and Kashmir. It will also correct the short-sighted policies of denying free and fair elections.

2. It will meet the subversion and violence of the militants with force.
3. It will hold open-ended public opinion on the issues of strengthening Article 370 and guaranteeing autonomy to the State. It believes that would create an acceptable solution within the Indian Union.
4. Human rights violation by the security forces shall be strictly dealt with.
5. Conditions of democratic civil society shall be created by holding elections at all levels. Discussions with Pakistan will be held to resolve the dispute, keeping in view sentiments of people of the State.

Above were what the Dal assured people before the hustings for the Eleventh Lok Sabha. Its confidence in people-oriented approach having paid some divident, as is well-understood from its being enthroned to power today, the Dal had offered checkered baits for the state of Jammu & Kashmir. Obviously its ally will be some like-minded party or parties, maybe National Conference by Sheikh Abdullah's son, Farooq Abdullah. The assurances Janata Dal has given to the polity in the State are briefly as under:

1. Construction of 290 km. rail link between Udhampur and Baramula. Survey of the Udhampur-Banihal sector has been completed. Construction work is being started on the Udhampur-Katra sector and Rs 200 crore are to be spent to complete it in the next four years.

   The creation of this rail link will connect the State from one end to the others, open opportunities for trade and industrial development and generate massive employment.

2. The Dulhasti Power Project closed since 1992 is to be reopened as the French company with which there is collaboration has now agreed to restart it.

   After completion of this project, provision of electric power for irrigation and industrial development will increase greatly.

3. Power generation will also be vastly augmented by the commissioning of the Uri Hydroelectric Project of the capacity of 4 × 120 M W by early December.
4. Moghul Road—as an alternative Highway connecting J & K with rest of India, and Jammu, Rajouri, Shopur, Pulwara with Srinagar with a length of 85 kms.—will also be completed.
5. Orders have been issued for a special grant of Rs 2 crore for the purpose of drinking water supply for Kargil town.
6. In addition to this, for providing drinking water in the rural areas in Leh and Kargil districts, Rs. 2 crore will be released as outright Central grant.
7. Keeping in view the remoteness, inaccessibility and difficulty of terrain of Leh and Kargil, the Central allocation under the Desert Development Programme for each district is being raised to Rs 5 crore for each district.

   Orders have been issued for all these programmes today. All these will cost the Centre Rs. 16 crore in all.
8. Orders have also been issued for release of Rs 2 crore for the development of infrastructure like roads and drainage in the Leh town.
9. The Centre has decided to provide a special Central Plan Assistance of Rs 352 crore to balance the State budget during the current year so that the entire Plan outlay of Rs 1050 crore can be utilised for development schemes without having to divert any part of it to meet the non-Plan gap.
10. For improving facilities provided for 27000 migrant families in 13 camps in Jammu like latrines and bathrooms, construction of more one room tenements, buildings for schools being run in the camps, improvement of drainage of facilities in the camps, etc, Government would be providing an additional sum of Rs 6.6 crore to provide the aforementioned additional facilities in the camps to be completed during the current year.

11. A amount of Rs 2.40 crore has been allocated for setting up of a Convention/Conference Centre at Leh.
12. For the development of an Airport at Kargil allocation of at an estimated cost of Rs 25 crore has been made.
13. In the meanwhile, a weekly helicopter service to Kargil in the Winter months instead of the present arrangement of a fortnightly service is being provided.
14. The Government is committed to give maximum autonomy to the State. Once an elected Government is in place, consultations will be held with them to arrive at a consensus. While doing this, the aspirations of all regions in the State, namely, Ladakh, Kashmir Valley and Jammu shall be taken into account.
15. Green cards will be issued to the poor families which will entitle them to receive 10 kg of cereals per family per month on half of the normal price.
16. Cancellation of loans upto Rs 50, 000 for all rural people.
17. Establishment of an Agricultural University in Ranbir Singh Pura.

There are several socio-economic issues which remain and which will be dealt with by the new State Government. The Janata Del would strive to raise these issues and if it comes to power, it promises to resolve them.

PEOPLE'S CHARTER

The poverty of the Kashmiris,—apple growers, cultivators of land, rural and urban artisans and all those working people who live by the tourist trade—is well-known. During the last seven years, their economic plight has only intensified. They have to be provided immediate as well as long term relief; hence Janata Dal's pledges are as under:

I AGRICULTURE AND ALLIED OCCUPATIONS

i) Small and medium irrigation schemes including lift irrigation to provide perennial irrigation to all farmers will be promoted.

ii) Subsidy on Fertilisers which had been reduced by the former the Congress Government and has been partly restored by the present United Front (UF) Government shall be made available for all types of fertilisers in use in the State.

iii) Various concessions provided by the Union Government in its annual budget to the Kisans will be implemented with necessary modifications to benefit the farmers in J & K.

iv) Pesticides for prevention of spread of diseases in apples and other horticultural and agricultural produce shall be made available.

v) Apple growers shall be given liberal credit facilities and other inputs shall also be subsidised. Export of apples will also be promoted.

vi) Credit to apple growers and other horticulturists and farmers will be advanced for construction of godowns.

vii) The State Government's assurance given to the JD during the peaceful agitation for issurance of pass books to the farmers shall be fully and expeditiously implemented.

viii) The minimum programme accepted by the recent conference of Chief Ministers shall be adopted by the State Assembly, if JD is voted to power, and implemented on priority basis with liberal assistance from the Centre. It includes provision of safe drinking water, shelter for the houseless, approach roads in all villages, universal primary education, primary health facilities in all villages and towns.

II INDUSTRIAL DEVELOPMENT AND TOURISM

i) Those engaged in tourist trade like houseboat pliers shall be given the same loan waiver concessions, as the farmers.

ii) Oil drilling in the Sunisar lake area abandoned without full exploration shall be resumed as prospective studies have confirmed the existence of oil fields in the area.

iii) Mini training industrial, institutes shall be established at Bloc level, for imparting training for self-employment.

iv) Sheel rearing, silk and wool production, dairy farming and allied occupations shall be given the fullest support.

v) Tourism shall be promoted by giving incentives in respect of comfortable but reasonably cheap accommodation and travel facilities. Tourist resorts shall be developed in several new places.

III WOMEN AND YOUTH

i) The State Assembly shall adopt legislation for providing reservation of one-third of the seats in the assembly to women.

ii) A State Human Rights Commission on the lines of National Human Rights Commission and district level Human Rights Courts shall be appointed.

iii) State, regional and district level youth and student councils shall be set up to youth in ensuring their participation in rebuilding the State and its developmental and power structure.

IV REGIONAL AND LOCAL ISSUES

i) Jammu city shall be given 'B' status.

ii) Dogri language shall be included in the Schedule VIII of the Constitution.

iii) Separate regional committees for the three regions of Srinagar Valley, Jammu and Ladakh will be established.

iv) Elections to all local bodies and Panchayati Raj Institutions shall be hell expeditiously after adopting the requisite legislation on the line of the 73rd and 74th Constitutional amendments.

v) All pending cases of industrial relations shall be resolved by negotiations and free trade union activity shall be encouraged. All court cases pending against trade union leaders of State Government employees shall be reviewed for withdrawal or speedy trial. All disciplinary actions against them for activities shall be reviewed.

V GENERAL WELFARE

i) Ration cards for all citizens issued over a decade ago and not renewed thereafter shall be renewed exhaustically.

ii) Efforts shall be made that the age limit exemption provided to migrants in eligibility for Central Government jobs is fully implemented and extended to all residents of J&K. The same exemption will be done for the State Government services.

VI SOCIAL JUSTICE

i) Recommendations of the Mandal Commission for Socially and Educationally Backward Castes (SEBCs) shall be implemented in letter and spirit. For this purpose the Malik Commission has already been urged to finalise the list of SEBCs on the guidelines of the Mandal Commission.

ii) Migrants who were forced by circumstances to leave their homes shall be encouraged to return to their homes by providing full security. They shall be given credit and other facilities as well as incentive schemes to improve their economic status. Rehabilitation Programmes shall be initiated on a large scale. Grants for construction of houses and shops shall be given to those whose properties have suffered damage or destruction.

Janata Dal would appeal to all people in the State to forgive and forget the traumas of the past. There have been terrible mistakes which have played have with the peace, prosperity well being and unity of the people and State. Attempts have been made to separate J&K from the rest of India, to separate the Jammu region from the rest of the State and to divide the people on communal lines. All such attempts have however failed miserably. However, they have fouled the social relationships fraternity and amity.

On the other hand, absolute power enjoyed by regimes ruling the State decade after decade, "elected" by fraudulent hustings in the absence of the Legislature, has engendered as climate of corruption at all levels—more particularly in high places. Administrative sensitivity to needs of the people have been totally missing for most of the history of J&K after Independence. People's well-being could hardly be promoted under present circumstances.

NORTH-EAST STATES

1. The region beyond Siliguri, the chicken's neck, offers problems both complex and delicate. This region is important geographically as well as politically. It was particularly affected by the partition. Continuous influx of people from Bangladesh and other areas has created tensions. Insurgencies based on various historical and ethnic interests have added to the confusion. Sense of injury, neglect and exploitation which have given expression through insurgent activities, require deeper understanding. Janata Dal promises sensitive handling of the entire problems. It ensures that it will secure North-East's emotional integration with the rest of the country.
2. Janata Dal understands that problems of the North-East cannot be properly comprehended unless placed in a larger regional setting.
3. Janata Dal also appreciates that its each territorial entity has its own ethnic problems, each ethnic group has its own sense of identity and aspirations. Hence, there has to be a policy for which it will go beyond conventional thinking.

4. It would not let matter drift any longer or be content adhoc responses to periodic eruption.
5. As did the erstwhile National Front government, Janata Dal also will take keen sympathetic interests in problems of Assam. It can legitimately claim that during its brief tenure it did meet more aspirations of people than its previous Congress Government. Its achievement included substantial rise in oil royalty, sanctioning of a refinery and other economic and financial benefits.
6. It will also consider sympathetically the demands for application of the 6th Schedule of the Consitution of India to some North-Eastern states like Manipur.

POLICY ON HUMAN RIGHTS

1. Janata Dal will ensure all assistance to the National Human Rights Commission so that it continues to act independently without any problems.
2. State and district level Human Rights Commission will be constituted.
3. In order to ensure that they act independently, the prosecuting counsels who assist them, will be recruited by the National and State level commissions from among lawyers committed to human rights.
4. Human Rights education will be given at school, college and University levels. It will include the message of human dignity and fraternity.
5. It will revise to delete the references in Indian Penal Code which are not found to accord with human rights.
6. The Dal is particular about the misuse of Sections 107, 109 and 151 of the IPC which will be stopped.
7. Special laws to handle extraordinary situations in the insurgency-prone areas will be substantially reviewed to remove any possibility of their misuse. United Nations' conventions on torture and refugees will be ratified.

JANATA DAL'S POLICY ON PUBLIC HEALTH

1. Janata Dal believes that preventive, promotive and curative health care requires inter-sectoral approach and represents a primary investment of human development.
2. It will, therefore, lay special emphasis on reducing infant mortality, universal immunization malnutrition.
3. On top priority will be preventing the spread of diseases like AIDS through mass consciousness programmes and controlling of drug prices.

POLICY ON EX-SERVICEMEN

1. The National Front government had announced on 13 October 1990 adhoc increase in pensions for JCOs, and ORs and their equivalents in the Indian Navy, Air Force who had retired before 1 January 1986. This ad hoc increment in pension was to be effected from 1 April 1990, and proposed similar benefits to officers too.

   The subsequent governments did not implement the decision and the announcement went a-begging.

   The Janata Dal reaffirms its commitment to implement the announcement without further delay and also to sanction similar increase for officers with effect from 1 January 1990.
2. It will make the welfare of ex-servicemen a joint responsibility of State Governments and the Central Government. Earlier it was exclusively a responsibility of the concerned State Government.
3. It also plans to take effective monitoring steps to provide meaningful post-retirememt employment to defence personnel.

5

Backgrounder: Janata Party

THE JANATA PARTY is a child of the most epoch-making struggle in the history of Indian democracy. In March 1977 the people of India, under the inspiring leadership of Jayaprakash Narayan, elected the Janata Party to power and entrusted it with the task of restoring democracy and freedom to the people and constructing an egalitarian and decentralised social order based on the Gandhian perspective. In this perspective political and economic tasks involve a common approach, that of providing the people themselves—above all to the poor and deprived among them—both the opportunity and the power to shape their own lives and destiny.

In the first Election Manifesto (1977), the Janata Party, had declared: "The Janata Party is dedicated to the values and ideals of Gandhiji. It is dedicated to the task of building a democratic State in India, drawing inspiration from our rich heritage, and the noble traditions of our struggle for independence. In other words, the Janata Party's ideology is to foster democracy in all its dimensions—economic, political, social and cultural. This has to be done by learning from our ancient history and the Freedom struggle; within the Gandhian framework."

The Janata Party was ushered into power in 1977 on the strength of the youth (who constitute over seventy per cent of the electorate). However, this mandate of the youth was soon betrayed through splits and defections. The Janata Party has bled through defections in the 1980s, but it is still alive and kicking today. The mission of the Party, given to it by JP, is still unaccomplished and yet relevant. Those of us who are remained steadfast and suffered the wilderness for it, have kept this historic Party alive. In 1977, the nation's democratic structure was under seige and the nation was in crisis. Today, the nation is on the throes of a deep identity crisis and ideological bankruptcy. At the crossroads of history today, the future of our country is crucially dependent on making the right choice on the direction for the country. While the Freedom Struggle had given the people a clear identity and the underpinning of its ideology, the last one and a-half decades have thrown up anti-national and anti-social forces which now seriously threaten our national integrity, and have sown doubts in the people's mind about the nation's future. Organizations such as RSS, LTTE, Hizbullah etc., are all equally responsible for today's atmosphere. No political party has come forward to provide an answer.

The political parties of today have in fact failed so far to formulate a concept of our identity and relevant ideology. The continued inability of political parties to formulate an acceptable concept of identity and ideology is dangerous for our democracy. No wonder, our people are confused about the future, and the youth gone astray. If this continues, the ensuing disorder may threaten the collapse of the Indian Union, which, in the Soviet Union and elsewhere has become a reality. But still no political party today is thinking along these futuristic terms. The Congress Party of today cannot provide the frame work for our identity and ideology because the Party itself is suffering from a crisis of identity and ideology. There is a wide gap between policy and practice in the Congress Party. With the collapse of Communist rule in the erstwhile Soviet Union and Eastern Europe, the ideology of the Communists stands discredited.

The BJP which frequently, albeit intermittently, talks of Hindu Rashtra, has essentially a negative outlook. The Party has defined India's identity and ideology in purely anti-

Muslim terms, and not in positive terms. Every Hindu concept formulated by the BJP has a predominantly anti-Muslim content. It thus believes in a zero-sum society. That is, Hindus can gain only if the Muslims lose. In practice, the Party is anti-Christian and anti-Sikh as well. There is nothing of a 'Renaissance' in their view of Hindu Rashtra. It has a strong fascist streak. BJP does not envisage, as we do, disbanding the caste system by enforcing the equality of sexes, or abolition of castes, taboos and superstition. It fact, BJP wants to fossilize the inequalities accumulated in Hindu tradition. Furthermore, a united India is impossible if we leave out Muslims, Sikhs and Christians of the population in our reckoning of the nation. But this is precisely what the BJP is doing, much the same way that the Hindu Mahasabha did before Partition. Fanaticism divided India in 1947. It can do so once again and therefore patriots should join together not to allow it.

All the Left parties—like CPI, CPI(M), Marxist-Leninist groups and the other constituents of the National Front like Janata Dal, Samajvadi Party etc., and above all the Congress Party by passionately advocating the cause of State- controlled Socialism until recently—have only laid solid foundations for raising a superstructure of mega corruption which has only lured hundreds of thousands of criminals and anti-social elements into the noble arena of politics and public life.

The Hawala Scandal in New Delhi, the rapacious greed of top-notch politician in Bihar graphically brought in to focus by the multi-crore scandal of animal husbandry department in Bihar, and the Himalayan corruption in Tamil Nadu should all be viewed as the logical culmination of State-sponsored Socialism which was most appropriately described by Rajaji as "A Licence-Permit- Control and Quota Raj."

The Congress Party which has been enjoying power and authority most of the time after Independence has failed to wipe out poverty. Janata Party believes that the only hope of redemption of the country is in the replacement of the present Government, by leaders whose ideal is integrity in public and private life, whose ambition is to use their high authority for the amelioration of the common man's condition, whose patriotism is above temptation of any kind and is not prostituted for perverse ends and personal gain. *This is not an easy task, but all long journeys begin with a first step.*

Janata Party is pledged to the establishment of **minimum government and maximum welfare for all.** Janata Party stands for social justice and removal of disparities of opportunity and equitably distributed welfare. Statism is not the road to socialism. It is the way to authoritarianism at the top and serfdom at the bottom. Janata Party wants to create a society with a political government powerful in its legitimate domain and minimal elsewhere, a government that governs but does not dabble in business, arts, media, justice, religion and piety.

Drawing on the inspiration of Jayaprakash Narayan, with adherence to the moral edicts of Mahatma Gandhi, the philosophies of Swami Vivekananda and Sri Aurobindo, the poetry of Iqbal and Subramania Bharathi, the patriotic fervour of Bankim Chandra Chatterjee, the courage and conviction of Mahatma Phule and Dr Ambedkar, and the social reform zeal of Periar EV Ramaswami Naicker, the Janata Party rededicates itself to a virile concept of national identity and a nationalist ideology embodied in an implementable Agenda. This is the Janata Party's Agenda for National Renaissance, representing the ideological framework of the party.

Manifesto: Janata Party

POLITICAL: DECENTRALISATION

1. For qualitative change in political management through principled rational distribution of political powers between the Centre and States, and for taking that to village grassroots level, Janata Party would:
   a) review Central, State and concurrent lists of all subjects;
   b) establish an effective Inter-State Council as envisaged in the Constitution for harmonious, speedy and productive outcome of Centre-State issues,
   c) ensure through various constitutional, legal and fiscal arrangements economic viability of States,
   d) effectively implement the Article 40 of the Directive Principles of State Policy in the Constitution regarding decentralisation through "units of self government" upto the village level,
   e) reorganise states appropriately to improve administration and enhance citizens' satisfaction.

ELECTORAL REFORMS

1. Janata stands for substantial reforms of structure of political parties and the electoral systems.
2. It wants political parties should have inner democratic structure based on periodic elections as part of Constitution.
3. They shall be made to submit audited accounts regularly.
4. It wants that State shall contribute to election expenses.
5. It wants voters must have identity cards.
6. It wants voters' list should be annually updated and displayed permanently at each polling booth.
7. It will initiate a review of the existing system of political and administrative divisions, and thereafter will evolve

to make political constituencies coterminus with administrative divisions. This will presage formation of multiple tiers of democratic institutions to oversee the implementation of policies.

8. It will make administrators responsible to local and regional political institutions and not to the distant masters.
9. In short, it wants that top down parental system of the colonial era go for ever and true democratisation of Indian nation begins.
10. Janata Party will take care to induct honest efficient and qualified people in the arena of public life and thereby rescue the nation from clutches of thieves and goons who have almost usurped the Independence. Indeed, it believes that the task is one of metamorphosis of a nation.
11. Janata Party promises to all patriotic Indians that they will soon have a good fortune, and participate in the task of resurrection of their great nation, thereby vindicating their honour of the martyrs whose sacrifices brought us freedom.
12. Its overall objective is to enhance responsiveness and accountability of nation's managers — both elected and administrative.
13. It will gear them to meet the challenge of providing a vibrant government that protects life, upholds the Constitution and leads them on the path of growth and social justice.
14. It will amend Articles 102 and 191 of the Constitution to make any appeal to voters in the name of religion a cause for disqualification from Parliament and Legislatures.

Inculcating Basic Moral Values

1. It will encourage inter-caste and inter-religious marriages in its aim to build up a casteless India.

2. It will educate masses on equality of religions and fostering equal respect for the theology of all religions.
3. It will restructure education system and include the basic precepts of all religions to promote truthfulness, courage and austerity.
4. Emphasis on character building will be given by Janata Party if voted to power. At the same time it will give governmental assistance to voluntary organisations which conduct classes, programmes, camps to promote character building through approved syllabus.
5. It will publicise through Doordarshan and other media concepts of casteless society, equality of sexes and inculcate general concern for the poor and the under-privileged.
6. It will promote festivals, cultural events, get-togethers for social interaction based on equality.

POLICY ON ECONOMY OF THE NATION

Globalisation, Liberalisation

1. There is a broad consensus today on merits of freeing nation's economy from the shackles of the State, by process of deregulation.

   Janata Party believes although there is great controversies over how much to open up to foreign participation, India combine foreign capital and technology with Indian human talents. This is best illustrated in the Computer and Software industries.
2. It believes that in the eagerness to join global bandwagon of liberalisation and privatisation, the Congress Government of PV Narasimha Rao has abandoned responsibilities and vacated space. It hardly amounts to process of economic reforms.

   Also, that, the government had been hesitant and ambivalent commitment to reform process, despite its acceding to demands of giving up its monopoly in practically all infrastructural areas except railways, energy, telecommunications and civil aviation including foreign areas.

Janata Party pledges itself to the cause of deepening widening and broadening the vistas and processes of globalisation, liberalisation and privatisation in India with focus on maximisation of production, employment and exports.

3. Janata Party wishes to create an economic environment in which the business community in India can get behind the government to keep up the momentum. It will thus help in accelerating the process of liberalisation in India.
4. If voted to power the Government's major economic role will be to use taxation and set interest rates which would eventually raise the rate of savings.
5. It will induce investments that will promote employment, modernise agriculture, encourage efficient small industries and encourage grassroots capitalism to improve life of both rural and urban poor.
6. To achieve better results, Janata Party will have to transform our economy to one of low-cost employment generating economy, it feels.
7. Janata Party pledges itself to the cause of full privatisation of public sector in accordance with suitably drawn time bound programmes.
8. In this context its concern will be to redefine the role of the government both Central and State, in cases of power, roads, irrigation and telecoms.
9. Also, government's role has to be redefined with regard to power, roads, irrigation and telecoms to provide appropriate legal, regulatory and administrative framework for them.

This is important for ensuring smooth and accelerated flow of private investment. Janata Party will take on the above issue on war footing.

10. Janata Party will transform the rural economy by according the status of "Industry" to agriculture and also by opening the scope of export to the agricultural and bio-technological products.
11. Rates of interest for the investment in agriculture, agricultural export, agro-based products, biotechnology etc would be brought down to the level of 5 per cent.
12. Janata Party believes that Free Ports are the gateways of international trade and commerce. Keeping in view the examples of Singapore and Hongkong, the Janata Party pledges itself to the policy of declaring Bombay and Tuticorin ports as Free Ports.

Control of Inflation, New Programme of Food Stamps

1. Janata Party will take effective steps not only to bring down the prices of essential commodities but also to introduce a new and revolutionary public distribution system. The existing system of public distribution is marked by total inefficiency and absolute corruption. The party will introduce a new system which will make it possible for poorer sections and the middle class get all their essential commodities at very reasonable prices.
2. It will introduce a novel system of Food Stamps in place of the existing one which only ensures large scale procurement, massive storage and a large network of distribution.
3. The Food Stamps programme ensure higher food consumption and food-based income for the locals without entailing administrative burden. It also cuts the costs associated with a system of general price subsidies.
4. Food Stamps transfer income not as cash per se, but as food purchasing power to vulnerable households. It fosters better consumption, boosts up local production by raising demand for basic local products.
5. Once the Food Stamps programme gets going, the Party government would be able to do away with the existing networks of Food Corporation of India, State Civil Sup-

plies Corporation and the fair price shops. By withdrawing these agencies of food distribution, the government will be successful in cutting through the cost overhead of commodity handling and the resultant economic costs to the society.

6. It will suitably target the New Food Stamps Programme to meet the requirements of the most impoverished and vulnerable sections of the society.

Tax Reforms

1. Janata Party will bring about a radical transformation in the existing taxing system, so that it can become objective, transparent and non-discretionary.
2. Personal income tax accounts for only 2 per cent of the Central revenue. It is the fountainhead of corruption in India. Janata Party will abolish personal income tax, and liberate citizens from the tyranny of the income tax officials.
3. It will simplify and rationalise massively the existing system of indirect taxes.
4. It will allow tax deductions for every expense of the corporations which will promote social welfare of employees by schemes for housing, transportation, medical care, education and training.

REFORMS IN LEGAL SYSTEM

1. It will review all legislations and abolish the redundant Acts and provisions.
2. It will bring together diverse amendments, notifications, ordinances, orders etc. to reduce them into four broad areas, namely, civil, criminal, economic and social.
3. A veritable legislative jungle has been created by the socialist epoch and the licence-permit-inspector Raj in the past.

   Janata Party will review the entire body of law, and weed out such laws that does not serve any rational purpose but only creates harassment for the litigants and citizens and also indirectly helps the criminals.

4. It will edit in four volumes all the gamut of the valid legislation so that even the common man of the street comes to know what law exactly is. These volumes will be published every year on the FIRST DECEMBER to make them effective from the following FIRST JANUARY.
5. All future legislations, whatever be the dates of adoption, will be effective from the FIRST day of the following year. Exception, however, will be only when a legislation is needed to be adopted with immediate effect.
6. Systematic arrangements for updating the codes so that the presumption of knowledge of law applies only to what figures explicitly in the latest edition of the code concerned.
7. It believes that presumption of knowledge of law should be limited only to such legislations that appear formally in print in systematic updated volumes.
8. It will computerise all recognised jurisprudence.

Restructuring the Education System and Reforms

The destiny of India is being shaped in class rooms. On the quality of people coming out of our schools and colleges will depend India's success in all aspects of national reconstruction. In India, while the most children enroll at the beginning primary schools more than 50 percent drop out from schools before completing the cycle because of poor quality of schools and inherent poverty. Among those who stay back in schools, quality of education achievement is abysmally low. Taking into account these critical problems of disparities, which also include regional disparities, Janata Party has adopted far-reaching projects on educational reforms.

1. It will implement broad-based functionally relevant educational programmes to remove adult illiteracy.
2. It will launch mass movement involving entire administrative and political apparatus, utilize the services of NGOs to achieve universal literacy.

3. It believes that vocationalisation of higher secondary level of education and vocational training through special institutions are essential to provide manpower for the maintenance of infrastructure. This is also necessary for developing production technologies.
4. In order to attain that goal care would be taken to make the school system integrate with its immediate environment and the community in which it is located.
5. It will take measures to double the teachers' salaries. For, the party believes that without ensuring economic security of the teaching community the educational system cannot be improved.

POLICY ON SOCIAL JUSTICE

1. Towards the goal of social justice and equal opportunity, the Party will introduce special programmes for welfare of the minority, the physically handicapped, the aged and the infirm. It will take special care of the handicapped women, the destitute females and other impoverished people under the poverty line.
2. The Janata Party will take human beings as both the means and means of development. It doesn't take people as convenient fodder for materialistic machine.
3. It will, therefore, promote a concept of human development with emphasis on four essential components: (a) Productivity, (b) Equity, (c) Sustainability, and, (d) Empowerment.
4. It will specially work for effective implementation of programmes for upliftment of Scheduled Castes and Scheduled Tribe members of the society. To attain this goal, the cornerstone for the Party will be the Constitutional provisions and the National Human Rights Charter.
5. It will fully implement the Eliaperumal Commission Report (1969).
6. The Party is committed to people to abolish the heinous

practices of child labour, bonded labour and other forms of labour exploitation by the year 2000.

7. For the purpose it will adopt measures outlined by the Subramanium Commission on Labour Standards Report (1996).
8. The Party would seek to enact a National Labour Standards Act to integrate all the various labour laws in force since 1855 so as to meet desirable International Labour Conventions of the ILO, as recommended by the commission.

Effective National Security Doctrine

Janata Party will ensure the following:

1. It will raise the Defence Budget to 7 per cent of the GDP.
2. It will allot 30 per cent of the Defence Budget to the Navy to set up an effective naval monitoring section in Car Nicobar. It will also develop a Blue Water Navy.
3. It will work for making South Asia a terrorist-free zone by asserting the right of Indian Armed Forces to cross the national frontiers with a view to put down terrorism and terrorist camps.
4. It will work out close diplomatic relations will Israel and China based upon principles of mutual accommodation and interests.
5. It will declare that India will effectively defend human rights of people of Indian origin violated in any part in the world.
6. It will work to promote Democracy as a system in South Asian countries.

Strong Law and Order Machinery

Towards the goal of strong law and order atmosphere in the country. The Janata Party has some indepth visions. It believes that mandate to people prone to become political criminals and/or criminal politicians has become more effective than the law and order machinery itself. It pains to notice that the police administration has been subverted by corrupt recruitment, plethora of laws and criminal-politician axis. To tackle these and other related issues effectively, the Party will take following measures:

(a) Ruthless suppression of gangsterism, terrorism and bellicose fundamentalism.

(b) Re-establishment of Rule of Law.

(c) Revamping the Intelligence system.

(d) Effective Interpol Interaction and Coordination.

(e) Computerisation of Criminal Record History.

WOMEN RIGHTS AND ELIMINATION OF GENDER DISCRIMINATION

1. With a view to quell the ill-effects of the male dominated societal norms, the influence of outworn tradition, prejudice, ignorance which had been always the dominating factor in atrocities and violence against women, particularly against the economically weaker sections like SC and ST members, Janata Party vouchsafe to activate the State law and order enforcement body to the best ever effective form.
2. For the purpose it will effectively reorganise the State law and order enforcement body like the Police, the Judiciary and the Bureaucracy, so that they cannot afford to remain indifferent to the condition of women.
3. It pledges to give importance to women's education and female literacy as the mother is the primary teacher of the child.
4. The Party feels that the literacy of women lags behind that of the men. Janata Party will strive to bridge the gap by expanding opportunities for women's education in rural areas, opening Child Care Centres, Hostels for Working Women and Students.
5. The Party will create new institutions and formulate newer programmes to strengthen potentials of women for training and employment.

6. It will streamline the fora like National Policies and Programmes of Health, Nutrition and Population Control so that the benefits from these institutions can reach women to the remotest areas.
7. Special steps it will take to see that benefits from science and technologies reach to all women, particularly, to the rural areas.
8. It will work to create special programmes to develop political awareness among women and involve them in policy decisions at various levels. In this task voluntary agencies will also be made to play important roles through various streamlined incentives.
9. The Party will suitably amend the existing laws affecting security and life of women with special accent, "Equal Rights for Women."

REFORMS IN BASIC HEALTH FACILITIES

1. Janata Party commits itself to the cause for correction of existing gross anomalies in our medical education and health care delivery system. It notes with concern that 75 per cent of the population who are low middle class or the poor live in rural India, where adequate or proportionate PHCs do not exist. We do not produce doctors for the PHCs.
2. Janata Party has noted that an average MBBS doctor after passing seeks for his post-graduation and instead of joining a PHC, tries to become a specialist and seeks his career in urban set up Janata Party will check this tendency.
3. A National Programme for training village level workers in the Science and Art of treatment of common ailments will be launched through well-known medicines in rural areas.

POLICY TOWARDS ENVIRONMENT PROTECTION

1. Janata Party notes with deep concern that forces of economic growth have unleashed continuous threat to our

environment. These forces are Primarily urbanisation, industrialisation and the like. These have correlated human health care and the ecosystems. The hazards include presence of pollutants in air such as suspended particulates, in water such as coliform that have outreached the level of healthy balance.

Janata Party pledges that with a view to keep the environmental balance it would call for an integrated enrichment of village ecosystem and systematic "greening" of rural India.

2. The calculus of proprieties for conservation of forests, bio-diversity and wildlife is inherently not quite clear cut. This will be rectified.
3. The task is however doubly difficult in India as hard, quantitative data and information are constantly scarce as to what exactly is happening to India's ecosystem and why. Party's priority therefore will be to build up more and more information and data.
4. Janata Party will introduce a suitable Environmental Action Programme (EAP) creating a comprehensive regulatory and strategic framework for control of pollution and conservation of forests, wildlife and bio-diversity.

SUMMARY

The salient features of the Janata Party Programme therefore are as under:

a) Inducting honest efficient qualified people into politics.
b) Opening export opportunities to agriculture and dairy products.
c) Setting up free ports in Bombay and Tuticorin.
d) Privatisation of public sector units.
e) Controlling inflation by food stamps systems for providing essential commodities at low prices.
f) Southern River Grid for adequate water supply.
g) Abolition of personal Income Tax.

h) Restructuring education system by giving priority to primary education.

i) Vocational training option to be introduced in education.

j) Doubling of teacher's salaries.

providing basic health facilities through environment protection measures.

k) Training village level workers for treating common allments through well-known medicines.

l) Strong law and order machinery by revamping the intelligence system.

m) Inducting research studies.

n) Formulating a counter-terrorist strategy.

(o) Developing efficient Interpole Interaction and Coordination.

p) Computerisation of criminal record history.

q) Effective national security doctrine.

r) Building up better social justice and women rights.

CONCLUSION

Janata Party will rededicate itself to grand vision of Mahadev Govinda Ranade, as is outlined in his own soul stirring words;

> "With buoyant hope, with liberal manhood, with a faith that never shirks duty, with a justice that deals fairly to all, with unclouded intellect and with all her powers fully cultivated India will take her proper rank among the nations of the world and be the master of the situation and of her own destiny. This is the cherished home. This is the Promised Land. Happy are they who see it in distant vision; happier those who are permitted to work and to clear the way onto it and happiest those who live to see it with their own eyes and tread on the holy soil once more."

All voice and power to the People.

6

Backgrounder: Left Front Parties

COMMUNIST PARTY OF INDIA (MARXIST)

Congress (I) Rule

THE LAST FIVE years of the Congress rule has been a period of chronic instability for the people of our country.

The economic policies of unbriddled liberalisation has led to large scale privatisation. Multinational corporations have gained entry into the core sectors of telecommunications, power, coal, steel, oil etc. The public sector is being sold off. The financial sector—banks, insurance, etc.—is sought to be privatised. At the same time, the country's total debt has crossed Rs 6 lakh crore. The interest payment on this in the current year is over Rs 60,000 crore equivalent to our entire fiscal deficit in the current year. The net result has been the mortgaging of the economy and undermining its self-reliant basis.

These policies have meant bonanza for the big business and misery for the mass of the people. Companies like ITC, Reliance, Larsen & Tubro, Mahindra & Mahindra have seen an increase in their profits by over 300 per cent. At the opposite end every aspect of a common man's existence has worsened.

The conditions in rural India, which houses two-thirds of our population has distinctly worsened. The real wages of agricultural workers has fallen. Their cost of living index has risen the sharpest. There are widespread reports of starvation deaths. The refusal to implement land reforms has kept the vast mass of peasantry in conditions of abject poverty. The growth of foodgrain production is just about keeping pace with the population growth. Coupled with the scuttling of the public distribution system, this implies a grave threat to food security for the most needy. The refusal to evolve a national water policy results in crores of rupees worth of property and precious lives being lost due to annual floods and drought. On top of this come the burdens of the new economic policy.

Price Rise: On the economic front the Congress (I) had promised in 1991 election manifesto that within the first 100 days the prices of essential commodities will be rolled back to levels of July 1990. Daily experience shown all of us that the results have been to the contrary. Rice costs double of what it cost in 1991; the prices of pulses (*dal*) have risen nearly twice and in some cases three times; edible oil has become more expensive. So has wheat, sugar, tea and even salt. During these five years, the Central Government resorted to unprecedented administrative price hikes. In fact every single item that constitutes the daily consumption basket of millions of Indians are today much more expensive, nearly double of what it was five years ago.

Unemployment: The Congress (I) had promised that it will create 10 million new jobs per year. Instead what is the situation today? In January 1995, 36,737,000 people were registered at the employment exchange an increase of 444,000 from January 1994. Over four lakh industrial units that employed lakhs of people are today either closed or sick. In fact instead of increasing employment even those who were employed earlier are on the streets. Additionally the privatisation of the public sector is reducing the employment potential. The Government's plans would result in some 6,46,000 people who were employed in the public sector being eventually retrenched. According to the Government itself 1.4 lakh public sector employees had already had to face the axe. Many schemes have been announced by the Government with much fanfare. But they have miserably failed to provide any relief to the people. Of the allocation made only 14.3 per cent reaches the needy.

Education: The Congress (I) had promised expanding investment in primary and secondary education. Instead, in real terms there has been a contraction of Central Government's expenditure. Privatisation and commercialisation of education have been highlights making both the access to and cost of education beyond the reach of the common man.

Health: The Congress (I) had promised an increase in allocation for public health to achieve Health for all by 2000. Instead there has been an actual decline in the per capita health expenditure from Rs.120 to Rs.116, on the public health system from Rs 103 to Rs 94 and on disease control programmes from Rs 103 to Rs 89 (between 89-90 and 92-93). The withdrawal of the government from its obligations in this sector resulted in skyrocketing of cost of health facilities with privatisation which is keeping the health requirements of the people beyond their reach. At the same time the prices of medicines have shot up drastically, keeping them beyond the reach of those who need them most. This has resulted in a massive outbreak of diseases and the death of lakhs of people due to completely preventable and curable diseases like Malaria and TB.

Poverty: It had promised the reduction of poverty. According to the Planning Commission's own figures, the number of people below the poverty line increased from 35.6 per cent in 1990-91 to 39.6 percent in 1994-95.

Food security: It had promised expansion of the public distribution system and its greater reach to feed the needy. Instead what we see during these five years has been a sharp decline in the quantity bought by the people through the public distribution system. This has been primarily due to the fact that the prices of rice have been doubled and that of wheat increased by 75 per cent in the ration shops during this period. The threat of food security is bound to aggravate in the coming years with the shift from foodgrain production to commercial crops as a result of the new agricultural policies.

Foreign Debt: It had promised to prevent India falling into a debt trap. During these years India's foreign debt has risen to over Rs 6,00,000 crore. In 1993-94 the indebtedness of the country increased by Rs 244 crore every day or over 10 crore every hour. India today is the third largest debtor in the world.

It had promised to curb conspicuous consumption and tackle the menace of black money. On the contrary these five years have seen the illegal and immoral enrichment of the ruling politicians businessman-bureaucrat nexus and maximum growth in corruption and black money.

Threats to secularism: It is in this sphere that the Congress (I)'s betrayal to both India as a nation and people has been exposed.

It had promised that it will protect the Babri Masjid and firmly implement the status quo of all existing places of worships as of 15th August, 1947.

The despicable destruction of the Babri Masjid by the BJP-RSS-VHP combine and the continuously compromising positions taken by the Congress leadership has contributed to worsening of the communal situation in our country. The Congress (I) had promised in its manifesto last time that all parties must "respect the order and verdict of the court".

Yet it allowed the demolition to take place. Subsequently, instead of clubbing all pending cases and bringing them before the Supreme Court for speedy disposal as suggested by the CPI(M), it deliberately stalled the issue even after the demolition and adopted the wrong method of a presidential reference on whether the mosque was built on any Hindu religious structure. The Supreme Court refused to rightly entertain such a reference. The net result is that till date there has been no solution. Thus, its abject compromise with the communal forces led to the worsening of the situation where casualties in the communal riots during the last five years and the loss of property has been the highest in recent memory.

Kashmir: It had promised that a political solution to the problem. Despite the change in mood of the people in the Valley who are getting increasingly alienated with the extremists, the last five years have seen the total absence of a political initiative to solve the problem.

Women: It had promised a better deal for women of India. Instead what we have seen during the last five years has been a sharp rise in all forms of atrocities perpetuated against women. The brunt of the negative impact of the economic policies is being borne by working women.

Electoral Reforms: It had promised electoral reforms to curb both the excessive use of money and muscle power. It has singularly failed to bring forward any proposal during these last five years.

Foreign Policy: It has promised the strengthening of the non- aligned foreign policy of our country. The last five years have seen unashamed succumbing to pressures of US imperialism in matters of defence including the beginning of hitherto unknown military pacts with the USA. Its vacillation in the foreign policy have seen Indian troops acting under UN/US commands in various parts of the world violating the accepted Indian principles of non-interference in the internal affairs of other countries. In fact, at a time when US imperialism is attempting to impose its New World Order, India's traditional anti-imperialist voice in international fora was missing. As one of the leaders of the NAM, India during these five years, miserably failed to discharge its anti-imperialist duties.

In short, on each and every promise that the Congress had made to the people five years ago the results have been quite opposite. As a consequence the living conditions of the people have worsened, the country's unity and security further threatened and economic sovereignty and self-reliance further jeopardised.

Corruption — Order of the Day

These five years have seen totally unprecedented levels of institutionalised corruption. The hallmark of the Narasimha Rao regime has been the exponential growth of both the number of scams and the amount looted through them. No area was left untouched, no stone unturned to loot public assets by the criminal-ruling party politician-business man-bureaucrat nexus.

The Rao Government began its tenure by stalling the Bofors investigation that is not complete till date. Then came the bank scam, the disinvestment of public sector scam, the sugar scam, Bailadila mine deal, Enron deal, Railway-ABB deal, telecom scam and finally the Hawala scam. For the first time since Independence, as many as 15 ministers of the Rao Cabinet were forced to resign under a cloud. There are many other scams as well — St. Kitts, Goldstar etc. Criminal activities of Chandraswami under political clout of Congress Government, which are now, subjudice. The very fact that the Rao Government that assumed office as a minority government turned itself into a majority by organising defections using its money power speaks volumes. Moral and material corruption has become the order of the day.

The Congress party is now a political party with no internal democracy and plagued by internecine quarrels; it has turned itself into an organisation whose leadership is abandoning all commitment to the national cause.

The only answer to redeem the situation is to prevent the return of the Congress (I) to the helm of affairs. Defeat of the Congress signifies the safeguarding of the vision of modern independent India that we shaped during the freedom struggle.

THE COMMUNAL DANGER

Never since the partition of the country, have the communal forces mounted such an offensive as has been witnessed during the last five years. Violating all assurances to the National

Integration Council, Supreme Court and to the people the BJP went ahead and organised the dastardly demolition of the Babri Masjid. This was followed by a period of worst social instability with large scale spread of communal riots, wanton killings and destruction of property. The BJP brazenly defended this action. In order to consolidate the communal forces it struck an alliance with the rabid communal and chauvanist Shiv Sena in Maharashtra.

During these five years, the BJP sought to project itself as responsible opposition claiming to be a party with a difference. On each of the planks, it has been exposed before the people. With great fanfare it announced adherence to its policy of "Swadeshi" and even promised the electorate before the assembly elections in Maharashtra that it would cancel the dubious deal with Enron and in fact expel the MNC from the country. But as things have turned out it has not only renegotiated with Enron but has in fact facilitated greater penetration of the multinational corporation in our power sector. On every other matter of importance, policy prescription, it has gone along with the Congress (I) in introducing this policy of unbridled liberalisation that is undermining the economic sovereignty of our country. Its State governments pursue the same policies leading to the worsening of people's living conditions.

It has projected itself as a party with a different culture distinct from the self-seeking politicians and opportunistic elements that have gathered in the Congress. However, the whole exercise in Gujarat and the internal bickering in the Party in other states where it is in power have shown that its leadership is also replete with people of the same culture as that of the Congress whose self-seeking opportunism precedes the interests of the country.

Similarly, with its highest leadership involved in the Havala scandal it has shown itself as a party that is no different from the Congress as far as looting the country is concerned.

With this track record, the communal forces in the recent period once again seek to mount an offensive head spreading deeper the poison of hatred against minorities in order to garner more votes. The Vishwa Hindu Parishad has issued a blue print for Hindu Rashtra while whipping up the campaign for the destruction of the mosques in Kashi and Mathura. The other outfits of the RSS are also active in organising various activities towards this end. Its State government in Maharashtra has abolished the Minorities Commission. It also wound up the Srikrishna Commission enquiring into the Bombay riots, brazenly patronising criminal-communal elements.

In the background of these developments and considering the fact that the BJP had emerged in the last elections as the major Opposition in Parliament in power in four state legislatures, it still represents the most consolidated danger to the very unity and integrity of our country. It is out to destroy the very social fabric that composes India. It is therefore necessary that this communal challenge be squarely met with and that these forces be defeated in the coming elections.

ROLE OF THE CPI(M)

The consistent, principle and firm role of the CPI(M) and the Left in maintaining the unity of our country against all divisive and communal onslaughts is there before the people.

The CPI(M) has been the in forefront in the struggle against communalism. West Bengal and Kerala, are like oasis of harmony in the otherwise desert of communal strife. CPI (M) has been the staunchest defender of national unity. In Punjab alone more than 200 CPI(M) members, the best of patriots in contemporary India, were martyred in the struggle against terrorism. In Kashmir and elsewhere, the CPI(M) has been in the forefront championing the unity of India in countering the separatist forces. It has earnestly defended the concept of social justice and the rights of the backward castes, scheduled castes, scheduled tribes. During the last five years, the CPI(M) and the Left have been in the forefront in opposing the new economic policies that are bartering away the sovereignty of our country.

The CPI(M) initiated the strengthening of Left unity in the present situation. The Left alone with its consistency and firmness can meet the challenges before the people. During these years, this unity in people's struggles, whether on the question of the opposition to the GATT 1994, privatisation of public sector or the question of attacks on the rights of the working people, it is the Left-led mass organisations that have led the united resistance including four all-India industrial strikes and big mass actions.

Role of CPI(M)-Led Left Front Governments:

In stark contrast to the record of the Congress (I) and the BJP governments has been that of the Left Front government in West Bengal which for 19 long years has been in power with its mandate being renewed in every subsequent election. It has provided the most stable government independent India has ever seen and during this period working people of West Bengal have achieved unprecedented gains. It has been the outpost of communal harmony staunchest protector of the rights of the minorities. Its record in the implementation of land reforms, protection of the rights of the working people, decentralisation of power to the panchayats, consolidation of the panchayati raj structure and taking democracy to the grassroots have all been achievements unparalleled elsewhere during the last five years.

Tripura, under the Left Front rule has emerged distinct from the rest of the North East because of the role of the CPI(M) in maintaining the unity of the tribal and non-tribal people in Tripura, protecting interests of the tribal community and safeguarding their rights.

If Kerala today has some of the best social development indicators in India like literacy, health etc., it is because of the foundations laid by the communist-led governments in the past. Of particular significance are the land reforms initiated and implemented by the Left. Whenever the CPI(M) led governments were voted to office they have their mark through their policies and practice.

Above all, in the existing morass of corruption, criminalisation and moral degeneration it is the CPI(M) and the Left that have emerged most credible. It is with the above record that the CPI(M) is appealing to the Indian people to rise to the occasion in these grave circumstances to defeat the Congress (I) and the BJP.

Manifesto of the Left Front

Taking into account the multi-dimensional crisis that is afflicting the country and the people, the CPI(M) places before the electorate following 'programme of demands' as parts of its election platform. The electoral platform must be a part of the wider political struggle to achieve these 'demands' which will strengthen democracy, secularism, national unity, strive for economic and social justice for the toiling masses and to eradicate the curse of corruption.

Unlike the most other political parties, however, who declared on the pre-election campaigns what exactly they would like to do if they are voted to power to form the Government at the Centre, the Left parties led by CPI(M) and the CPI, tell what they would 'demand'. Thereby, they discount themselves of the claim to form the Government if given the electoral mandate to govern. The question is: they would 'demand' from whom if they are ruling the nation? Opposition demands from the Government that rules. If they are to govern, of whom they would 'demand'? The very idea seems basically miscued. This spyche of placing 'demands' also indirectly tells two things: their long-standing roles in the Opposition, and their mentzl unpreparedness to rule, wherein a great deal of tact and craft is inherently required. A party or its allies who fail to muster confidence to win and convince on that line, can perhaps never really succeed in winning the power to govern.

However, the LF has a formidable ally in Communist Party of India.

PROGRAMME ON ECONOMY

1. Safeguard the country's economic sovereignty and strengthen its self-reliance; reverse the politics of unbridled liberalisation which undermine our sovereignty.
2. Stop privatisation of public sector, revise telecom, power policies, stop privatisation of financial sector enterprises,

provide them autonomy from bureaucratic controls and ensure workers' participation in management.

3. Curb price rise and ensure food security by expanding the public distribution system bringing into its ambit 14 essential commodities and reduce prices by 50 per cent; reduce issue price of foodgrains.
4. Reverse the present industrial policy; new policy to strengthen indigenous industry and domestic capacities, end to preferential treatment to foreign investors, entry of foreign capital to be decided on national priorities and technology needs.
5. No amendment of the Indian Patent Act of 1970 which will erode India's sovereign right to develop domestic R & D.

Right of the Working People

1. Ensuring need-based minimum wages for the workers; protective legislation for unorganised workers; protection of labour from severe exploitation and emoluments and inflation linked increase in wages; report of the fifth pay commission for Government employees to be expedited and implemented.
2. Recognition of Trade Unions through secret ballots.
3. Granting of pension to working people as a third benefit; one-rank one-pension for; ex-servicemen; upgrading pensions of all categories of pensioners in consonance with the cost of living-protection of rights of handicapped employees.
4. Handloom weavers; yarn to be provided at control rate for weavers and provide adequate infrastructure for the marketing of their goods.

IMPROVING LIVING CONDITION

1. Guarantee right to work as a fundamental right; release accumulated food stocks to start food-for-work programmes to generate employment.

2. Increase allocation for basic health and sanitation. Stop privatisation of health facilities; ensure provision of drinking water to all villages and for the control of preventable diseases.
3. Increase allocation on education and mass literacy; stop privatisation and commercialisation of education; the allocation must be at least 10 percent of the national budget and 30 per cent of the state budgets; free and compulsory education must be guaranteed by law for all children upto the age of 14 years; syllabus and curriculum to strengthen scientific temper, secularism, national unity and integrity.
4. Housing to be accorded the status of basic right; housing schemes for urban and rural poor to be implemented as an urgent priority.
5. A proper water resources policy to prevent the annual scourge of floods and droughts; immediate and adequate relief for those affected by these.

AGRARIAN SECTOR

1. Implementation of land reforms by plugging loopholes in the law and distribution of land; reversal of laws brought in due to new economic policies diluting the land reforms provisions; creation of authentic land reform records; security of tenure of tenants; provision of homestead land for the rural poor.
2. Greater Plan allocation for the spread of irrigation; proper schemes for crop insurance.
3. Central legislation protecting the rights of agricultural workers, their wages living conditions and social benefits.
4. Proper facilities for assistance to producers of traditional crops and protection of markets and sources of raw material.
5. Expansion of credit facilities for the poor peasantry and agricultural labour.

6. **Fishermen:** No licences for deep sea fishing to foreign companies and joint ventures. Protect rights of fishing people.

SOCIAL JUSTICE

1. Prevention of atrocities against scheduled castes; end to discrimination and strict implementation of laws guaranteeing equality.
2. Prevention of atrocities against tribals; protection of land, culture and language of tribal people; granting of autonomy for compact cintiguous tribal majority areas within the framework of the existing States.
3. Implementation of reservation for scheduled castes, scheduled tribes, and other backward classes. Within reservation form OBCs, implement the creamy layer principles so that needs sections are benefited the most. If vacancies exist after application of the creamy layer principles then they should be filled up by candidates from within the same communities. Reservation to be extended to Christians from converted scheduled castes.

WOMEN AND CHILDREN

1. Protection of the rights of women, stringent measures against atrocities and crime against women, implementation of legal and democratic rights guaranteed by the Constitution; increasing opportunity for employment and ensuring no discrimination in the pay; recruitment and promotion; equal rights in property and land for women; issuing of joint pattas for ownership.
2. Equal legal rights for women of all communities; joint matrimonial property rights; registration of marriage to be made compulsory.
3. One-third of the seats in legislatures and Parliament be reserved for women.
4. **Children:** Suitable legislation to prevent sexual abuse of children; abolition of child labour; adequate child-care

facilities at work place.

STRENGTHEN SECULARISM

1. Immediate legislation separating religion from politics.
2. Transfer of all cases connected with the Ayodhya dispute to the Supreme Court under Article 138 (2) for a speedy verdict which will be binding on all sides.
3. Strict implementation of status quo of religious places as of 15 August, 1947.
4. Protection of just rights of the minorities; implement the provisions of the Constitution to prevent discrimination; strengthen security of the life and property of the minorities; backwards amongst the minorities given be OBC reservations; protection of Urdu language.

STRENGTHEN PARLIAMENTARY DEMOCRACY

1. Immediately set in motion the process of bringing forward a legislation for comprehensive electoral reforms to ensure the elimination of money and muscle power from elections on the basis of Dinesh Goswami Committee report; amend Section 77 of the Representation of People Act to plug loopholes in enforcing ceiling on election expenditure of candidates.
2. To check corruption, the immediate setting up of Lok Pal bringing in its purview the Prime Minister; to be appointed by an authority constituting representatives of the executive, legislature and judiciary; streamline functioning on investigation agencies, protect them from political interference; ensure speedy disposal and appropriate action.
3. Strict action against all manifestations of criminalisation of politics.
4. Proportional representation in the electoral system.
5. Reforms in judicial system to provide easy and speedy relief to the common people.

FEDERALISM AND DECENTRALISATION

1. Restructuring the Centre-State relations with more powers to the States; legislative measures to ensure balanced economic development to overcome regional imbalances.
2. Devolution of finances to the states ending over-centralisation of resources at the Centre.
3. Protection of the Rajya Sabha as the "Council of States" to defend the federal structure of our Constitution; its members must belong to the States they are elected from.
4. Decentralisation of democracy to the grassroots; proper devolution of power to the panchayats; strengthen panchayati raj institutions; financial assistance to panchayats to flow through State governments.

DEFEND NATIONAL UNITY

Immediate announcement of political solution for the Kashmir problem which must include defence of Article 370 and a review of the erosion which has taken place since 1953 by the elected State assembly; granting maximum autonomy within the framework of the Indian Constitution; compensation and adequate measures for those displaced from the state and a comprehensive economic package for development, generating employment opportunities.

FOREIGN POLICY

Defence of the non-alligned foreign policy; world peace and spirit of national independence; firm resistance against US imperialist attempts to impose its New World Order; strengthen international anti-imperialist solidarity; strengthen South-South cooperation; rebuff imperialist efforts to subvert our independent development and resistance to its attempts to impose its NPT and CTBT; cancellation of its military cooperation pact with USA.

CULTURE AND MEDIA

1. State support for expansion of cultural facilities, encouraging of activities aimed to take democratic culture to the mass of the people.
2. Implement autonomy for the official electronic media updating the Prasar Bharati Act provisions; legislation to prevent growth of monopolies in print and electronic media; which is inherently undemocratic; no foreign ownership of print media; ensure States have say in media policy and control on Doordarshan and AIR.

SCIENCE

Science and technology policy which encourages creative work; scientific temper and strengthens the self-reliant basis of India's development.

ENVIRONMENT

An environment policy which is integrated with the needs of rapid and sustainable economic development; stringent action against contractions illegally cutting down forests; strict pollution control against industries using hazardous technology which affect health of workers, the neighbourhood; provision of adequate rehabilitation package for persons displaced by development projects; particularly for adivasis who are most affected.

BACKGROUNDER: COMMUNIST PARTY OF INDIA

CONGRESS NO LONGER FIT TO RULE

The Congress regime which started as a minority government, and later acquired a majority by engineering defections has thrown the country into a deep and alround crisis.

The Rao Government's economic policy has unfolded itself as 'pro-rich' and 'anti-poor', as aggressively pro-multinationals and monopolies and anti-public sector, industries and local industries.

Despite the Government's tall claims of declining inflation, the common man finds the prices of foodstuff and other daily necessities soaring beyond his reach. The market remains within the clutches of profiteers and blackmarketeers. Yet the Rao Government, when it came to power in 1991, had solemnly pledged to bring down prices to the level of the previous year. This turned out to be nothing but a hoax to deceive the suffering people.

Foodgrains production and stocks were at a record level, but per capita consumption was declining and offtake from public distribution system had fallen due to lack of purchasing power of the masses.

The value of the rupee was sliding sharply and trade deficit was growing.

Budget deficit continues to be high and unchecked, chiefly due to squandering of public funds and profligate spending by the powers that were.

Domestic savings stagnated at a low level.

The country's debts have reached astronomical figures.

The problems of poverty, unemployment, illiteracy and disease, were so far from being tackled, were getting aggravated as a result of structural adjustment programme dictated by the International Monetary Fund and the World Bank, and the new regime imposed by the World Trade Organisation. The worst victims of the new economic policies were the people below the poverty line.

The policy of liberalisation, globalisation and privatisation had struck a heavy blow at the self-reliant path of development for big country like ours with abundant resources. Public enterprises built with the sweat and toil of our people were being privatised, and public assets were being given away to private parties, both foreign and Indian. MNCs were acquiring grip over vital sectors of our economy and in consumer industries, depriving large sections of our people of their livelihood. In collaboration with local monopolies they were capturing large space in our markets, pushing aside local artisans, small scale industries, and even some medium and large scale ones.

The much tom-tomed figures of growth do not reflect a picture of development with social justice, but a distorted picture of affluence for the top 7 or 8 crores of our population, and misery and insecurity for the rest 85 crores.

Under the Rao regime heavy blows were struck at the secular foundations of our Republic. A sense of alienation and insecurity overtook the minorities, who do not look upon this government as a protector of their life and property.

Corruption has reached new qualitative dimensions under the Rao Government, with every passing day exposing a new scam, each bigger and more scandalous than the one earlier. Securities scam, sugar scam, disinvestment scam, Bailadilla deal, telecom scam, railway gauge scam, Purulia arms-drops scandal, the defence scam, and now the havala racket have polluted our democratic system and life. Even the country's security has been at stake in some of these scams.

There is today a growing nexus between money power breeding corruption and the latter breeding criminals and mafia elements who manoeuvre politics with the help of their benefactors. The growing criminalisation of politics, the politicisation of criminals and criminals rising to high positions represent a grave danger to democracy and social life.

A creeping paralysis has overtaken the executive pillar of our democracy during Rao's tenure allowing grave issues to remain unresolved and for unsolved problems to become festering sores. The legislative pillar has been rendered ineffective and blocked due to the insensitiveness and total lack of accountability and transparency of government and its unabashed partisanship. Several times, it had to be the third, the judicial pillar which had to take decisions and issue directives because of the executive's failure to discharge its own duties and responsibilities.

The Congress is clearly unable and unfit to rule the country any longer according to Constitutional imperatives, with 7 serving ministers having to resign and chargesheeted for corruption, with 2 more ministers who had resigned earlier being similarly indicated, and with the Prime Minister himself under a cloud. It is itself in a state of disarray, having suffered a split. The country is no longer safe in Congress hands. Its chances of gaining a majority on its own, are non-existent.

The slogan : "Give me stability, and I will give your progress" hides the truth that unless there is real progress in eliminating poverty, unemployment and other urgent problems of the poor in this country, there can be no stability.

BJP is no Alternative; It is Nowhere Near Power

The BJP has been loudly claiming to be the 'party in waiting', the alternative to the Congress. But its claims have come a cropper. Much before the polls, it stands thoroughly exposed.

With an eye on power, it took recourse to out and out communal propaganda, distorting the humane essence of religion and is misusing religion for garnering votes. In an act of mediaeval frenzy it demolished a place of worship. Its action stirred up communal hate and poision on both sides that led to a spurt of riots and took hundreds of innocent lives.

It has attempted to put up a new face by talking of 'cultural nationalism'. But getting desperate after corruption and inner dissension caught up with it, the BJP has started openly espousing the so-called 'Hindu Agenda' of the Vishwa Hindu

Parishad. Every single element of the BJP's cultural nationalism is aimed against the minorities, and is a denial of the pluralism and multifacetness of Indian society and culture, which is the basis of our secularism.

Its so-called 'economic nationalism' is a crude mixture of swadeshi demagogy and actual support to liberalisation policy of the Congress. After bravely denouncing Enron and threatening to throw it into the sea, it quickly struck a fresh deal with the self-same Enron.

Caught in the havala net, the BJP has no face to talk of a crusade against corruption and of upholding high moral values and probity in public life. Its State governments notched up a record of scandals that match that of the Congress — the tendu leaf scandal, the saal seeds and opium husk scandals in MP under the BJP Governments, the dal scandal in Maharashtra, the tractor scandal in Rajasthan, the land grab by BJP-RSS outfits in UP, MP and Rajasthan, and others, too numerous to be mentioned. The Congress rulers sank into the mire of corruption through four and a half decades of power. The BJP Governments did so in less than four and a half years. Its crusade against corruption has ended in fiasco.

It is the same with dissidence and violent faction fights within each State outfit of the BJP. The Khajuria-Hajuria fight in Gujarat has caught the attention of the whole country. It has torn to shreds the BJP's boast that it is a 'party with a difference', a disciplined party. With only a whiff of power, its power-hungry members are at each other's throat.

A grave aspect of the havala racket is the fact that it was a conduit for siphoning money to the Kashmiri miltants, as also to BJP leaders and Congress ministers. This came out 4 years back, yet the patriotic conscience of these honourable gentlemen did not speak up. And now it is revealed that Dawood's criminal associates and hitmen found shelter both with a BJP MP and a Congress minister. The Congress and the BJP are thus tarred with the same brush.

In Maharashtra, the BJP-Shiv Sena Government unceremoniously wound up the States Minorities Commission and the Srikrishna Commission. It withdrew 1500 cases filed under the Prevention of Atrocities (Against Scheduled Castes) Act. All these expose the BJP and its allies' ingrained hostility to minorities and dalits.

The reactionary ugly face of the ruling BJP was also seen in the shameful rally organised by it in Jaipur 'honouring' the five rapists of Bhanwari Devi.

The BJP and its allies cannot therefore be an alternative to the Congress. The Indian people will not agree to jump from the frying pan into the fire. The BJP can hardly expect to better its earlier performance at the polls.

Country Needs: A Real Third Alternative

What the country needs today is a functioning Government at the Centre—a broad coalition of Left, secular and democratic parties and forces which will keep both the Congress and the BJP away from power, and which is sworn to carry out an alternative programme corresponding to the most urgent demands and aspirations of the common people for eliminating poverty, unemployment, illiteracy and disease.

The awakening of the hitherto oppressed and deprived masses, the dalits, backward classes and women, has raised the question of their empowerment in political and social life. Only a coalition of the Left, secular and democratic parties and forces can pave the way for this.

The Left parties have a decisive role to play in forging such an alliance, and in carrying through their programme. People have seen that it is only the Left parties which are not tainted by any scams and scandals. The Left has always stood up for the people, for their demands and grievances—organising and leading struggles outside Parliament and acting as 'people tribune' inside Parliament.

It is only the CPI and the Left who have firmly opposed all attempts by imperialism, their agents and proxies to subvert our economic and political sovereignty or threaten our national security and integrity.

The CPI and the Left has consistently fought against all brands of communalism and upheld our best traditions of humanism, tolerance and brotherhood. The CPI and the Left have made tremendous sacrifices for defending national unity against all divisive and separatist forces.

Upholding accountability and transparency in public life, the CPI has been regularly submitting its audited accounts to the authorities for scrutiny and demanding that all registered parties do the same.

The CPI will work for the victory of such a 'Third Alternative', which alone can meet the requirements of the situation and the aspirations of the common people. Only this can prove to be the salvation of the country. The 'Third Alternative' has to become the first inside the 11th Lok Sabha.

The CPI puts forward the following programmes and tasks in the present situation and will strive for its implementation.

The CPI believes that this is a package of programmes for national revival, for development with social justice, for defence of the country's unity and integrity, for defence of our democratic values and institutions which require clean political parties and untainted leaders as pre-requisites.

- These are programmes for solving the problem of poverty, unemployment, illiteracy and disease that beset our country.
- These are programmes that meet the most urgent demands and aspirations of the common people, of our dalits and *soshits*, of our children and youth who are our future.
- These are programmes that can be implemented and fulfilled in the present circumstances.

The forthcoming elections have to lead to a radical chance in the balance of forces in our country. The decadent and corrupt Congress regime must be thrown out of power if the road to progress is to open for the people. The voters must demonstrate their firm belief in those forces and parties which will stand unswervingly against Congress misrule and BJP's divisive threat to national unity and integrity.

Only the democratic, Left and secular forces, acting together, can lead the people to a new order capable of defending our economic and political independence based on social justice for all.

Menifesto : Communist Party of India

ECONOMIC PROGRAMMES

1. The party believes in economic development based upon self-reliance and democracy. According to the party, Indian economy needs reforms for ending bureaucratic controls and cutting of red tape, but not by introducing liberalisation, globalisation and privatisation. For, it believes, these approaches, erode the economic sovereignty and weaken its self-reliance. Such policies it feels must be halted and reversed.
2. Public sector has to be defended from the wholesale attack of privatisation. Cure for the ills of the public sectors units should be sought from within the public sector enterprises and not by automatically privatising them. In all cases care must be taken to protect interests of workers through adequate compensation, retraining and redeployment. Management of public sector enterprises shall be professionalised and democratised through workers' participation, and made efficient and accountable.
3. The party wants to discontinue vandalising of public assets by handling them over to private parties or disinvesting them invariably below par.
4. The party wants that the funds already acquired by disinvestment should be utilized for revival and modernisation of the concerned units.
5. Indian industries and agriculture shall be given all encouragement and help to utilize scientific and technological know-how within the country and constantly upgrade it. The know-how should be geared towards areas of health, environments, food, shelter and energy.
6. It will defend interests of medium and small scale industries through easily available credit, greater market accessibility and so forth.

7. Opportunities for smaller entrepreneurs and the self-employeds shall be expanded.
8. It will work out for balanced development to prevent discrimination and large scale migration from one region to the other.

PROGRAMMES ON AGRICULTURAL DEVELOPMENT

1. The party shall set aside fifty per cent of the budget allocation for development of agriculture, horticulture, pisciculture, animal husbandry and so forth.
2. It would ensure irrigation and supply of inputs at reasonable prices to the peasantry.
3. It would extend the subsidised inputs such as irrigation, power, credit and other help especially to small and marginal farmers.
4. It will fix remunerative prices for the agricultural produce and reasonable prices for the consumers.
5. A rational land and water management shall be undertaken through a national water policy, which safeguards agriculture from droughts and floods, and helps to solve inter-State disputes on water sharing.
6. Crops and cattle insurance shall be extended all over the country.
7. Land reforms have to be carried forward. There must be vigorous implementation of land ceiling laws and distribution of surplus land, degraded forest lands, and cultivable waste land for the agricultural workers.
8. All attempts to reverse land reforms shall be halted and opposed.
9. It will fix and implement the need-based minimum wages for agricultural workers and for other sections of unorganised workers.
10. It shall adopt the comprehensive Central legislations, which provide social security and labour protection, to

agricultural workers and construction labour.

11. It shall protect the artisans, weavers, fishermen and the self-employed who are threatened by the Big Business and MNCs. Natural resources for their livelihood shall be safeguarded.
12. It believes that strong efforts should be made to unearth the black money, check tax evasion and mobilise to the full domestic resources for productive investment and prevent their misutilisation for speculative purposes.
13. It believes that rate of domestic savings has to be raised by curbing Government extravagance and checking unbridled consumerism.
14. It also believes that planned efforts must be made to reduce our external and internal debts within a time-bound period.
15. It wants that foreign investments are to be sought and the MNCs to be permitted in specified areas of economy where there is need for high technology and resources. This should be done within an overall plan of national economic development.
16. It believes that foreign capital can be desirable for productive investment on selective basis but not for speculative profits, or for grabbing shares and ultimate control of local industries.
17. It shall retrograde amendment of all patent laws which obstruct our R & D and are harmful to national interests. The party believes that to promote the R & D there must be a cess in industries.

PROGRAMMES ON ENVIRONMENT

1. Protection of our land water, forests, air and public health from growing environment, hazards is the party's paramount environment policy.
2. It will stop predatory actions arising from greed for profits.

3. It will promote nature conservation through community efforts and people's participation. It will undertake the afforestation by actively involving the village dwellers in and around degraded forests.
4. The party will provide safe drinking water to all villages and localities of urban poor.
5. The party shall evolve a national scheme for supply of domestic fuel.

PROGRAMMES ON JOB FOR ALL

1. The party is for expansion of educational and employment opportunity for the youth.
2. It will enshrine right to work as a fundamental right in the Constitution and provide the unemployed dole.
3. It will evolve a comprehensive youth policy which takes into account the right to work and education.
4. It believes that employment guarantee schemes should be for a minimum of 200 days in a year at national minimum wage.

PROGRAMMES ON EDUCATION FOR ALL

1. The party's stand is: there should be free and compulsory education for all upto the age of 14 with training into productive skills.
2. It agrees that charitable institutions and private societies have important roles to play in development of educational fields, but it opposes privatisation and commercialisation of education. It wants six per cent of the GNP should be allotted for education.
3. The party will launch National Literacy Campaign for achieving total literacy within a time-bound period. For the campaign it will mobilise students and the youth.

PROGRAMMES ON LABOUR AND THE BONDED LABOUR

1. It believes the child labour and the bonded labour systems are shame on the society and must be eliminated.
2. Children must be in schools and not in jobs. To ensure that, network of schools whereto children can easily get admission has to be created.
3. It shall implement 'Food for Education' scheme to ensure presence of children in schools and guard against drop-outs. For the purpose it will provide one kilo of foodgrains per day for every child for his daily schooling.
4. It will severely punish child abusers, particularly sexual exploitation of girl child.
5. It will rescue the bonded labour and rehabilitate them. It will also enforce the national minimum wages for them.
6. It will definitely constitute a national commission on Child Labour and Bonded Labour with powers for implementing and enforcing suitable measures.

PROGRAMMES ON FOOD SECURITY FOR ALL

1. The party believes that food security should be made a fundamental right, with nearly 40 per cent of our people below the poverty line. It is therefore an important step, which means that all people must be ensured economic access to balanced diet, safe drinking water, and access to resources to life.
2. The new economic policies and the WTO trade regime are today further jeopardising this food security, the party holds. This must be prevented, it believes.
3. It believes that public distribution system must be strengthened and must cover all items essential for life, of good quality and at prices pegged for a period of 4 to 5 years.

4. Food Security programmes should not jeopardised in the name of encouraging exports, which particularly hit the poor.
5. It will undertake vigorous price control measures and all reliefs given in the budget it will transfer to the consumers.

PROGRAMMES ON HEALTH CARE FOR ALL

1. The Party believes that private hospitals and nursing homes are not substitutes for the chains of health centres both in urban and rural areas.
2. Similarly, it holds, Government and ESI Hospitals and dispensaries must be set up with necessary equipments and all essential drugs, medical as well as para-medical staff.
3. It will ask for panchayats and municipalities to run the maternity and child welfare centres in every village and urban ward.
4. It will allot special financial grants to these bodies for the purpose and will also see that provision of old age homes and medical care for the aged be well-organised.
5. It will also set up Homes for Abandoned Women.
6. The party will control the drug prices and counter the monopolistic grip on product of drugs by developing production of basic drugs by the public sector.
7. It will see that Anganwadi and village health visitors be paid reasonable wages and allowances for discharging their vitally important tasks.
8. It will vigorously carry out campaigns against menace of liquor, drug abuses, HIV/AIDS and all communicable diseases.

PROGRAMMES ON SOCIAL SECURITY

1. The party would work out for social security and labour welfare measures to cover rural and urban workers in

all sectors, providing for medical facilities, pensions and other benefits.

2. Towards that end, identify cards will be issued to members of the work force in unorganised sectors including rural labour, so that they can claim social security benefits.
3. The party has noted with concern that with growing longevity and increased number of retirees from different services including industrial and other establishments the number of pensioners are getting inflated fast. This has made pension the most important element of any scheme of social security. Therefore, the party is principally committed to evolve and implement a well-through-out policy on pension.
4. The pension policy would include the following aspects: (i) the adequate pension, minimum not to be less than the minimum wages fixed in different employments, (ii) a parity in pension between employees of similar cadres and length of service, (iii) same-rank-same-pension principles in the Army and other services, (iv) creation of a pension fund attracting reasonable interest on investment, (v) pension linked to cost of living index, (vi) a machinery to begin payment promptly on retirement.
5. The party has noted that handicapped, disabled, blind persons constitute no less than 10 per cent of the entire population in the country. They have to be given special facilities for education and reservation of at least 3 per cent in jobs.
6. The party will ensure proper rehabilitation and pensionary benefits for ex-servicemen and their dependents.

SOCIAL SECURITY: SC, ST, WOMEN, MINORITIES AND OTHERS

1. The party stands for firm defence of the rights of the SC, ST, OBC, minority communities, women, children and other weaker sections.
2. It wants the policy of reservation must fully be implemented.

3. It will also do efforts to extend reservation to the private sectors which has become imperative in the context of liberalisation of our economy.
4. It will firmly oppose the BJP-VHP stand that "the rights and privileges accorded to SC and STs will be withdrawn on their conversion".
5. The party will resist atrocities against SC, ST, women, and the guilty shall be punished.
6. It will set up a special court in each sensitive district in keeping with the spirit and purpose of the SC, ST (Prevention of Atrocities) Act, 1989.
7. The party will organise people's resistance to growing atrocities on women.
8. The party strongly believes there must be provision for free legal aid by Government to women in all cases of dowry death, abduction, rape.

SOCIAL SECURITY : GENDER EQUALITY

1. The party believes "Equality between women and men is a matter of rights and a condition of social justice and is also necessary and fundamental pre-requisite for equality, development and peace", as it is mentioned in the Beijing Platform adopted at the World Conference of Women, 1995.
2. The party wants that having made the beginning in the panchayat and municipal committees, the next step should be to reserve one-third seats for women in the State assemblies and Parliament.
3. It will ensure women's access to credit, diversified vocational training, information on legal rights, and other facilities to further the advancement of women and girls.
4. Equal regal and social rights for women of all communities should be ensured.
5. It will strictly ensure equal remuneration for women and men.

6. It will ensure safety of women in public and private spheres of life by vigorously combating sexual harassment, and by creating a violence-free society.
7. It will set up hostels for working women and creches for their children.
8. It believes that ownership of land and houses should be registered in the names of both husband and wife.

SOCIAL SECURITY: TRIBALS

1. The party thinks on the line that tribal majority areas should be guaranteed autonomy under special provisions of the Constitution. Wherever is viable, separate statehood can be extended as in the case of Jharkhand.
2. It believes scheduled areas have been excluded from the operation of the Panchayat Acts.
3. The Party believes that the present vacuum should be filled by implementing Bhuria Committee recommendations so as to give them the right to village self-governance as are democratic custom of the tribal people.
4. It wants that tribal land must be protected from alienation by non-tribals. At the same time, lands already alienated from the tribals must be restored to the original tribal owners.

SOCIAL SECURITY: HOUSING

1. There should be a democratic housing policy and popular control over real estate transactions which generate black money.
2. The party believes that a vigorous house construction programme, both in rural and urban areas, should be undertaken by distributing house-sites and building materials to the landless.
3. By similar process it will like to undertake housing constructions for slum-dwellers with arrangement of all civic amenities in the slums.

4. The party will work to extend cheap housing land to the middle classes and control prices of building material.

SOCIAL SECURITY : DEMOCRATIC RIGHTS

1. It will repeal all democratic and repressive laws.
2. It will defend democratic rights and liberties.
3. It will reform and overhaul the police forces.

SOCIAL SECURITY : PLURALIST CULTURE

1. It will pursue democratic and secular cultural policies, incorporate humanist and tolerant teachings of the social reformers. It will uphold pluralist culture of this great nation.
2. It will resist ideological and cultural invasion that might threaten our traditional, cultural, moral and literacy values.
3. It rebuff any drive to spread feudal and unscientific ideas, obscurantism, mysticism, superstitions, obscenity, glorification of crimes and violence.

POLICY ON LANGUAGE

1. All languages in India shall be developed as the modern languages and if voted to power, it will give due recognition to the rights of Urdu and Sindhi under Article 345 or 347 of the Constitution.

POLICY ON SECULARISM

1. It will defend secularism as the basic tenet of our Constitution from attacks by all brands of communal forces.
2. It will ensure effective intervention of all secular and administrative forces and the administration in fight against communalism so that people from minority can feel sense of security.
3. At the same time, it will see that genuine grievance of the minority regarding discrimination in matters of jobs and other economic rights be given priority for implementation.

4. It will ensure more avenues for education and bring end to mismanagement of Waqf properties, et al.
5. If voted to power the party will refer all cases related to Ram Mandir and Babri Masjid dispute to Supreme Court under Article 138 (2) and its decision shall be binding.

PROGRAMME OF RESTRUCTURING CENTRE-STATE RELATIONS

1. The Party feels that Centre-State relations should be restructured in real spirit of federalism, giving greater powers and financial resources to States, as recommended by the Sarkaria Commission.
2. It holds that fate of any State Government should be decided on the floor of the House, and parties and arbitrary use of Article 356 for dismissing State Governments shall be stopped.
3. It will revive and make the Inter-State Council function.
4. It will carry out real decentralisation by conferring more power and financial resources to elected bodies at district, block and panchayat levels.
5. It will defend Article 370 of the Constitution in connection with Jammu and Kashmir. It will also rectify the erosion that had taken place in it.
6. It will evolve an economic and political package on the basis of consensus among all national and State parties.

POLICIES ON NORTH-EAST AND UTTARAKHAND ISSUES

1. CPI believes that the Government of India should take initiative for dialogue with the insurgent or militant movements in the north-eastern part of our country without any pre-condition from any side so as to find lasting solution to the problem.

2. The party firmly believes that Constitutional as well as administrative steps shall have to be taken to form a separate state of Uttarkhand without which its backwardness and neglect cannot be overcome. The CPI, as the first national party to support the demand, shall strive for it in all possible ways.

CORRUPTION TACKLING AND PROGRAMMES ON IT

1. The CPI wants that Lok Pal Bill, which accommodates within its scope legislators and also the Prime Minister should be adopted.
2. It also believes that the Lok Pal institutions should be set up at the Centre and in the States to investigate corruption charges against the ministers and bureaucrats.
3. It feels that transfers and postings which are fertile source of corruption should be done by a committee of senior officials.
4. It will set up at different levels Citizens' Committees composed of personalities of well-known integrity for rousing public opinion and with right to initiate proceedings before Lok Pal institutions and for resisting extortions of money and other mafia-type crimes.
5. It will neither put up nor allow candidates with criminal background or records contest elections.
6. It will work out to ensure there be more transparency in government, in all deals of contract and supply. It will also ensure that right to information be established so as to make administration more accountable to the people and their elected bodies.

PROGRAMMES ON ELECTORAL REFORMS

1. It will carry out, if voted to power, the electoral reforms comprehensively not in piecemeal suiting to occasion.
2. It will amend the Representative of People Act to (i) curb

money and muscle power, (ii) ensure state funding specially in form for necessary election material, (iii) enforce model code which bans communal propaganda and appeal for votes in the name of religion, and (iv) ensure that everybody can exercise his or her right to vote.

PROGRAMMES ON FOREIGN RELATIONS

1. It will oppose defence link-up with the US and joint naval or other forms of military exercises.
2. It will firmly oppose the armed intervention or economic blockade and blackmail by imperialist powers, mainly the US against socialist and other developing countries.
3. It believes that the non-alignment movement should be reinvigorated especially in the present context of the world.
4. It wants that India should remain firm in her principled refusal to sign the nuclear non-proliferation treaty, which permits the legitimisation of weapons of mass destruction.
5. It will actively and positively develop South Cooperation between all developing countries, and extend cooperation among the SAARC nations.

Backgrounder : AIFB

TOWARDS A VIABLE ALTERNATIVE

Eversince the installation of the Rao Government in 1991, the country has been faced with a number of threats and challenges. Of these the principal ones are: (a) threat to the economic sovereignty, (b) threat to secular fabric of the Nation, (c) threat to national unity and integrity, (d) threat to political sovereignty and Parliamentary democracy.

The dismal failure of the Government to meet these threats effectively, has given rise to the fear and apprehension about possible political instability in near future. The apprehension and fear are not without any basis. The flow of events in the recent years, do presage ominous political instability, if corrective measures are not taken to avert it.

The old system of governance has failed the multitude of the common masses. The old system here means the Congress system. India needs a new system of governance.

The Object of the new system must be construction of a political and ideological alternative which can lead to a social order which is more humane, more social judice-oriented, more balanced and sustainable. This can be achieved not by the continued pursuit but by total rejection of the Congress (I) policies and programmes based on outdated social and political perception. It further requires the rejection of the old organisation forms and social equations.

The Congress(I) policies were and are rooted in the Centrist consensus. In class terms, they correspond with the aspirations of the emergent bourgeoisie and upper middle class. The essence of the Centrist consensus is the compromise between the conflicting interests of the Indian bourgeoisie and Indian people, including the aspirations and interests of the socially and economically depressed groups. This resolution of conflicting interests through the mechanism of Centrist consensus, worked till late sixties. In economic terms, the Centrist consensus meant increasing statiation of the economic activities (Nationalisation moves). This also did not work because it was not even substitute for State welfarism as conceived of and implemented in some Western countries. But the rising social and political consciousness among the depressed, under privileged, dispossessed segment of populace, disturbed the social equilibrium resulting in the emergence of Non-Congress State Governments in different States in the late sixties.

The Congress(I) system even did not strengthen the Parliamentary system of Westminister type and allow it to bloom unhindered.

The system did not create socialism, nor deeply institutionalised welfarist capitalism. It created industrial elite prospering within the domestic space being protected by the State. International political and economic environment provided space for this Congress system.

The system began sliding in the late sixties and early seventies and finally collapsed in the late seventies when the first non-Congress Govt. came into being it 1977 led by late Morarji Desai.

The reasons for the Congress (I) decline are many. Among them the following are of crucial importance.

a) Rise of rich farmers outside the Congress orbit.
b) Significant conflict of interest between industrial and agrarian elites.
c) Growth and consolidation of Indian industrial elite, not committed to the development of indegenous industrial base and technological self-reliance, always eager and keen for greater and greater collaboration with foreign capital and surrender to the conditionalities.
d) Alignment with a section of bureaucracy linked with corrupt businessmen and under-world meaning the politician-businessmen-bureaucracy nexus as mentioned in the Vohra Commission report, and recently revealed havala

scam, preceded by chain of scams beginning from Bofors to Telecom.

e) Awakening among various segments of populace namely the women, students, youths, peasants, working class and urban poor, especially among the Dalits, OBCs and minorities, has led to the new equation of social forces which are committed to usher in new era of social justice. Social justice means right to participate in the decision making process and governance.

The decline of the Congress influence and end of the Congress as the dominant party in the national policy has given rise to regional formations, which has had stints of ruling party in different States. The emergence of the regional parties as substitutes of the Congress has resulted in the regionalisation of Indian polity. The advent of regional formations and the support they enjoy among the masses of the region reflects the people's aspirations and urges for the replace of the Congress(I).

The cumulative effect of this flow of events, has created a profound vaccum generating the politics of flux and instability.

The Continued existence of the Left Front Government, in West Bengal in synonymous with the light at end of the tunnel. While other non-Congress Governments in other States could not survive for long, West Bengal Left Front Government continues to serve the people and provides continuity and stability. The key to this success and stability is that the Front Government is the harvest of united struggles of the people of West Bengal on the basis of agreed common minimum programme. The Left Front Government is run by common understanding and consent of each constituent parties. Differences surface, but resolved through mutual understanding.

Erosions into Congress base continues. Its base has increasingly been becoming narrower and narrower. Congress base under Smt Indira Gandhi was narrower than Nehru's. It was still narrower during Rajiv regime. Congress base under Sri Narasimha Rao has further been narrowed, particularly, because of the anti-poor thrust of the new economic policy adopted by Government under the diktat of IMF-WB-WTO.

It has been further narrowed because of the repeated compromises with the communal forces. The failure of the Government to protect the Babri Masjid has alienated the Muslim minorities from the Congress. It has its impact on the psyche of other minorities.

The break-away of Arjun Singh-ND Tewari faction, has been the last straw for the Congress camel.

The Congress(I) has ceased to remain as a dominant party in the national scene today. It is now a regional formation—divided, dejected and frustrated.

The profound vacuum, thus created needs to be filled. The main questions arises, "who fills the vacuum".

With the question of filling the vacuum, the important question of stability is linked. 'Wave election' does not ensure the required stability; nor the 'family loyality' does guarantee it. The voting pattern in the Lok Sabha elections in 1977, 1980, 1984, 1991 does hold out the prospect of the emergence of any kind of stable two-party system of alternation at the Centre.

In so far as the Left is concerned, it has to be admitted that its capacity to influence the politics is very limited and is incapable of filling the vacuum by itself alone.

The BJP is striving to fill the vacuum. 'Parivartan Yatra' is on throughout the country.

The BJP projects solution of the country's ills from the right. It seeks to answer the growing cravings of a section of the upper-caste, upper middle class elite on the plank of *'Hindutva'* which does not correspond to the hopes and aspirations of the multitude of the poor urban and rural, Dalits and under-privileged. In their approach to the economic problems faced by the nation, the Congress (I) and BJP have by and large the identical position. In class terms both of them belong to the same pole. They are twin of the both sides of the coin.

Secularism and democracy go together. Both are interdependent. One existed because of another. Secularism and democracy is the lifeline of India. India cannot survive without secularism and democracy. *Hindutva* is an assault on secularism. BJP plank of *Hindutva* is, therefore, not acceptable. The havala scam, which followed the Gujarat power struggle, had badly soiled the image of the BJP. The BJP myth today stands exploded.

The vacuum can be filled by combination of social forces which provide an ideological and political alternative to both the Congress (I) and BJP. Political stability does not depend on number alone. Stability depends upon entirely on the soundness of the programme and the degree of the successful implementation.

That alternative can be provided by the Left, democratic and secular parties, wedded to compatible ideologies. Compatible ideologies can alone provide the framework of common minimum programme.

What India needs today is the emergence of a third front against Congress (I) and BJP.

In the changed context, coalition of like-minded parties of compatible ideology, has become an urgent need of utmost importance.

The coalescence and new political equation is possible only within a well-defined framework of programmes and polices, short and long-term, covering most vital aspects of citizens' life. These necessarily pertain to (i) required political reforms, (ii) macro-economic policies, (iii) minimum needs programme, (iv) infrastructural capacities.

MANIFESTO : ALL INDIA FORWARD BLOC

POLITICAL REFORMS

1. All India Forward Bloc sincerely thinks that there is urgent need to bring forward political reforms to provide a qualitatively different Government other than the ones by Congress (I) in the past.
2. The new Government must ensure the greater democratic accountability, promote genuine transparency in decision making and institutionalise the right to information as fundamental right, and subject major policies to Parliamentary scrutiny.
3. If voted to power, the AIFB Government shall pass the Lok Pal and Lokayukta Bills to provide effective machinery to fight corruption at high places. Legislators and senior public servants must disclose their assets for public scrutiny. There shall be no immunity for Legislators and public servants from prosecution on charges of corruption and malfeasance.
4. AIFB will take adequate measures to eliminate evils of 'money' and 'muscle' power to ensure free and fair election.
5. It will also work out for state funding for the election campaign. The electoral reforms must include the introduction of the system of proportional representation and 'right to recall' the elected representatives.
6. It also wants that reforms must aim at providing opportunities for greater participation of the people in the day to day administration and policy farming. The administration should be accessible to people, it believes, to the maximum extent to give proper meaning to the 'participatory democracy' and 'grassroots' democracy.
7. It voted to power, AIFB Government shall protect Human Rights and its approach should be positive and sensitive. It will codify Human Rights and incorporate that into Constitutional law.
8. Its Government will give teeth and power to the Human Rights Commission, and towards that goal the present

Act would be suitably amended.

JUDICIAL REFORMS

1. It will ensure that In Constitutional Law secularism be properly defined. The party believes that secularism actually means separation of religion from politics and respect for plural composite culture of India. Its Government, therefore, shall make efforts to promote rational, scientific and modern nation of secularism as well as human values of all religions.
2. The party believes that Uniform Civil Code is a part of the Constitutional directives. It must be wrought out on broad consensus among members of all communities, and be adopted voluntarily.
3. It shall make lawful arrangements to decriminalise and democratise the political party system; ask the parties hold organisational elections regularly, maintain list of members and office bearers and have their accounts properly audited.
4. The party feels there is great and urgent need of judicial reforms. Inability to provide elementary timely justice is the major cause of social apathy and cynicism, it maintains. The AIFB will work out to this regard to effect proper implementation of the relevant reports of the Law Commission, consolidate and speed up disposal of cases.

ADMINISTRATIVE REFORMS

1. AIFB believes that civil services need appropriate reforms. It shall work out mechanism for proper recruitment, training and reviewing of performances of the candidates, and shall also devise suitable novel system for awarding promotion, transfer order and punishment.
2. In view of present day's police image, that of exploitative and oppressive instrument of the State apparatus, the party considers a reform in the police administration also. It will weed out criminalised, communal and corrupt elements, re-educate the Police force on constitu-

tional, secular, democratic and humane values.

3. The party shall recruit more Dalits, Muslims and Women in the police force.
4. It shall speedily implement the recommendations of the National Police Commission. It will also definitely punish the police officers indicated under the Commission of Enquiry Act.

CENTRE-STATE RELATIONS, J&K AND OTHER PROBLEMS

1. The party firmly believes that it is imperative to restructure the Centre-State relation by devolving greater administrative and fiscal powers to the States. Autonomy of States, it holds, must be protected and further extended to give the meaning to the federal principles enshrined in the Constitution.
2. If voted to power, it as a constituent of the Left Front, would pursue a peaceful, democratic and just solution of the Jammu and Kashmir problems that should arrived at without non-participation by any third party. This will be the priority responsibility of the party.
3. AIFB will not allow abrogation of the Article 370. It feels, it is necessary to grant J & K the maximum possible autonomy under the Constitution of India. It also believes while working out the solution to problems of Jammu and Kashmir all sections of people of the State must be involved to the extent practicable.
4. It is imperative, the party feels, to revive cooperatives at grassroots level to ensure local participation. It will give top most priority to comprehensive decentralisation in it agenda of democratisation process in India.

REFORMS IN CONDITION OF WOMEN, LABOUR, DALITS & OBCS AND MEDIA

1. AIFB believes women's empowerment is the basic instrument to ensure gender equality, which in real terms means, equal opportunities, equal rights in land and

property, enhanced representation in Government legislatures, measures to out-law and punish discrimination tests, female foeticides and infanticides dowry-taking and sexual abuse and harassment in schools, colleges, offices and streets.

2. It will address the inadequacies to fill up the gaps in existing schemes for reservation.
3. At the same time it will adopt enabling measures such as providing for free books, special coaching and income support schemes, to enable Dalits and economically weaker sections of the society like under-privileged OBCs avails themselves existing opportunities to fill their quotas.
4. The party will restructure the State-controlled Television along the lines of Prasar Bharati Bill and would create autonomous corporations accountable to public.
5. It will regulate entry of the foreign satellite Television so that their programmes do not adversely affect our national cultural heritage.
6. The party must prevent the entry of foreign print media too.

MACRO-ECONOMIC MEASURES

1. The Left Front and its qualition partners would consider to address a number of economic problems which are the outcome of the economic mismanagement and pursuit of wrong, anti-national and anti-people economic policies since 1991.
2. It will give top priority to the unbridled inflation and slide of rupee, compared with dollar. It is imperative to take appropriate measures to reduce inflation rate. It is also highly necessary to arrest the slide of rupee in order to protect the national economy, policy of the self-reliance and independent economic growth with distributive social justice. For, the party is convinced that inflation hits the poor the hardest and fattens the rich.
3. The party feels there is wide scope for reduction of

the wasteful State expenditure may be, to the extent of 5 pe rcent or more of the GDP. Expenditures on paramilitary forces and defence may be put under judicious cut.

4. The party will work to reduce the gap between direct and indirect taxes, and lay more stress on progressive, equitable taxation while improving the efficiency of the collection machineries.
5. The party will see that tax net be further widened to cover the rich. It will also make the tax-evasion a criminal offence.
6. It will make efforts to reduce the Centre's fiscal deficit, particularly the revenue deficit, which is currently 3.4 per cent of the GDP. For it rejects, the Congress Government's practice of reducing deficit by divesting public sector equity to finance the deficit, as it is fraught with grave danger.
7. It will aim at creating economic policy conducive to build up a dept-free India. The party notes with concern that today our total public debt stands at nearly 4,50,000 crore as foreign debt.
8. It feels that it is highly essential to ban excessive and indiscriminate imports. It shall ban imports of luxury goods.
9. If voted to power the party will promote export growth not through rupee depreciation but through strong, competitive domestic economy which can export high-value added manufactures and services.
10. It will, if voted to power, selectively accept foreign collaboration proposals, only when they are unavoidable.
11. It will accept foreign investments and technology choice strictly on selective basis. Terms of that will be commensurate with India's potentials for strengthening self-reliance.
12. It will subject to fresh scrutiny all commitments made by the Congress Government to international bodies. Such scrutinies shall be made by experts.

13. The party sincerely feels it imperative to fight against the present unequal international economic order and seek equitable set of trade and investment arrangements.
14. It is highly essential to reject, the party feels, the fraudulent view that 'globalisation' under the present exploitative and unequal international order can be equal or even-handed.
15. India's industrial policy should be restructured with the object of creating indigenous capacities in the wide range of industries, the party feels. India will thereby achieve technological self-reliance, discourage and ban monopolies and end preferential treatment to foreign investors. It is in fact rejection of the present Government's New Economic Policy.
16. It will work to reverse the policy of the Congress Government to discriminate against the public sector coupled with privatisation. However, the party feels that the public sector has to be reformed and functional autonomy should be given to them.
17. It will provide the Public Sector Units (PSUs) with strong R&D thrust, all round help and assistances, financial or otherwise, to enhance their efficiency, and make them more accountable to people. It firmly believes that workers' participation in the management is another route to revitalise the PSUs.
18. The Party feels that reversing of 1991 policy of the Congress Government to prune the productive public investment, in the name of reducing deficit, is necessary. For, the party believes that policy has indeed become counter-productive. The capital expenditure and Plan-spending on the infrastructure must be substantially raised.
19. Top priority projects for the party will be building and expanding the roads, railways, ports, telecommunications and urban infrastructure.
20. It will invest in these sectors and enhance the investments to ensure speedy and balanced industrialisation.

21. It will do maximum efforts to generate power through judicious mix of thermal, hydro and atomic researches, whereas indigenous capabilities will be enhanced, to the maximum limits.
22. It will discourage and do away with dollar-dominated power agreements with foreign companies at exorbitant costs.
23. It will move to make for the State a Constitutional obligation to launch strong comprehensive anti-poverty programmes. Ideally, the state must provide gainful employment to every one who demands for it or unemployment benefit in lieu there of. This programme receive resources at least 5 per cent of the GDP of the country in addition to the budgeted spending on health, education and welfare.
24. It will modernise agriculture with liberals aids from the State. It will enhance public investment in agriculture and related ministries.
25. It will promote crop pattern suitable to our country, and that which does not affect the food security.
26. It wants producers must get remunerative prices for their produces. It will also expand purchases from markets by the agencies like Food Corporation of India and others.
27. It will be the party's endeavuor to provide minimum needs to propel. To fulfill that commitment, following measures shall be taken:
    a) It will expand employment generation schemes so that 300 man-days of work per year can be provided to all unemployed who want to work.
    b) This means current Jawahar Rojgar Yojana must be raised manyfold. The Yojana should be integrated into plans for building rural infrastructure, regeneration of land, water-shed, management, ex-pansion of irrigation potentials.
    c) Right to work shall be a fundamental Constitutional right.
    d) Ensure participation of youth in decision-making process.

28. It will provide clean potable drinking water on priority basis to all villages. The current Drinking Water Mission shall be restructured, reformed and galvanised. It will also ensure people's participation.
29. A major aim of the party is to/make Primary Health Care available to every citizen. This requires revitalisation, reactivisation and adequate funding of the existing primary health centres.
30. The aim of the party is to universalise literacy. It shall strengthen the National Literacy Mission with the motto "Nation for Literacy, Literacy for Nation."
31. The party will established for every village with 200 people a primary school, backed by need-based incentives such as mid-day meals, provision for free text books, writing materials and modest scholarship.
32. It would set up adequate budgetary allocations for education by the Central and State as well as the State Governments. Special education bank would be set up for the purpose.
33. It will get women and children involved in all these projects.
34. The party feels education is the super structure of the society. Therefore, it will work to get 6 per cent of the GDP and 10 per cent of the budgetary allocation spent for education.
35. It also feels that there should be a bank assisting students in matters of education by providing interest-free loans for continuing higher studies.
36. In the entire realm of rural development land reforms should be the highest priority goal, the party feels. Land reforms indeed includes:

    a) preparation of authentic land records,

    b) registration of tenants,

    c) security of tenure,

    d) elimination of rack-renting,

e) enforcement of ceiling laws,

f) acquisition and distribution of surplus land,

g) provision of home-stead land on which peasants can build his house and grow trees, vegetables and fruits.

37. It will give women effective land and property rights.
38. It will guarantee minimum wages to rural unorganised workers. Also, they are to be organised effectively. It is necessary to revise existing legislation on minimum wages.
39. The rate of minimum wages must be revised every two years in the light of inflation rate. The wages shall be equal for both men and women.
40. The party, if voted to power, shall enforce the Hanumantha Rao Committee's recommendation of national minimum wage. It shall also recommend for secure punishment for violation of Minimum Wages Act.
41. It will also bring an Act to the Parliament to pass Protection to the rights and interests of the agricultural workers.
42. The AIFB feels it imperative to provide adequate financial social security to citizens must include: (a) old age pension for all those above 60, (b) accident and life insurance for all citizens, (c) compensation in the case of death of a wage earner, and (d) pension for widows.
43. The party will expand and strengthen the Public Distribution System by lowering issue prices, ensuring adequate supplies, plugging leaks. The issue price it shall reduce by increasing subsidies.
44. It will also strengthen the Public Distribution System through Panchayats and local bodies.
45. It is necessary, the party feels, to introduce special assistance schemes for the Dalits, OBCs, SC/ST populace.
46. It will ensure special schemes for the migrants to protect their interests, safety and security.
47. It will launch housing and slum improvement programmes

base on sites and services.

48. It will pay highest attention to the protection and enrichment of environment, and would take it as fundamental criterion to effect viable development projects.

49. Every development project must draw up humanitarian rehabilitation plants.

50. The AIFB feels it highly essential to promote to range of rural industries in informal and small sectors, based upon local resources, skills and needs.

51. It also holds that cooperative route is very relevant and equitable means of sharing resources and developing common distribution strategies. This route shall be further expanded and strengthened. The party will democraties the management of the cooperatives, upholding a model cooperative legislation, enough so that they get a level-playing field vis-a-vis Corporate sector, shunning rich dominated cooperative which indeed defeat purposes of cooperative movement.

FOREIGN POLICY

1. The foreign policy of the party shall be an instrument of advancing national interests. Beyond this it would deploy for realising the broader objective of peace, disarmament and a just, fair and equitable world order.
2. Principal components of AIFB foreign policy will be:
   a) improvement of relations with neighbours on top priority,
   b) relation shall be marked by active partnership in all areas of cooperation and continuing dialogues at all levels,
   c) India has no intention of exercising hegemony in South Asia. On the contrary India has vital stakes in stability and prosperity of the countries of the region,
   d) It will not allow bilateral issues fester and make all efforts to resolve them peacefully and through negotiations.

3. The party shall take initiatives to promote people to people diplomacy.
4. AIFB will improve relations with all the countries including USA, however only after ensuring that India's security and sovereignty do not get any way com- promised.
5. India will take further initiatives to give momentum to the process for improving relations between India and China, AIFB holds.
6. AIFB will also work for improving relations among SAARC countries, particularly in fields of trade and commerce, science and technology, education, culture etc. AIFB shall not allow India cease its efforts to improve relation with Pakistan despite many irritants created by her.
7. AIFB shall safeguard against threats to security of the country may it come any side whatsoever.
8. AIFB will work for India unflaggingly pursuing its disarmament policy which seeks complete nuclear disarmament, within specific time frame. The party will seek freezing of production of fissile materials. Also, the party will seek for Comprehensive Test Ban Treaty (CTBT).
9. AIFB shall not allow India sign the NPT, instead would oppose it since the treaty is discriminatory.
10. AIFB identifies itself with Indian Government's concern about erosion of the role of United Nations which seem to have allowed itself highjacked by the United States of America and its allies. AIFB shall seek democratisation of United Nations.
11. AIFB will pursue for India the multilateral diplomacy through instrumentalities of Non-Aligned Meet, G-77 and G-15 groups apart from UNO.

7

Backgrounder: All-India Indira Congress (Tiwari)

AS A TRUE successor to the Indian National Congress founded in 1885 and rejuvenated in 1969 and 1978 under the leadership of Shrimati Indira Gandhi, All-India Congress (Tiwari) represents continuity with change in the best tradition of the Congress.

Indira Congress pays homage to all the leaders of India's freedom struggle and renaissance specially those who sacrificed their lives in the noble cause of service to the nation. It believes that the rich heritage bequeathed to us by Mahatma Gandhi, Gurudev Tagore, Subhash Chandra Bose, Sardar Bhagat Singh, Bal Gangadhar Tilak, Annie Besant, Jawaharlal Nehru, Sardar Vallabhbhai Patel, Maulana Abul Kalam Azad, Ambedkar, Pattabhi Sitaramaiah, G. N. Bardoloi, Lal Bahadur Shastri, Kamaraj, Smt Indira Gandhi, Babu Jagjivan Ram and Rajiv Gandhi will strengthen the resolve required to discharge our responsibilities to the present and future generations of India.

Indira Congress is wedded to the basic values enshrined in the Preamble and the Constitution of India. Above all, it is committed to social and economic justice to all and alleviating the condition of women, the Dalits, backward society, downtrodden and economically weaker sections of our people.

Indira Congress symbolises the ethos of India. It is a party with a vision. Its vision is that of a modern, self-reliant, progressive, proud and prosperous India. It is confident of taking the country out of the present morass of gloom and despair and bring it back to its pristine glory and greatness by restoring national pride and self-respect.

Indira Congress gives high priority to providing a clean, transparent and efficient administration guaranteeing security of life and liberty for all, therefore, it is for a government that governs.

The present national scenario is disturbing and distressing. Times are critical and challenging. The entire administration is in a shambles. The leaders at the helm of affairs have failed the people. We are, for all practical purposes, sitting on the debris of the dreams of the founding fathers of our Republic. People are losing faith in politicians and political parties. There can be nothing sadder or more tragic in a representative democracy than the spectacle of the representatives of the people themselves losing their credibility with the people. Conscious of the dismal state of affairs, Indira Congress is determined to remedy the situation and restore the confidence of the people in the political system.

Indira Congress is truly the people's party. Its doors are open to all the citizens of India without any discrimination of any kind. The only requirement is that they accept the basic tenets enshrined in the Constitution of India and are prepared to work for their realisation under all circumstances.

What does Indira Congress stand for?

Indira Congress says what it believes in. It means and does what it says. There is no dichotomy in its precepts and practice and no place for hypocrisy, double speak or false promises.

Indira Congress believes in value-based politics and politics for service to the people. Politics for the party is not merely the art of somehow getting to power and staying in power through whatever means. For India Congress, means are as important as the end.

Party and the People

Indira Congress stands for internal party democracy — full freedom of expression and right of dissent within the party and expression periodic elections at fixed intervals for all party posts and bodies. We believe that political parties which are not democratic in their own functioning cannot play any relevant or legitimate role in the consolidation of our democratic polity.

Indira Congress would like to regulate the functioning of political parties by law and to ensure fullest transparency and openness in their activities. Indira Congress stands for all political parties and aspirants for party or public offices being required by law to declare their assets, the annual returns, maintain full accounts of receipts (with sources) and expenditure. Accounts of all the parties should be duly audited and the audited accounts made public.

Indira Congress believes that whether in office or out of it, the party exists for serving the people and fighting the battle of socio-economic development and justice for all. Elections are not an end all and be all of public life.

Indira Congress believes that there should be a national consensus on how to (a) address issues of paramount importance to the nation especially foreign policy, (b) defence policy, (c) population policy, and (d) plans for fighting the evils of criminalisation of politics, corruption and ensuring security of the life and liberty of citizens.

Security of the nation and its citizens: The present situation is so dismal that there seems to be no functioning government at all in large parts of country.

The security establishments which protect the integrity and sovereignty of the country have been allowed to become so porous and vulnerable in vital areas that foreign aircraft violate the air space of India at will and scatter sophisticated and deadly arms for use by anti-national elements to disrupt the peace of the country. The Purulia aerial arms dropping security disaster probe still remains a mystery with all its ramifications. Indira Congress demands a judicial enquiry into this serious issue of national security.

The State exists most primarily for providing security to the nation and protecting the life and liberty of its citizens. Today the security of the nation is under threat and the situation of internal law and order has so deteriorated that no citizen feels secure. Ordinary citizens are under savage by criminal and anti-social forces. There has been a spurt in the white-collar crimes. Faith in the law and order machinery has been eroded almost completely so much so that sometimes the forces of the State are themselves seen indulging in violation of human rights and acts akin to those of terrorists. Often citizens live under the fear of mafia gangs and the police and they find it safer to seek the protection of the local goons. Kidnapping for extortion or for others ends, murders and rapes have become matters of daily occurrence. Indira Congress believes that unless a semblance of the sense of security of the citizens is ensured, all talk of fancy socio-political programmes and so-called stability would remain meaningless.

*** Your own party — party for all Indians, join it, guide it, improve it.**

*** It stands for service and certain principles, for relentless fight against (1) communalism, (2) criminalisation of politics, and (3) corruption and for deterrent punishment for misuse of public funds for personal ends, for exposing the guilty in various scams, for (4) unmasking the conspirators behind the assassination of Shri Rajiv Gandhi.**

* It gives high priority to clean and efficient administration an guaranteeing security of life and liberty for all citizens, if necessary by changing the system. It is for a Government that works and works better.

* It is for genuine transfer of power to the people at grassroots, true federalism, decentralisation of power, small States, conceding statehood to Pondicherry, Uttarakhand, Vidharba, Chhattisgarh, Bundelkhand and others.

*** It shall fight against rising prices, unlimited borrowings, unproductive and wasteful expenditure and surrender of economic sovereignty to multinationals.**

*** It stands for providing within 10 years.**

(a) 100 per cent literacy,

(b) reformed judicial system with justice made affordable and speedy,

(c) free education and job opportunities for girls and severe penalties for crimes against women, and

(d) foodgrains to the poor at subsidized prices, promotion of cottage and village industries and remunerative prices for farm produce, subsidised availability of inputs agriculture to farmers.

*** It promises to provide within three years.**

(a) 10 lakh additional jobs - *also one job in every family,*

(b) safe drinking water to all villages,

(c) electoral reforms,

(d) one rank one pension for the armed forces.

The Party believes theirs is the original INDIRA CONGRESS, hence names it as Indira Congress. We, however, would call it Tiwari Congress because the party was started by Mr N D Tiwari, primary and actively shaped into form by Mr Arjun Singh, both former Union ministers during Mrs Indira Gandhi's tenures; and also because Mr Tiwari held the office of Uttar Pradesh chief minister for quite sometime in the past. Another reason why we would suggest so, is, the entire concepualizing of the party, form of their dissent to AICC chaired by Mr Narasimha Rao initially was done by Mr Narayan Dutt Tiwari. The party came to its present format only after Mr Arjun Singh, the former Union minister of Human Resource

Development, resigned his post and was expelled from the Party's primary membership. As a consequence to the episode, Mr Singh forsook his intention to stage a come back within the Congress I Party and decided to join hands with Mr Tiwari to form the what they wanted to name, 'Indira Congress'. Its broad areas of reforms, as suggested by its manifesto are given here after.

Manifesto: All-India Indira Congress (Tiwari)

ELECTORAL REFORMS

1. Tiwari Congress would like to regulate the functioning of political parties by law ensuring fullest transparency and openness in their activities.
2. It will ask all political parties and aspirants of party and public offices to declare their assets, file annual returns, maintain full accounts of receipts (with sources) and expenditure. It would ask for all accounts of all political parties should be duly audited and the audited accounts be made public.
3. It believes whether in office or out of it, the party exists for serving the people to fight its battle for socio-economic development with justice for all. It also believes that elections are the end in all and be everything of the public life.
4. Tiwari Congress believes that there should be national consensus on how to address issues of paramount importance to nation, —especially of foreign defence, population policies and of plans to fight the evils of criminalization of politics, corruption, with a view to perfectly ensure security of life and liberty of citizens.
5. Its electoral reforms, however, are wedded to the basic values enshrined in the Preamble and the Constitution of India. Above all, it is committed to social and economic justice to all and alleviating the condition of women, the Dalits, backward society, downtrodden and economically weaker sections of our people.
6. Tiwari Congress believes that the Anti-Defection Law has not achieved the objective of preventing unprincipled defections. It has been misused in particular in shielding, promoting, buying and selling defectors in groups for consideration of money and office. The party promises to reform the law and ensure the twin objectives of morality and ethic in public life.

7. It believes that the loyalty of legislators elected on a party ticket is to the party policy and programmes and not to an individual leader, who might manipulate the people's mandate for his personal ends.
8. Tiwari Congress will check communalism, criminalistion of politics and commercialisation of politics which inhibit voters right to exercise their franchise and even stop them from going to polling booths.
9. As Tiwari Congress stands for free and fair elections to the Union and the State Legislatures, it will, therefore, try to introduce far-reaching electoral reforms to prevent use of money, muscle and mafia power to influence the poll process and results.
10. The party, therefore, will seriously consider for immediate implementation the recommendations of All Party Goswami Committee Report.

POLICY ON SECURITY

1. Its prime concern will be security of the nation and its citizens. The present situation is so dismal that there seems to be no functioning government at all in large parts of country.
2. Tiwari. Congress will demand judicial enquiry into serious issues of national security, like Purulia aerial arms dropping .
3. It believes that the State exists most primarily for providing security to the nation and protecting the life and liberty of its citizens.
4. Tiwari Congress believes that unless a semblance of the sense of security of the citizens is ensured, all talks of fancy socio-political programmes and so-called stability would remain meaningless.
5. ORGANS OF THE STATE, AUTHORITIES AND INSTITUTIONS: There has been serious erosion in the boundaries defining and delimiting the functions of three organs of the State, viz, the Executive, the Legislative and the Judiciary. Tiwari Congress believes that during the last

five years the Constitution and its basic principles have been eroded and the various Constitutional functionaries have become dysfunctional. It is necessary to restore the scheme of checks and balances enshrined in our Constitution. The party will also ensure that there organs function in harmony.

Apart from other steps, attention would have to be paid to strengthening the legal framework. It will not like that the Constitutional authorities like the Election Commission should be tampered with in any manner.

6. Investigating agencies like the CBI and other intelligence agencies should be allowed to function without interference by the Government in order to ensure both impartiality and effectiveness.
7. UNITY OF INDIA : Tiwari Congress is fully committed to the unity and integrity of India. The party will ceaselessly strive to prevent disintegration on grounds of religion, caste or language. It believes that citizens of India in all parts of the country are all equally patriotic and wedded to the unity and integrity of India. It also thinks there cannot be any wrong they seek to fulfill their ethnic, regional and linguistic identity and aspirations. All legitimate movements in that direction should need encouragement. Tiwari Congress, therefore, accepts several demands for creation of Small state units as legitimate and reasonable.
8. SMALLER STATE: The party agrees with the political experts and scientists that bigger States are not desirable in respect of (i) effective administration, (ii) balanced regional development, (iii) social justice, and (iv) implementation of schemes of socio-economic development designed by the States.
9. It, therefore, doesnot find any objection in demands for separate statehood for Vidarbha in Maharashtra, Chhattisgarh in Madhya Pradesh, Jharkhand in Bihar, Uttarakhand in UP and Bundelkhand.

10. UNION-STATE RELATIONS: Tiwari Congress is convinced that the desire to dominate over others or to centralise powers is at the root of most of the present day aberrations in our polity. Strong local units are imcompatible with a strong Union. For Tiwari Congress, unity doesnot mean uniformity, or diversity doesnot cannot division or divisiveness.
11. It would work to build up healthy relationship states and the Union, to justify the concept 'strong States in a strong Union' both in theory and practice. It would take steps to remove the present imbalances and the backwardness of States.
12. THE NORTH-EAST: The Tiwari Congress party believes that the problems of North-East States in the country has to be settled through political processes. Unlike attempts so far, which were mainly viewed as a mere law and order problem, it will appropriately assimilate hopes and aspirations of the people in that area in the specific policy and administrative actions. For, a volatile situation is fast developing in that part of the country where a large tribal population reside with ethnic plurality as distinct feature.
13. The party believes that a pragmatic overall policy on North-East has to be formulated with paramount importance to effectively check funding of insurgency and terrorism by the international narcotic drug cartels.
14. If voted to power the Tiwari Congress promises to review comprehensively all laws which have been brutally imposed by the Rao Government in violation of human rights. It will draw the final solution to all political problems through a process of negotiation with all concerned.
15. Tiwari Congress believes a judicious action plan has to be evolved in consultation with people on the twin objectives of economic development and protection of distinct local institutions of culture, customs, law and land tenure systems.
16. It reiterates the Constitutional commitments of protecting some special provisions in certain areas and safeguarding the personal laws prevalent in those areas.

17. In each case in North-East, the party will consider : (a) nature of development and cost input for employment, social services, to the locals, (b) upholding that which doesn't challenge the traditions of the states, and effectively, and (c) that no model of economy be imposed on the States from outside, without evaluating typical problems and potentials of the area.

INFLUX

1. With regards to migration and problems of continuing influx of refugees and infiltrators in the north-eastern border States, Tiwari Congress believes that it is a matter of grave concern to all the Seven Sisters. If these migrations and the influx continue unchecked, the laws protecting the North-East will become countre- productive which has well been evident by insurgent activities getting firmly rooted due to feelings of insecurity of the indigenous people.
2. Tiwari Congress will look after these problems very-well.

PROBLEMS RELATED TO JAMMU & KASHMIR

1. Tiwari Congress believes that Jammu & 'Kashmir is a part of our country and people of India look upon it as the crucible where secularism, tolerance and unity were born during the most trying times when partition of India took place.
2. The party has noted this part of our nation is tormented by mental militancy, insurgency, unabated violence often aided and abetted by a neighbouring foreign power. The party pledges to break the vicious circle by adopting bold policies and postures to restore rule of law and order.
3. The situation in Jammu & Kashmir is also due to utter lack of perception and appreciation of sentiments and aspirations of people of Jammu & Kashmir on the part of administration which has proved to have become un-

responsive and unimaginative. The administration has created the sense of alienation fairly widespread among citizens there. Instead of playing a role of protector and promoter of common people there, the apparatus of the administration has often become one of oppressive with harsh and unjustifiable measures.

Tiwari Congress will remove meticulously the causes that have led to the alienation of the people of Jammu & Kashmir. This can be brought about, it believes, only by frank and candid dialogue with the people at all levels. It would bring about a truly participative government and administration that would provide an atmosphere for democratic functioning of all institution provided for by the Constitution.

4. Tiwari Congress makes a commitment to people of Jammu & Kashmir that it will espouse their just and legitimate causes as citizens of this great nation. It would work determined to realise their rightful place in the Republic of India.

POLICIES ABOUT SOCIAL AND ECONOMIC JUSTICE

1. The Tiwari Congress is committed to render social and economic justice to all the deprived sections of society, specially the Scheduled Castes, Scheduled Tribes, Backward Classes and other weaker sections of the society.
2. The party believes, though some amenities and advantages are already accruing to these sections of the society through various policies and programmes, yet there are much left to be done for them further. Hence, the party commits itself to: (a) further expand educational facilities by providing them high quality schools, (b) enact legislations conferring the right of ownership of minor forest produce in the country, so as to enable them derive economic benefit as owners and not labours, (c) ensure that reservation conferred on them in services and education institutions are in effect given to them.

3. The party feels the necessity to enact legislation to provide deterrent punishment to the bureaucracy that might thwart proper implementation of reservation process.
4. It would amend the Constitution to provide for further reservations above 50 per cent mark wherever necessary.
5. It would amend reservation laws to accommodate more tribes and castes to the SC & ST category.
6. The party adopts the Dalit Manifesto incorporating the "Rights and entitlement of Scheduled Castes and Scheduled Tribes and Backward Classes" prepared by the National Action Forum for Social Justice under the chairmanship of Sri P S Krishnan, IAS (Retd.) The idea is to give reservation advantage to the "Dalit Christians" on par those for the SC and ST members.
7. Tiwari Congress believes all economic planning and policies are meaningless if they donot help to ameliorate conditions of the poor and fail to improve the quality of life for the disadvantaged and the downtrodden.
8. It wants like Mahatma Gandhi to wipe every tear from every eye.
9. It believes like Nehru that its task would be incomplete as long as single man is without food or clothing.
10. Tiwari Congress, therefore, maintains that alleviation of socio-economic inequalities is the basic commitment of the party.

ECONOMIC POLICY

The Tiwari Congress begins with the innate reality of the nation that at the time of restructuring the country's economy after Freedom (August 1947), the nation had been beset with innumerable hurdles and drawbacks. We had shortage of resources. Lack of Capital formation, dearth of technology and the growing legions of the poor and the downtrodden. It must be recognised, it believes, that what India was able to achieve between 1947 to 1987 was the result of this imaginative approach to industrialisation in the country.

Tiwari Congress, therefore, totally rejects the premises propounded by certain people that all the achievements of the Nehruvian model of development has to be abandoned, if India needs to embark upon a new economic policy. It firmly believes, that we indeed need to build upon these achievements and improvise upon them vis-a-vis standard of the global economic realities.

It also believes that after the 1991 General Elections, the Narasimha Rao Government went about implementing a policy of most reckless and self-centred economy which created grave misgivings in the minds of people. Especially the weaker section of the society, and also allowed aberrations develop giving rise to corruption and unrestricted entry of multinationals to the detriment of indigenous industries.

Tiwari Congress therefore commits itself to wider range of real economy, as detailed under:

1. It will continue with the economic liberalisation regime which is totally in tune with our national development in the last 45 years.
2. It will regulate the economy and expand it without any hindrance allowed.
3. It will fix priorities for foreign investments keeping in view larger national interests.
4. It will provide a level playing ground for foreign and the indigenous industries for a fair competition.
5. To avoid creating any regional imbalance in the country, it will provide adequate incentives for industrial development to backward regions.
6. It will ensure basic values of social justice as enshrined in the Constitution to enable the deprived section of the population get economic, social and quality opportunities without discrimination.

7. It believes that socialist approach adopted by India does-not in any way imply monopoly or capitalism of the State, nor does it imply a mere regulation by licence and permits. On the contrary, socialist approach is essentially an approach to effect all round development without discrimination, keeping in constant view the needs and aspirations of the poor.
8. The party, therefore, feels that overriding need today allow unfettered scope for expansion of Private Sector, while the Public Sector has to be further strengthened.
9. Tiwari Congress will ensure wide ranging consolations and consensus to attain strong economic base so that India is one equal footing with the world and not as a subordinate player.

POLICY ON RISING PRICES

1. Tiwari Congress attaches top priority to control rising prices of essential commodities for the common man.
2. Earlier, Narasimha Rao Government did everything to prove the wrong thing right but failed to control the prices. This party will not manipulate statistics, not would create any false impression about it.
3. It will not allow hoarding of foodgrains while offtake from public distribution systems go down and millions remain hungry.
4. The party will channelise all its energies to bring about drastic change in the present gloomy picture, with the interests of the common man in mind.

POLICY ON RURAL ECONOMY

1. Power to People: The party stands for a meaningful genuine transfer of power to the people at the grassroots. Although two Acts — Panchayati Raj Act and Nagar Palika Act — were passed in 1993, yet much more is still to be done to give the real power to the people. The

party will see that socio-economic life of the villagers are changed by way of mutual help and cooperation and proper education and training.

2. It also believes that laws along cannot bring in changes in villager's lifestyle. Each village is to be made self-sufficient and self-supporting unit with small and cottage industries linked to agriculture and forest. It will work to that direction, if voted to power.
3. It also holds that Panchayats being units of basic democracy should be founded on moral principles. It will see that intensive training to various functionaries of Panchayati Raj institutions be provided to the villagers.
4. Tiwari Congress will also ensure that money meant for Panchayats and rural development programmes actually reach the people and be properly used.
5. The party believes that the rural economy will be based on the status of farmers, farm labourers and other artisan in villages. Special attention has to be given to agriculture sector also because it is the highest employer in the country.
6. The party is aware of the fact that *Roti, Kapra* and *Makan* are constantly haunting the rural poor. Hence, it will, if voted to power, provide amenities like water and power enough to create employment in agriculture and also remove thereby situations like under-employment and partially employment.
7. The party will reduce in fertiliser prices and also of those of improved varieties of seed by 25 per cent. This will be possible by plugging loopholes and artificial escalation of prices.
8. It will wave the excise duty on electric motors upto 5 HP thrashers, power tillers and 25 HP tractors, tyres and other agricultural implements and their spare parts.
9. It will abolish sales tax on agricultural equipments, seeds and insecticides.

10. It will allow 50 per cent subsidy on sprinklers, drip irrigation equipments, and all tractor-driven or traditional agricultural tools including bullock-driven implements.
11. It will allow no electricity cuts for agriculture and to restore the policy of the eighties in this regard.
12. It will pay adequate compensation for agricultural land acquired for irrigation projects and the like.
13. It will assist farmers in crop planning and make provisions for more comprehensive crop insurance whereunder compensation for loss is real and adequate and covers everything.
14. It will rationalise and streamline the procedures for bank loans for farmers, and abolish penalty interest provisions.
15. It will increase minimum wages for landless labourers and ensure that these are actually paid and that minimum wage laws are passed in all States.
16. It will waive agricultural loans as also those to artisans, weavers and others.
17. It will provide the landless peasants and labourers right of shelters at the place of work.
18. It will provide a comprehensive scheme for helping village artisans financially and organise marketing of their produce through suitable incentives.
19. It will review the issue of conferring ownership title on farmers holding agricultural land as tenants' intention will be to amend the laws in the country to ensure this.
20. **Export of Essential Commodities:** Tiwari Congress believes that export of essential commodities like edible oils, vegetables, fruits, lentils, sugar, and the likes should be okayed only after Government satisfied itself that there is a surplus and not just to earn foreign exchange at the cost of the common man in the country.

COOPERATIVE MOVEMENT

1. The party will strengthen the cooperative movement particularly for agro-products.
2. It will aim at vesting real economic powers in the village upon the village panchayats and ensure that the funds meant for rural development actually reach the villagers.
3. This is all for protecting cottage industries and establishing cooperatives of artisans so that the middle men are eliminated in areas like marketing of handicraft and their exports.

UNEMPLOYMENT PROBLEM

The Tiwari Congress believes that unemployment in such mammoth number in all parts of the country is the root of poverty and of all social evils. The large number of unemployment may even create explosive situation in the near future.

The party, therefore, wants to provide one job in every family. To that direction it will create 10 lakhs additional jobs within next five years.

POLICY OF WATER RESOURCES AND DRINKING WATER

1. Availability of pure drinking water in rural areas is a constant problem in the country, especially as its absence or scanty availability is the cause for many diseases. Tiwari Congress promises to boost up the existing programmes and add up to realise the objective of providing pure drinking water to all villages in India by the turn of this century.
2. Though India is fortunate to have vast of water resources, the party has records to prove that 60 percent of water flows down to the sea unharnessed and utilised. The party seriously views this for timely utilisation.

3. The party believes Hydro-electric Power is the cheapest to harness from excess flood or rain water, but it is not available for industry and agriculture. It is, therefore, necessary that small Hydro-electric multipurpose projects should be constructed throughout the country, especially where rain water can be stored, from Kashmir to North-Eastern Hilly areas. This could turn out to become a novel step towards solving various socio-economic problems in the rural areas.
4. If voted to power the Tiwari Congress would construct multi-purpose Hydro-electric projects.

POLICY TOWARDS CHECKING OF CORRUPTION

1. Tiwari Congress is intrigued by the spate of scandals at high places in the Narasimha Rao Government during last five years. Apart from personal corruption charges which are yet to be unearthed gradually, there are such sensational ones as the Gold Star, Harshad Mehta's Scam, Sugar Scam, Telecom Scam, Purchase of MPs. The party believes all these and many which are likely to follow are to be investigated and the Prime Minister's responsibility be fixed in each of these.
2. Tiwari Congress makes a solemn commitment to introduce transparency in the decision-making process to eliminate favouritism and arbitrariness in finalising economic deals.
3. It pledges that all decisions involving foreign parties in projects in India will be taken through international competitive bidding along with defined parameters so that import of "Crony Capitalism" can be eliminated.
4. In case any indiscretion is committed, they will be dealt with by well-defined legal processes, streamlined as and when necessary.
5. The party would go in for immediate legislation to set up institutions of Lok Pal and Lok Ayuktas to consider

complaints of delay, corruption etc. In the administration and Government including all ministers, the Prime Minister, the chief ministers. It will ask for enquiries and even impose punishments.

6. The party stands for comprehensive laws effective for deterrent punishments for corrupt practices irrespective of the status of the person involved.
7. Corruption in electoral process is also another aspect, expressed in forms of criminalisation and commercialisation of politics, to which the party is witness. It believes that such turn into political activity has been brought about by the corrupt, criminal and communal elements in the body politic of the country. The party promises to make very determined meticulous attempts with strong political will to arrest pernicious influence of such elements. For that adequate changes in the system will be made.
8. The party commits itself to speedy resolution of investigation in Rajiv Gandhi Assassination case, unmask the conspirators, and punish all those who aided, abetted and inspired the dastardly crime. It denounces the callous approach of the Narasimha Rao Government towards the Commission of Enquiry, which even at times in the recent past was on the verge of termination, after the Rao Government had soft-pedalled the enquiry process of the Commission.

APPROACH TO UNPLANNED GROWTH OF INDUSTRIES

1. The Tiwari Congress plans to adopt a programme linkage plan by which the backward and remote areas of the country are to be provided with industrial estates linking each estate by 100 to 200 villages. This will stop exodus to towns and cities, which in turn creates slums, pollution, unhealthy lifestyle. This will provide gainful employment to rural masses.

2. The party will see that people of these villages are provided short term training in a centre to be set up in the industrial estates, provided work in the linked industries and in their native places.
3. They are to be provided with cooperative transport systems of their own which will take them to the place of work and return.
4. They are to be helped in matters of housing in their respective villages and they are not to migrate to the place of work.
5. Thus problem of creation of new slums will be solved.
6. Their children will be provided with education in their villages where Government will provide facilities for them.
7. The party will work out for a Five Year Plan for this and employ the entire rural job-seekers, thereby would solve the unemployment problem.
8. Tiwari Congress wants that the master plan for development be made not alone for towns but also for the villages under their purview. That will provide water supply, sewage disposal, street lighting and other community facilities to the villagers. Such master Plan will also accommodate low-cost housing for the poor living in jhuggis and jhonprhis and slums within a targeted period of 1996 to 2001.
9. The party will pass legislation conferring ownership rights on slum dwellers of the land on which the slums have been built.
10. The party will provide civic amenities to residents of unauthorised colonies if they are inhabited by poor sections of the population. Half the cost of such provision of amenities (water and electricity, in particular) will be borne by the Government of India.
11. The party believes that the Technical Area Development programme should be revived and implemented in the right spirits it was started with.

POLICY ON GOVERNMENT EXPENDITURE

1. Tiwari Congress has noticed that non-productive administrative government expenditure for the last five years has shown phenomenal increase, highest in 1995-1996 fiscal year. It believes that such increase makes policy implementation half-accomplished, and eradication of poverty becomes ineffective. It also believes that government must introduce controlling measures to bring down this increase. If voted to power, Tiwari Congress will would consult the financial experts, fix the maximum control limits of unproductive expenditure in the budget in each department and will not allow that limit exceed in any condition.
2. Tiwari Congress is committed to reducing and controlling all wasteful unproductive expenditure of the Government through budgetary controlling devices.

CONTROLLING OF ECONOMIC STRUCTURE

Tiwari Congress thinks that the new Economic policy of the Congress Government, which is in operation these days, has mortgaged future of the coming generations and brought the nation closer to disaster. The party strongly believes that fiscal and revenue deficits have not come down. From being a savings-oriented society, we seem to be moving fast into a system of living loans and credit.

1. The party would attempt to rationalise the tax structure so that savings are encouraged and wasteful expenditure is severely curtailed.
2. As a positive step toward that goal Tiwari Congress would rationalise tax structure, provide for single point tax and raise the income tax limit to rupees one lakh.
3. It will allow HRA to all tenants below certain specified limits.
4. It will distribute all surplus public lands to the unemployed and landless labours.

5. It will institute a scheme for unemployment allowance.
6. It will transform the right to work envisaged in the Constitution a fundamental right.
7. It will reclaim all the saline land and distribute it among small farmers cooperatives and the unemployed youth.
8. Tiwari Congress is opposed to throwing Indian market open to multinationals without any reciprocal benefits to Indians in the matter of free entry for services and man power.
9. Tiwari Congress would stress upon basic values of India and Gandhian ethos of austerity and *aparigraha.*
10. It will not give preference, like Narasimha Rao Government, to developing an acquisitive and consumerist culture. Its sole objective cannot be, like Mr Rao's Government, enabling about 100 million strong upper middle-class elite society acquire purchasing power to live in selfish luxury.
11. Tiwari Congress, instead, will first attend to the basic needs of foods, drinking water, clothing, shelter and primary education for the 800 million people.
12. In areas of opening up of Indian market, it will first try to acquire the latest State of Art Technology from the multinational foreigners.
13. Tiwari Congress has noted with serious concern that India is now facing an unsavoury spectacle of moving into the category of the most indebted nations of the world with prospect of having to pay 50 per cent of its revenue receipts in debt servicing.

To permit this continue means courting national disaster, which might even jeopardise India's existence as a sovereign state.

Tiwari Congress will not allow this to happen under any circumstances.

POLICY ON EDUCATION

1. Tiwari Congress will provide free primary education to all in the age-group of 4 to 14 years by the year 2005.
2. It will eliminate illiteracy in next 10 years.
3. It will provide free education to girls upto post-graduation level.
4. It will provide avenues for the best quality education for Scheduled Tribes and Castes in special institutions created for them by the State.
5. It will reorient educational programmes to make them employment-friendly, through vocationalisation at all levels.
6. It will lay down wholesome guidelines for improving the quality and content of higher education.
7. It will provide adequate safeguards and incentives to promote the education of the minorities as laid down in the Constitution of India.
8. It will ensure that 6 per cent of GDP is spent on education.

POLICY ON HEALTH

1. Tiwari Congress will give top priority in creating basic infrastructure to provide health services to the vast majority of the people, which the party feels is a daunting task.
2. These infrastructure will be done both in public as well as private sectors.
3. The party will make every effort to regulate the prices of the drugs and medicines, as they have gone practically beyond the reach of the common man.
4. To this effect it well work out on the line of Hathi Committee appointed by the former Prime Minister Late Smt Indira Gandhi in the past.

AGENDA FOR WOMEN

1. Tiwari Congress attaches highest importance to the women causes; for, the woman in India have always played a historic and decisive role in the shaping the nation's destiny.
2. It will take all effective measures to ensure that women of India are given their rightful share in every walk of life in the country.
3. It will enact suitable laws to prevent the exploitation of women in any form and to provide deterrent punishment for offences committed against women in the country.
4. It will provide 33 per cent reservations to women in all public office in the Panchayat to Parliament.
5. It will enact legislation to give women full rights in matters of property adoption, guardianship and to remove all discriminatory clauses in the divorce laws.
6. It will enforce the principle of "equal wages for equal work" in the organised and unorganised sectors.
7. It will initiate steps including enactment of women who have become victims of immoral trafficking.
8. Tiwari Congress will take all necessary steps to protect the rights of the girl child in all aspects and provide for free education for girls in their entire educational career.

POLICY ON MEDIA

1. Tiwari Congress recognises the crucial importance of the Fourth Estate in consolidation of democratic and secular content of our polity.
2. In order to play this role effectively there should be complete freedom of the Press, which the party would ensure, and any attempt by individuals or corporate entities to influence it should be checked through legal processes.

3. Tiwari Congress believes that if there is no free Press there could be no democracy. The party has witnessed in utter dismay the attempts by the Narasimha Rao Government to influence both the print and electronic media for his political ends. Tiwari Congrees will make suitable amendments to prevent such occurrence for anyone's benefit in future.
4. Tiwari Congress will protect the basic values and ethos of India's cultural heritage from the adverse effects of Western TV channel. It will specially keep vigil over attempt to exploit women and children for commercial advantage.
5. Laws in this regard the party will make in consultation with the representatives from the Fourth Estate.

REFORMS IN JUDICIAL SYSTEM

1. Tiwari Congress believes that some basic reforms are desirable to make the judicial system of India more in tune with requirements of the changing Indian society.
2. Also, the party believes that our Constitution rightly recognises the prominent position of the judiciary in reform processes in this sphere, and this has to be approached in a very sensitive manner.
3. Tiwari Congress will try to enter into dialogue with all political parties in this regard to arrive at a consensus on an approach to this matter. Thereafter the resolution would be presented to the Honourable Supreme Court of India for guidance and directions in order to make the reform a reality.

POLICIES ON COMBATTING COMMUNALISM

1. Tiwari Congress gives solemn commitment that it shall fight relentlessly against all communal, divisive and sectarian principles and ideas that are bedevilling Indian polity today. For, it believes communalism has been the

bane of Indian Politics and poses the gravest danger to the future of democracy itself in the country.

2. The party will work ceaselessly to bring about an atmosphere of amity and goodwill amongst all communities of the country.
3. It is opposed to the exploitation of religion, language or caste issues for any purpose.
4. The party holds that minorities have equal rights, must be protected and promoted in every manner permissible under Constitution.
5. Tiwari Congress deplores the failure of Mr Narasimha Rao as Prime Minister to protect the Babri Mosque from destruction. His inability to act has given rise to the legitimate suspicion that he connived in the destruction of the Mosque. The party believes that the Prime Minister should have publicly apologised to the nation for this lapse on his part, but the brazen manner in which he and his ministerial colleagues continue to refuse to do so is a pointer to their frame of mind.
6. Tiwari Congress firmly believes that the unity and integrity of India depends solely upon its secular character and any tampering with this fabric could lead to unimaginable consequences for the nation. The party commits to preserve this basic character of our polity and would not hesitate to make any sacrifices in this regard.

POLICY TOWARDS OUR ARMED FORCES

1. Tiwari Congress stands for a strong Army, Air Force and Naval Force. The indifference shown by Sri Narasimha Rao to the defence needs of the country has weakened in key areas our preparedness to face any threat to the security and integrity of the country.
2. The party believes a close examination and review of the entire defence scenario is called for, more so in the changed global context to ensure that we maintain the

highest standard in this regard that has been our pride for all these years.

3. Tiwari Congress also promises the implementation of "one rank one pension" principle for all the retired personnel of our armes forces.

MANIFESTO IN BRIEF: HOW IT'S DIFFERENT FROM OTHERS

* Tiwari Congress is truly a people's party, open to all and firmly wedded to inner party democracy, periodic elections, freedom of dissent and expression of views.

* A no-nonsense, no hypocrisy, no double speak party.

* A believer in purity of means and value based politics, politics for service and not for money and power.

* It realised that corruption, criminalisation and communalisation have become ingrained in the system and that probity in public life cannot be brought back without systemic changes across the board.

* It is opposed to sale and purchase of legislators, corruption, communalism, politicalisation of religion, caste, language and the like and pure vote bank politics.

* It accepts the legitimacy and relevance of ethics, regional and linguistic identity aspirations.

* It deprecates the tendency to dominate and to centralise powers and would like the widest possible decentralisation to lower and lower levels in 3-4 tier system of governance.

WHAT DOES IT STAND FOR?

Polity

Faith in the basic values enshrined in the Preamble and other parts of the Constitution.

Restoring confidence of people in political process and in the representative system.

Regulation of political parties, maintenance and audit of party accounts etc., declaration of assets by all public functionaries.

Giving the highest priority to removal of poverty and illiteracy and meeting the basic needs of people with a time-bound programme.

** Ensuring life, liberty and security of citizens which are everyday threatened by criminals, mafia gangs and sometimes even by State forces.

Strengthening legal framework and investigating institutions like the CBI so that they can function honestly and without fear and favour.

Genuine transfer of power, including financial power to Panchayats and grassroots level and more meaning flux and real multi-tier federal polity.

Negotiations with sections seeking recognition of ethnic identities without preconditions. Constitution can be amended in the interest of national unity.

Immediate setting up of Lok Pal and Lok Ayukts. Providing deterrent punishment upto death penalty for corruption, implementation of Benami Abolition Act, publication full Vohra Committee report, fully exposing and punishing the guilty ruthlessly, taking stringent action against all misuse of public funds for personal ends.

* Strengthening secularism meaning equality of all citizens being an article of faith, launching countrywide crusade and launching mass movements against political culture of crime, politician-bureaucrat-businessman-criminal nexusand against all communal, casteinst and reactionary forces endangering the integrity of the nation.

* Protecting the composite Indian culture form adverse effects of Western channels, implementation of Prasar Bharati Act ensuring freedom of media from censorship etc. preventing the blatant misuse of TV and Radio for personal publicity and image building of the leader of the ruling clique.

* Time-bound action plan for ameliorating social and economic conditions of the deprived and underprivileged, high quality education and training, allocation of higher resources etc.

* Summary trials and enhanced penalties for atrocities against women and children.

* Compulsory elementary education for all, free education upto post-graduation level for girls, opportunities of vocational education for the needed manpower in various areas, and right to work as fundamental rights.

* Free and fair elections, drastic electoral reforms to prevent use of money, muscle and mafia power.

* Reforms in the judicial systems to bring justice nearer to the people.

* Reforming the ineffective anti-defection law with a view to prevent its misuse of sale purchase of legislators and rule by parties which buy their majorities through horse trading.

ECONOMY

Basic values of socialism as enshrined in the Constitution and implying equality in opportunity of status, non-discrim- ination, socio-economic justice and not allowing concentration of wealth and means of production and distribution in a few hands to the detriment of the common good.

* Protecting and promoting cottage and village industries.

* Strengthening the cooperative movements in the agro-products, distribution of foodgrains among the poor on heavily subsidized rates.

* Creation of 10 lakh additional jobs and safe drinking water facilities for all villages within five years and 100 per cent literacy within ten years.

* Giving the highest priority to resolving problems of the farmers and the rural India, to improving quality of life in the villages, to assuring remunerative prices and free movement of farmers' produce, to supplying agricultural inputs at affordable prices and ensuring benefit of subsidies and welfare programmes actually reach the villagers.

* Liberalisation of economy without giving up principle of self-reliance and Swadeshi, without sacrificing interests of the poor and without surrendering national interests and economic sovereignty.

* To ensure that the new economic policy doesnot become devoid of all social content and economic justice, become anti-democratic, inconstitutional, anti-people and discriminatory against Indian entrepreneurs.

* Rationalistaion of tax structure encouraging savings, and penalties ostentatious or wasteful expenditure.

* Launching a mass movement against constantly rising prices of essential commodities, shameful philosophies of larger left-overs and trickle down benefits for the poor or of the rich getting richer before the poor get a little less poor.

* Bringing about greater transparency in international deals, exposing and punishing the guilty in various scams and scandals and reforming NEP to bring back the poor on the top of the agenda.

HIGHLIGHTS

* Tiwari Congress will pass legislation conferring ownership rights to the slum dwellers of the land upon which slums have been built.

* Basic civic amenities like water and electricity will be provided to residents of unauthorised colonies inhabited by the poor sections of the people. Half of the cost incurred for this will be borne by the Government of India.

* List of those eligible for reservations under ST, SCs will be revised to include those seeking inclusion for long time. Dalit Christians too will be included in the list.

* To confer ownership rights of minor forest produce to the SCs, STs and other poor people working in the forests. They will be entitled to get full profit accrued from these business.

* The issue of conferring ownership title on farmers holding agricultural land as tenants will be reviewed with the intention of amending the laws to ensure this.

8

Manifesto of Bahujan Samaj Party

BACKGROUND

THE ONLY MAJOR party that seems reluctant educate people through pre-declared pleadges in form of manifesto is Bahujan Samaj Party. A conglomerate of heterogeneous traits both in habits and lineage, occupation and intellectual alignments, ethnicity and mind-set, the party, as is claimed by its leaders, belongs to the majority of Indian polity. Clear-cut marks for identification of their exponents would always slither away, however, as long as the party remains in the wilderness away from the powers that make ruling practicable. Majority of its members whether politically active or not had remained mute onlookers of ways of men in power in India eversince dawning of Indians' sectarian societal divides and the standpoints on these lines got firmly rooted. They have given a name to these divides, which is general though rational, 'Manuawadi' society. Going by its programmes, this party exudes deep entrenched hatred towards all leaders of India and heartfelt aversion to all parties. They have been for centuries oppressed and exploited by almost every echelon of power, they feel; and it is a realisation which in turn has made members of this party equally ruthless and revengeful towards members of all other political parties and classes.

'Bahujan' signifies assembly of heterogenous people, more powerful in connotative latency than Gandhiji's sanctified 'Harijan'. The very name is also a sharp example of departure from Gandhian concept of social upliftment of the downtrodden. The idea is very important for analysis to a political scientist, whose job is to trace the watermarks of ideological and conceptual development in the post-Independent Indian political realm.

The concept of identifying their brethren and eagerness to bring all of them under one common umbrella has developed firm roots when their frustration in day-to-day life got admixed with awareness of repressed existence. Their existence incessantly clashed with their aspirations. For hundred of years they have been subjugated in Brahmin ordained 'Manuwadi' societal divisions. They always felt and aspired to quell such evil influences of the system, so that they can groom themselves upto the status of affluence and dignity. Their aspirations generally emerge from apathetic treatment they received from the upper caste social rulers for centuries. These aspirations are more an expression of revolt, than mere striving for betterment. Their aspirations also dawn unto themselves after they educate their palates from affluent lifestyles and dignity of the upper caste. This is a natural byproduct, and is correctly humane. However, this is also a sad commentary on psyche of members of this party which is well explicit in their inability to grab whatever preferential opportunities they are given in realms of education, job and self-style entrepreneurship. For, not all upper caste people are bad. There are millions who have worked hard to uplift the downtrodden and offered them opportunities.

Nevertheless their incapabilities in utilizing the offered opportunities, the party expresses a hostile mind. In its pre-election pamphlets it interprets and observes what it feels about its members.

It explains: Bahujan Samaj means a gathering of people of heterogeneous traits and mind-set such as members of scheduled castes, tribes and other backward classes like is barbers, *garherias, telis, gujjars, kashyaps, sainis, kumars, yadavs, kurmis, et al*; communities, religious minorities in India like Sikhs, Muslims, Christians, Parsis and Buddhists. In its election appeals, therefore, it targets voters from the converted Muslims, Sikhs, Christians from the backward classes primarily along with the non-converted members of the SCs, STs and OBCs, and not a Sikh from upper class echelon or a Muslim of a Gulf country, or a Christian from the Western nations. The minority yet rich Parsi community is automatic incumbent of favours from them. The external worlds ofcourse would find their religious affinities nevertheless. They would also feel encouraged in case BSP comes to power. Advantage in BSP lies, however, in its innate concern to win self-respect. In its papers the party chief Mr Kanshi Ram clarifies quite clearly:

"Our organisation is not against anybody on the basis of caste or creed. This is for agitation against the prevalent social system based on inequality which deprived us of all human rights."

There is therefore no honest reason why the members of this party would not feel that 'Bahujan' Indians comprise 85 per cent of the entire population, who are ruled by 15 percent of the minority polity consisting of Brahmans, Banias and Thakurs. The members of this party also realise the fact that the Brahmanical societal system is based upon unequal and differential craftiness. It is a system whereby 15 per cent of the populace gains at the cost of perpetual loss to 85 per cent of people of India.

They have no other option therefore than resolving, as they claim in their party papers, to uproot this Brahmanical societal system and empower the majority of the populace enough to enthrone and rule the country. Many a great souls have been born to the mother India to fulfill this task. Many an enlightened talents have worked hard to inseminate the real idea, of whom the members of this party recall with reverence, pioneered by Baba Saheb Dr Bhim Rao Ambedkar. Though Bahujan Samaj Party is the fruit of Baba Saheb's brain wave, the party was officially christened and started by Mr Kanshi Ram. The party has kindled in the members self-esteem and oriented them onto a soul-searching process. To that goal, Mr Kanshi Ram has been able to bring them out of their ageold stupor and rather dismayed style of thinking. The party feels strongly that the Dalits today are able to "keep their heads up with great pride."

Mr Kanshi Ram's is not just a political guardianship, his foray seems quite as much sculpturing to a novel height of political wisdom, which is likely to be put to acid test in future elections in the country. The present elections in India being only the arenas of his steady rise to international prominence, the ensuing elections from the twelfth general elections would prove the authenticity and results of his conceptualising which are quite convincing as truths today. Presently, it is more his charismatic appeals that are working in favour of his party. He made some sacrifices which are great to his followers. Sacrifices donot alone build up a political organisation, had it been so, then considering the pivotal sacrifices done by Netaji Subhas Chandra Bose would have made his Forward Block mass-mobilising party in solid power base. However, this does not mean Mr Kanshi Ram would not be able to do what his people are looking up with great zeal to him to do, that is, weilding power to rule the nation. Here lies the genesis of the phenomenon of Kanshi Ram in the political scenario.

In 1965 he worked for Republican Party of India, which at that time was the only Dalit outfit in the country. His meticulous lode of the downtrodden was fired up by a thought in mind to upkeep to achieve the power first and thereafter the bountiful heavens would be their for ever. On 6 December of 1978 Kanshi Ram launched his first organisation on his intended line of building up awareness. It was All-India Backward (SC, ST, OBC) and Minority Communities Employees Federation (BAMCEF) consisting of educated employees and "For" educated employees. He made it a non-political, non-religious and non-agitational forum. The sole aim was to "strengthen the non-political roots" of the oppressed and exploited society. According to the party, BAMCEF is the "brain bank, a talent bank and a financial bank of the oppressed and the exploited of the society to accelerate its mission forward" to think beyond the visible time. The party claimed that BAMCEF has the "purposeful social cause", a movement of the educated employees, by the educated employees but not for the educated employees. In 1981, he formed an archetypical D-S4 which in fact is, Dalit Soshit Samaj Sangharsh Samiti (that is, an agitational committee for oppressed and exploited society). This committee was formed exactly on the third year, on the same day.

This Samiti, he formed as his movement's agitational wing. D-S4 was indeed a political force for agitation, and mass mobilisation programmes. The organisation comprised "the resourceless section of the society" — students and women as well as doctors and engineers.

One of the stark realities of Kanshi Ram's ideological forays is his D-S4 anti-liquor campaign which took the upper caste for a ride; even the Gandhian exponents was enthralled to find somebody able to catch the upper caste-dominated Government on wrong foot. BSP volunteers launched a nation-wide campaign by cycling all over the state of Uttar Pradesh, particularly agitating against liquor shops opening in the predominantly backward colonies and localities. In his habitual caustic commentary Mr Kanshi Ram said: " On one hand the Government is spreading the word of Gandhi, while on the other hand, it is opening wine shops. How do you reconcile the two? They want our people to remain helpless, worthless and hopeless."

Here lies the basic point that found concrete shape in formation of Bahujan Samaj Party on 14 April 1984. Symbolically enough, that was Baba Saheb Dr Ambedkar's birthday that year. Achievements hereafter were no mean. A chronological assay of the plus points favouring the party would spell the truth rather convincingly, particularly when it concerns Uttar Pradesh affairs of state. We can look into them in a nutshell below:

1. In 1984 Lok Sabha polling BSP polled 10.05 per cent votes.
2. The same year in the State assembly elections (UP), BSP singularly polled 7 lakh votes. 45 Lok Dal and 6 Janata

Party candidates won their elections defeating their Congress rivals during that elections which was possible owing to BSP's presence in the contest. BSP played catalyst there.

3. In Punjab, BSP captured 1.53 lakh votes in the Assembly and 2.15 votes in the Lok Sabha elections, which in turn helped the 30 Akali candidates win theirs.
4. In the following (December 1985) Bijnor (UP) byelection BSP polled 61,000 votes wherein such stalwart like Mrs Meera Kumar (daughter of Babu Jagjivan Ram) polled only 5000. BSP's polling was 95000 votes less than what Congress candidate had polled to win the seat earlier. That showed BSP's root was getting firmer.
5. In Harwar byelection that year the party came impressive second with 1,35,399 votes compared to 1,49,335 polled by Congress (I), while others lost their deposits. Notable parties and people whom BSP floored in this election were popular Lok Dal polling a poor third at 39,780 votes, 1977 world record holder Mr Ram Bilas Paswan having polled only 34,225 votes and the BJP a meager 4,578 votes to their kitty. Such was rising awareness among the Dalits and their brethren that they mustered massive support in a sort of wave.
6. The party conducted successfully year-long social action programme against untouchability, inhumanity, injustice, insecurity and inequality by launching well-publicised dharnas and cycle marches from 15 August 1987 to 15 August 1988.
7. The Allahabad byelection of 16 June 1988 is a pointer how BSP is advancing through grassroots awareness. The byelection results came as a stark revelation when BSP polled 71,586 to come third behind 90,000 by Congress (I) and 2,03,000 by V P Singh's Jan Morcha. There BSP had to depend entirely on its door to door grassroots level campaigns, whereas Congress (I) resorted to use money, Government machinery and muscle power, and VP Singh had to his side seasoned

political campaigners from 23 parties which included CPI, CPM, and five Opposition chief ministers—of Kerala, Karnataka, Andhra Pradesh, West Bengal and Haryana. The attitude, according to Mr Kanshi Ram, was as if "it should be either you Congress (I) or we (Opposition combine) but not Kanshi Ram of BSP under any circumstances."

8. This apart the party launched massive five-fold movements aiming at social transformation for one full year 15 August 1987 to 15 August 1988 for (i) self-respect, (ii) liberation, (iii) equality, (iv) for annihilation of caste and building up of brotherhood in the broken society, and (v) for struggles against untouchability, injustice, atrocities and terror. All these struggles brought rich dividends for the Party. These idealised struggles in fact were carried out by symbolic cycle marches to converge huge humanity from the downtrodden round the five sides of the country.
9. One epochal yet not quite rational concept it launched to bring about hundred per cent partisan allegiance is its starting of Welfare Conferences in 1989 throughout the country where the ideal was spread that "Bahujan Samaj is safe only with the Bahujan Samaj Party" etc. There may not be quite illegitimate claim in the ideal thus propagated though, the approach especially rejects universal partisanless brotherhood which the Communist Parties in particular and Janata Dals and Congress parties in general do expound.
10. BSP also created a sort of novel convergence programme, rather on the line of Mahatma Gandhi whom the party detested and are critical of, whereby it is regularly arranging get-togethers. This policy is aimed at cementing allegiance among its members. Through cycle marches, conferences, welfare meets, journeys round the country on routined periodicity the party is able to make majority of its polity aware of their existence and, what they call, of partisan slogans like, "Muslims are safe with

BSP in Muslim dominated areas, or so" or OBC's are safe with BSP" in areas where families of such groups are in majority. These activities also bring under the umbrella all people who are Dr Ambedkar's followers.

11. BSP's march to prominence in Indian Political Scene is well established by Mr Kanshi Ram's convincing win at the Etawa (1992) byelection by 19,000 votes over Congress (I). There also existed clandestine poll alliance between Congress (I) and BJP to defeat the BSP. The constituency being a general one and not a reserved constituency, Kanshi Ram's win proved the party's growing popularity among the downtrodden who could assemble under the BSP umbrella forsaking their earlier Congress(I) camp. On that 16th day of November in 1992 BSP convinced itself of its firm roots in Uttar Pradesh which ultimately might take to the Centre with amazing results in near future it thinks.
12. According to the party papers BSP scored established remarkable identity and a victory amidst what they called "State terrorism in Punjab." It felt aghast at the "Centre unleashed state terrorism and goondaims using police power all over the state in name of terrorism of Punjab militants." The party claims that under the protective covers of security forces, the Congress (I) pasted posters in the name of militants that read; if voters dared to participate in the elections, they would be shot dead mercilessly. According to their hand book, the BSF jawans pasted these wall posters in all villages carrying Bahujan Samaj Party's flags. All these were done to deny the BSP its natural victories in elections, and to allow Congress (I) win almost in all important places. Votes were rigged enmasse, it said. However, that could not apparently erode the bases of the BSP.

During the terrorism intrigued days, it was BSP which could hold its meetings in open public gatherings in all constituencies. Its workers went deep into interior villages for campaigning whereas the BJP and the Congress (I) had to contend by holding their meetings indoors. In 1992, elections results did not flay the BSP efforts. The party came second largest with one MP to the Centre and nine MLAs of whom five were Sikh and four non-Sikh candidates. BSP therefore has enough things to justify and boast for. It records: "The BSP, now regarded as a very powerful mass movement has received people's mass support in UP, Punjab, MP, Haryana, Delhi and in four other States. It is now to storm Maharashtra, Gujarat and all Southern States. Even the Election Commission has recognized BSP as a State party now in MP to start with. Sweeping the national scene is only a matter of short time."

However, in the absence clear-cut declared programmes, the Party's best stand in matters of management of Government would be well-founded on the following terms. For readers' meticulous pursuit to the truth, the entire blue-book it has published from its ABCDE Publications from SQ-133, North Avenue, New Delhi could be relevant. The most salient features of the party's avowed goal as mentioned therein can be short listed as under:

(1) SOCIAL TRANSFORMATION,

(2) ECONOMIC PROGRAMMES TOWARDS THE GOAL OF ATTAINING FINANCIAL COMFORTS AND PROTECTION FOR ALL ITS MEMBERS AND THEIR FAMILIES,

(3) ACQUIREMENT OF POLITICAL POWER IN THE CENTRE TO RULE THE WHOLE NATION.

(4) SETTLING UNDERSTANDING AND DEVELOPING EQUITABLE RELATIONS WITH OTHER POLITICAL PARTIES.

Above features are also the guidelines from Mr Kanshi Ram for the party workers. Hence the blue-book might turn out to become the party workers' Bible in the near future. To avoid controversies we have published the full text without much editing.

Programmes of Bahujan Samaj Party

1. SOCIAL TRANSFORMATION

i) Social System
ii) Self-respect
iii) Class and Caste Struggles
iv) Eradication of Caste
v) Dalits
vi) Other Backward Castes
vii) Minorities—Muslims, Christians, Sikhs
viii) Brahmins and Upper Castes.

i) Social System

In the present vertical system, the caste arrangement is Brahmin, Kshatriya, Vaishya and thereafter the Shudras. Being the lowest in the Society's order of priority, the first three castes have been oppressing the Shudras. This order has to be changed and it is time for the majority to vote itself to power so that a horizontal social order can be ushered in.

—The Times of India (Allahabad) 29.5.1988

What is the use of our hearing Abe sense in excess? Animals, though with one sense less, are casteless; we suffer degradation, in spite of our sixth sense, because of caste! Should we not contemplate on this?

—From his Speeches

No 'ism' whether capitalism, communism, liberalism or socialism will succeed in Indian so long as there is Brahminism.

—The Hindustan Times 7.4.1987

Socialism cannot be a success here as long as Brahminsim exists. Instead of exploiting the weaker sections of society we want exploitation of the natural resources for the benefit of the people.

—Weekend Newstime 26.4.1987

ii) Self-respect

Our organisation is not against anybody on the basis of caste or creed. This is for agitation against the prevalent social system based in inequality which deprived us of all human rights.

—*The Oppressed India, 1983*

The upper caste people are committing atrocities on the lower caste people reducing them to the level of slaves. So the BSP is the party of the exploited of the labourers to fight this system. We won't tolerate the tyranny of the upper class. They should not bear anymore of this exploitation. They should not live like goats and pigs.

—*Current, 18.6.1988*

Four decades after Independence, you all have remained animals. This is your chance to become humans. Get together and throw out the 'Upper Castes' domination.

—*India Today, 10.6.1988*

The per centage of inter-caste marriages is less than one percent between the oppressed elites and the higher castes. In the final analysis, we should encourage intercaste marriage. If not today, tomorrow we should convince all that they are equal human beings and they should inter-marry.

—*Link, 9.2.1986*

We are fit to think of self-respect only when the notion of superior and inferior caste is banished from our land.

—*From his Speeches*

If any one wishes to serve society on the basis of humanism, what he should do first is to make people think and conduct themselves rationally.

—*From his Speeches*

Brahminical Social order stands vertical, where all the castes are unequal. Brahminism represents perfect inequality. That is why Baba Saheb Ambedkar advised the victims of the system, "Let us uproot Brahminism, the spirit of inequality."

There had been many struggles in the past. We feel the need to continue the struggles till the unequal vertical social order is transformed to the horizontal social order where all are equals.

—*Pamphlet written by Kanshi Ram*

Please remember, our primary objective is not power at any cost, we want to achieve dignity as well.

—*The Week, 16.4.1989*

We are fighting for equality and self-respect.

—*The Hindustan Times, 1.4.1987*

iii) Class and Caste Struggles

When we come to power our endeavour will be to treat everybody on par. We stand for horizontal equality of all the castes. In the present system the whole thing is dominated by the Brahmins. It is only in this country that we have caste struggles rather than class struggles.

—*Onlooker, 1.1.1989*

My struggle is a caste and class struggle. I would like to say that class struggle is not succeeding in India because of the vicious hold of caste system.

Dr Ambedkar was of the opinion and I am also of the opinion that there cannot be a class struggle as long as there is a caste struggle. As long as there is a caste, it will not allow the building of class. When Brahmins and Scheduled Castes come together to building bricks or break stones or to work in a factory they come closer. But the vested interests bring religion into the picture, which brings in the caste and people get divided into castes. And the class struggle becomes a meaningless dream. Though people face the same economic hardships, social standing prevails over the economic situation. That is the crux of the problem in India, that is why everything has failed.

iv) The Eradication of Caste

The sizeable population today remains as untouchables, and another sizeable population exists in the name of Shudras and as serfs, coolies, menials and illegitimate children. Who wants an independence that cannot change these things? Who wants religious scriptures and God, which cannot bring about a change?

—From his Speeches

No man is inferior to me. Similarly none is superior to me. This means that each one should live free and equal. To creat this condition, caste should be eradicated.

—From his Speeches

We are doing openly what others are doing clandestinely. The caste system in India is like a cancer which has to be brought out into the open before it can be operated upon.

—India Today, 11.1.1986

Uptill now we have been expecting the higher castes to annihilate caste. Why should they? They are the beneficiaries. That is why it is not going. It is only when the victims, the oppressed, organise themselves that the caste system will be wiped out.

—Express Magazine, 24.5.1987

I did not create the caste system and I do not perpetuate it by keeping a surname which demonstrates my caste. My aim is to annihilate caste.

—Sunday Mail, 29.3.1987

So far the upper castes have the caste system as a single-edged sword to dissect the lower castes. Unless they put a stop to this I would use the same caste system as a double-edged weapon against them.

—The Sunday Observer, 21.8.1988

We want to break dependence. We want to make them (oppressed class) independent. That dependence you have talked about is the main feature of our fight. In Independent India, why should the lower castes be dependent on the upper castes? This is our ideology.

We are going to prove that the lower castes have decided to give up their dependence. Our social system decided who should be rich and who should be poor. Till 140 years ago, when the struggle was started, the situation was such that the lower castes were not entitled to education, they were not entitled to acquired property, build a house, and the land is not yours... So, Dr Ambedkar struggled in 1930s and got the right.

The struggle has been going on for the last 140 years. In 1848 Mahatma Jyoti Rao Phule from Pune started the struggle when we were slaves of slaves. The upper castes were slaves of the British but we were slaves of the upper castes. Phule wrote a book also on this "Gulam girl."

The fight continued upto 1956. Till Ambedkar died it was continuous. After him also some people continued the struggle. But now we have picked it up very seriously and have decided to take it to the logical end.

—*Sunday Observer, 29.5.1988*

For too long we have been knocking at the doors of the system, asking for justice and getting nothing. It is time to break down those doors. No sacrifice will be too great.

—*The New York Times International, 18.4.1990*

v) Dalits

Dalits have both bullet and ballot power. There are 85 per cent Dalit voters. Similarly, in the defence forces the Dalits are 90 per cent.

—*The Tribune, 18.1.1990*

vi) Other Backward Castes

The SC/STs have got various benefits, facilities and opportunities but those who have got nothing are the 52 per-cent other Backward Castes (OBs) who are the duped majority.

—*Surya India, May 1987*

Seats reserved for the Scheduled Castes and Tribes is 22.5 per cent. The Brahmins and Kayasthas, who form only 8 per cent of the country's population occupy 52 per cent of the seats in Parliament. The OBCs have only 8 per cent seats. They are the ones who are losing out.

—Surya India, May 1987

vii) Minorities— Muslims, Christians, Sikhs

Muslims

We feel that they are also becoming victims these days. They are also having problems. So these victims need our help. And we will be able to help them and protect their constitutional, social, human and political interests.

—The Telegraph, 28.4.1987

We are struggling to remove the unequal system and Muslims are the worst victims of it. Till 1947 they had one-third participation in the governance of the land, today it has been reduced to one per cent. They are supporting us in their own interest.

—Weekend Newstime, 26.4.1987

The Muslims I am organising, 90 per cent of them belong to groups which have been kept down by the Syeds, Sheikhs, Mughals and Pathans etc. You can call them the Brahmins amongst Muslims.

Christians

The Christians are also Indian and patriots. Christians teachers, medicalmen and women were so fully devoted to their professions that they were absolutely unwilling to be drawn into other attractions. Now suddenly we see an enormous change in their outlook and behaviour. Not only laymen, but teachers, professional and priests also have come in the streets. Uptill now they had been ignoring the unjust treatment meted out to them. But now, they are in revolt almost enmasse, from Kanyakumari to Kashmir, to towns and cities are witnessing well-organised and well-attended public demonstrations by the Christian community.

—Oppressed Indian, May 1979

viii) Brahmins and Upper Castes

Don't blame the Brahmins. We people have carried Brahminism on our shoulders, it is high time we threw away our burden.

—*Weekend Newstime, 26.4.1987*

The upper castes say why not include us. I say you are leading all the parties. If you join our party, you will block change here also. They, upper castes can join the party, but they cannot be its leaders. Leadership will remain in the hands of the backward community. My fear is that these upper caste people will come into our party and block the process of change. When this fear goes, they can join our party.

—*The Illustrated Weekly, 8.3.1987*

2. ECONOMIC PROGRAMMES

i) Bharatiya Kisan Mazdoor Andolan
ii) Bhartiya Safai Mazdoor Andolan
iii) Bharatiya Dastkar Andolan
iv) Bharatiya Sharnarthi Andolan
v) Bharatiya Bhagedari Andolan
vi) Land Reforms
vii) Employment Opportunities
viii) Reservation

(i) Bharatiya Kisan Mazdoor Andolan

The basic idea is that those who are tilling the land and producing foodgrains are starving and those who own the land are becoming wealthy though they do nothing. We are against this. We do not want higher wages. You see, whatever land is under cultivation, double of that is lying vacant, which can be cultivated by the Government. So we feel that people should only work in their own farms or the Government farms. If people work in other's farms, it will lead to oppression and exploitation.

—*The Telegraph, 3.12.1989*

We have launched the Kisan Mazdoor struggle because the farmers movement so far had been in the interests of the landed farmers. I divide the farmers into 5 categories;

a) Landless farmers (34%)
b) Marginal farmers (26%)
c) Peasant proprietors (22%)
d) Feudal Lords
e) Neo-Feudal Lords (18%)

40 crore of people who constitute nearly 50 per cent of the total agricultural population in the country fall under the first three categories.

All the existing farmers movement of the Congress or the opposition parties talk of an increase in the prices of the agricultural produce but none about agricultural workers in relation to the increase in the cost of their produce. The increase in cost which these farmers agitations are demanding is sought to be pocketed by the landlords, which is what we are opposing.

—*The Illustrated Weekly*

ii) Bharatiya Saafi Mazdoor Andolan

This is a conceptual idea. In India, sweepers, scavengers and washermen, who are responsible for cleanliness, are looked down upon whereas those who spread dirt are considered to be great. We are against this concept. Why should only some do sweeping, scavenging and washing? Every one should do it.

—*The Telegraph, 3.12.1989*

iii) Bharatiya Dastkar Andolan

Artisans have suffered a lot, their old businesses have gone because of the steel and plastic boon and so they have become rootless people, we feel that we must ameliorate their condition.

—*The Telegraph, 3.12.1989*

iv) Bharatiya Sharnarthi Andolan

As a result of the wrong agricultural policy of the Government, 10 crore people have been forced to leave their villages and land for the slums of cities and towns. They have become refugees in their own land—"Bharatiya Sharnarthi." The first thing we want is to check this distress migration; besides employment, they must get justice in their own villages. And those who have already landed in the slums of cities, the Government must undertake housing for them.

—*The Telegraph, 3.12.1989*

The Union Government had set-up a separate rehabilitation ministry for the rehabilitation of 50 lakh refugees who migrated from Pakistan at the time of partition. For the 5,000 odd families who migrated from Punjab because of terrorism the Government has spent more than Rs 5.30 crore in Delhi in 1987. But why is it that for the 10 crore rural migrants, the Government has not spent even a single paise or set-up any ministry for their rehabilitation? It is because most of them belong to the Scheduled Castes and backward communities.

The situation can only improve if the government changes its faulty agricultural policy, creates options in the villages and improves the condition of those who have already migrated to the cities.

—*Pamphlet written by Kanshi Ram*

v) Bharatiya *Bhagedari* Andolan

Bhagedari means sense of participation; in the governance of the land, all sections of society must have a share. Only then can they have a sense of belonging; otherwise they will feel alienated. And in this concept another thing is included—the people must have the "right to work, and the duty to work."

—*The Telegraph, 3.12.1989*

vi) Land Reforms

Life is a many sided affair. I am talking of the most important side—the governance of the land. When the British left, the SCs/STs formed barely 18 per cent of the landless labour in the country. Today they form 30 per cent. In this respect they have suffered most.

—*Surya India, May 1987*

In fact, we can give land to all of them. There is no shortage of land in the country. Lots of vacant land is in the Government's possession. We will distribute it to the landless or set-up state farms of it.

Notes Vs Votes

SC, ST, OBC and minority communities are the most dispossessed people. The assets of 20 per cent of India's population at the lowest rung of the economic ladder are less than those of Birla House alone. This gap between the rich and the poor has been widening ever since the British left India and the levers of power fell into the hands of the Brahmins, the Bania and the feudal Lord Trinity. Unfortunately, the gap between the rich and the poor keeps on widening more speedily even today and the future outlook appears to be extremely bleak. Now such disparity appears to be most dangerous in prevailing democratic system whereby the rich man's notes manipulate the poor man's votes.

vii) Employment Opportunities

Enough employment opportunities can be generated in the country by tapping and utilizing its national resources. There is no shortage of iron or coal in the country. Instead of giving employment to 30 lakh people in mines, the government has employed only 7.5 lakh people for obvious reasons. It does not want the Dalits to progress economically.

—*The Tribune, 18.1.1990*

viii) Reservation

The government is not sincere in implementing the reservation policy. It is because of this reason that Scheduled Castes and Tribes quota has not been filled up even after 40 years of Independence. There are about 3700 listed backward classes in the country and the Constitution has specific provision for their upliftment. It is under this provision that the Kaka Kalekar and Mandal Commissions were constituted but due to deliberate apathy of the Government, their reports were gathering dust. Our party will continue its crusade until the recommendations of the Mandal Commission report are implemented.

15 per cent of the population is ruling the 85 per cent majority of the poor, weak and downtrodden of this country and employing measures to crush them. This will not work now as the exploited have learnt a lesson from the past and are ready to sacrifice anything for enforcing their rights. Now these sections comprising 85 per cent people of this country are ware of their rights.

—*The Pioneer, 8.12.1986*

The reservation is not our demand but our right. Reservation is a matter of participation.

—*Indian Express, Lucknow 9.12.1986*

Scheduled Castes, Tribes and other backward castes should fight for the cause of reservation.

—*Blitz, 10.1.1987*

Reservation is a must as long as we are not ourselves ruling. After that, the situation will be different. To illustrate, Brahmins today hold over 50 per cent of the district magistrate posts in the country, even though they account for only 4 per cent of the population. There is no reservation for Brahmins, and yet they are on top, because since Independence it is they who have been ruling. Those who rule do not need the crutch of reservation.

—*The Times of India, 20.8.1990*

Who asked the British about their merit when they ruled the country?

—*The Tribune, 19.9.1990*

I am preparing my people to create conditions whereby they are in a position to grant reservation to others, not ask for reservations from others.

—*The Independent, 25.4.1991*

To be frank, I am against reservation because it can only be a temporary measure, a crutch which won't help us achieve much. What the people in power are doing is to keep us happy with crutches so that we do not compete for power.

—*Current, 6.4.1991*

3. POLITICAL PROGRAMMES

i) Politics-Political Power
ii) Political Philosophy
iii) Power Movement/Political Power
iv) About the Election
v) Rigging
vi) Fight Against Corruption
vii) Bharat Ratna Award
viii) Dr Ambedkar University
ix) Political Reservation
x) Urban Slum Dwellers
xi) Democracy
xii) Future
xiii) Parliament
xiv) Scheduled Caste President

i) Politics— Political Power

We want to use politics for social transformation.

—*Sunday Mail, 9.4.1989*

No one can purchase us.

—*The Hindustan Times, 31.3.1987*

Our people have now better understood that conducting the missionary activities is entirely different from contesting the elections.

—*The Oppressed Indian*

The social arrangement as Brahmin, Kshatriya, Vaisya and Shudra is vertical. This is unheard of in the history of any other countries. The 40 years of independence has only strengthened this vertical structure. We want a horizontal social order where all of us are equals. This will become possible by the emergence of a new vote bank.

—*The Week, June 1988*

ii) Political Philosophy

We are the victims of the social system that caused inequality among the people in the spheres of social life, economic, educational and everywhere. All political parties which are a product of this system will naturally try to sustain Brahminism. Our message has made a deep appeal to the masses because we are talking of smashing this system.

—*Weakened Newstime, 26.4.1987*

iii) Power Movement/Political Power

We are not interested in Dalit Movement or the RPI. We are more interested in Power Movement.

—*Dainik Bhaskar (Bhopal), 8.1.1990*

Political Power

The political power is the master-key with which you can open any lock whether it is social, economic, educational or cultural lock. Very shortly we will be holding this master key in our hands.

iv) About the Election

I go begging with the slogan 'One Vote, One Note.' I need not take more than one rupee from one person. If we get Rs 50,000 by begging we would get two lakh votes.

—The Week, June 1988

v) Rigging

Suppose a minister is responsible for rigging, he might now be killed on the spot. What can I do? I cannot visit every police station (chowki) and every polling both to prevent such things. Next time when these Ministers go for rigging, will they come back? I visualize a situation where the people will rise and not allow the riggers to go back. That is my fear.

—The Telegraph, 28.4.1987

Let us make it clear to those who indulge in these things (Rigging) that we can also go to any length. We surrendered 100 guns after Section 144 was imposed at the time of the byelection (Haridwar) and mind you, these were licensed guns only.

—Statesman, 7.4.1987

Meeting state terrorism is no problem for us.

—Indian Express, 7.4.1987

If serious steps are not taken to stop rigging, BSP will be forced to resort to the same offence and no one can do it better than us.

—The Hindu, 7.4.1987

It is very easy for us. Let them (Government) say that rigging is good and we will be super-riggers. No one can match us. I have already told the Election Commissioner and I am going to tell the President that if the Government resorts to rigging this time, it is not going to be good for its health. Rigging is, state terrorism and any kind of terrorism is bad.

—Week Newstime, 19.4.1987

vi) Fight Against Corruption

For the last two years, there was a continuous fight against corruption at the top. We were witness to a strange phenomenon. Barring a few exceptions, the very people who stand condemned before our eyes for corruption were proclaiming to fight against corruption.

The people of India are victims of corruption. The corruption has resulted into all-round price rise, unbearable inflation, poverty, illiteracy and unemployment. The life has become miserable and the burden unbearable. It is, therefore, the need of the victims of corruption to fight corruption at all levels, especially the fountain head of corruption. Fight against actors and agents is no fight. The real and genuine fight should be against the head of the Government—the fountain head of corruption.

I, therefore, on behalf of the victims of corruption have decided to fight corruption at the fountain head. I have, therefore, offered myself as a candidate at Amethi against the Prime Minister of India Mr Rajiv Gandhi. That is the main purpose of my fight at Amethi.

—From the hand out for. the Press
—My fight at Amethi and East Delhi
—Fight for a purpose, 1.11.1989

Corruption is everywhere but merely accusing someone of corruption will not be corruption. The government and the people's representatives should have the willingness to fight corruption.

—The Free Press Journal, Bombay, 28.9.1989

vii) Bharat Ratna Award (Dr Ambedkar)

M.G. Ramachandran, former Chief Minister of Tamil Nadu was awarded the Bharat Ratna within a year of his death while Ambedkar was given the same honour 34 years after his death. It is absurd to compare the two.

—The Independent, 7.1.1991

vii) Dr Ambedkar University

For 15 years, we had struggled for an Ambedkar University in Maharashtra. Our demand was ignored but in U.P. where the BSP is strong, the Chief Minister sanctioned an amount of Rs 112 crore for Ambedkar University.

BSP will not be satisfied with a University in U.P. and will stop at nothing short of capturing power. We demand the *Guru Killi* (Master Key) to the state. If they think they can hide it beneath a University they are wrong. We want the Master Key and we will get it after defeating them decisively.

—*The Indian Express, 16.3.1991*

ix) Political Reservation

I do not want reservations for a long time. Those who cannot stand on their own, they need crutches. But the Government is forcing them on us for the last 40 years, especially the political reservation. Now, actually the reservation suits those who are in the government. They are extending reservation to remain in the government. Dr Ambedkar wanted reservation only for 10 years. It has already lingered on for over 40 years. And the Government is saying that we should again increase it by another 10 years. But we are against such reservation. That is why we don't bother about reserved seats and unreserved seats, all are alike for us.

—*The Telegraph, 3.12.1989*

x) Urban Slum Dwellers

All these slum dwellers-10 crore in the entire country. Not more than that. Each would have to get a house.

Like all that stretch beside the Yamuna, first the bank where all our poor from the villages have built slums. And behind that all these burial grounds — Gandhi's, Indira's Nehru's ... it's one big grave yard. Ridiculous. We won't allow this. We would like to collect all these (graves) at one place and distribute the rest of the land.

We need a separate Ministry for this — for rehabilitating the urban homeless, the refugees from our own country.

—*The Times of India, 14.9.1989*

xi) Democracy

If the social and economic inequalities are not done away with, the victims of this inequality will pull down the edifice of democracy that has been painstakingly built.

Democracy means rule of the majority. In India, the majority comprises the SCs, STs, the other backward castes (OBCs) and religious minorities. However, this majority is ruled over by a few upper castes notably the Brahmins — who comprise a minority of 10 to 15 per cent of the population. The Congress has been their main political instrument but all other national parties are equally Brahminical. This is a ridiculous situation. The 85 per cent "have not", the Bahujan Samaj, can become rulers the day they align behind a party that stands for change—like the BSP—instead of running after the parties interested in preserving the status quo. The ballot system makes this possible, therefore, seize power by working within the system.

—*The Times of India, 2.4.1987*

Today, the democracy in India has become a tool in the hands of rich people who purchase votes of poor man.

Our main goal is to bring about social democracy along with political democracy.

—*The Hindustan Times, 28.3. 1989*

I am not interested in the talk of democracy—inner democracy and outer democracy—which then goes on to rig the votes of others.

—*Surya India, May, 1987*

xii) Future

Our ultimate aim is to rule India.

—*Weekend Newstime, 26.4.1987*

After coming to power, in six months, we'll put all those practising untouchability in prison. In four months, we'll see that landless labourers don't have to work any more on others' farms for a living. We'll see they get the required minimum wages for that at home.

—*The Times of India, 14.9.1989*

Land for Landless

In fact, we will give land to all of them. There is no shortage of land in country. Lots of vacant land in the Government's possession. We will distribute it to the landless. Or set up State farms of it.

—*The Times of India, 14.9.1989*

In another 10 years, India will be one of the most prosperous countries in the world—with a human heart and feeling, not willing to exploit others and not willing to be exploited by others. It will be something like Ashoka's India.

—*Surya India, May 1987*

xiii) Parliament

We do not attach much importance to the Parliament. In a country where votes are purchased and sold, in a country where votes are stolen and looted the Parliament does not represent the people.

—*Surya India, April 1992*

xiv) Scheduled Caste President

The President as it is only a titular head. If you start appointing the President under the influence of stooges, then what we will become of Presidential office is any person guess.

4. PROGRAMMES ABOUT OTHER PARTIES AND LEADERS

i) Gandhi
ii) Jagjivan Ram, Ram Vilas Paswan, Ram Dhan & Buta Singh
iii) Congress
iv) Communist Parties
v) Namboodripad-Jyoti Basu-Nayanar
vi) Janata Dal
vii) VP Singh-Devi Lal, Chandra Shekhar
viii) Mandal Commission And Its Implementation
ix) BJP
x) BJP-VHP-RSS
xi) Shiv Sena
xii) Advani Yatra
xiii) Ram Janmabhoomi-Babri Masjid Controversy
xiv) Punjab Problem
xv) Other Opposition Parties.

i) Gandhi

Gandhi is the root cause of everything. I want change. Dr Ambedkar wanted changes. But Gandhi was the custodian of status quo. He wanted Shudras to remain Shudras. Gandhi worked to keep the nation divided. We are working to unite the nation and erase all artificial divisions.

—*The Illustrated Weekly of India, March 8, 1987*

Harijan was a term used to describe the children of devdasis in Bombay and Madras Presidencies. Gandhi might have thought theses people (the Scheduled Castes) were bastards. I do not think so.

—*Indian Express Magazine, 7.4.1991*

ii) Jagjivan Ram

He was a stooge, he was not a leader. As long as he was stooging and he was saying what you just referred to, he was enjoying himself. But later on, the stooge wanted to become Prime Minister and no one will make a stooge the Prime Minister. So, there was a conflict and he declared that he will convert. He was to become a Muslim in 1981 : a hue and cry was raised in Parliament also.

Then he started his own party, first Janata (J) then Congress (J), he was almost finished.

—*The Telegraph, 3.12.1989*

Babu Jagjivan Ram was created by the force of status quo and he was dropped by the force of status quo.

The Week, 16.4.1989

Ram Vilas Paswan

Paswan is known among his own community people as "Thakur ka Thappa" (stamp of higher caste Rajput landlords). When the Thakurs want Paswan to be elected, they do not allow the Scheduled Caste people to vote, they go and stamp five or six lakhs votes in Paswan's favour. If the Thakurs do not want Paswan to be elected then Paswan will end up with 34,000 votes. Thus the Scheduled Caste people really do not matter in case of Paswan. Thakurs put words into his mouth and he keeps on repeating them like a parrot.

—*Surya India, April 1992*

Ram Dhan

Ram Dhan is a super stooge. He cannot even get 5,000 votes of his own Tribal people. Ram Dhan is another Ram Vilas Paswan.

—*Surya India, April 1992*

Buta Singh

I do not consider Buta Singh and Paswan as leaders.

—*Surya India, April 1992*

iii) Congress

The Congress (I) is the largest rallying point for the forces of status quo. Just like smaller magnets are attracted by a bigger magnetic field, the Congress (I) attracts the forces of status quo. The Congress is the main Brahminical force.

—The Telegraph, 28.4.1987

Closure of one Desi-liquorshop will be a minor achievement but closure of the Congress (I) shop a far bigger one. Let us struggle for big things for our big Samaj.

—Pamphlet published by Central Office, New Delhi, 30.8.1986

Congress (I) is our nearest rival as an oppressor which has done nothing for the poor people except for selling them dreams.

The Congressmen are coming to me because they need me and not vice versa. Suddenly, the Congress seems to have realised my worth, I have been offered a share in power but that is not what I want. My aim is to hold power on my own.

I pity the Congress party if it is guided by Shankaracharyas.

—The Illustrated Weekly

iv) Communist Parties

The communists have been saying all along that they are for revolution, but when will they bring it about? Seventy years are not sufficient for them. We will do it in seven months. Actually, they are blocking the path of revolution.

—The Telegraph, 3.12.1989

No party except the BSP want to change the political status quo. The "Left" is also no exception and has even stopped reciting their old slogan "Dharti bant ke rahegi" (Land will definitely be divided amongst all people).

—The Telegraph 16.3.1991

We think the communists are snakes in the grass.

—Current, 19.1.1991

They are also a Brahminical force. They are perhaps worse than the other because they (Communists) profess to work for change and yet work only for the status quo. All communist parties are dominated by Brahmins and Thakurs. When I decide to go to West Bengal, they will be in the Bay of Bengal.

—*The Telegraph, 28.4.1987*

Our party has nothing in common with the Leftist who cheated the people. Their true colour came out in the open when they declared the 'Raja' and other feudal elements as the real proletariat of India and gave him their full-blooded support. They declared that they were in favour of dictatorship of such a proletariat. Our proletariat comprise the have-nots.

—*Sunday Mail, 26.8.1990*

The proletariat of India can write off the Communist parties of India. We must have no illusions about them, we can safely name them, for our future record, as Russian Raja Parties.

What relevance do they (Communist Party) have when they ignore the biggest reality in Indian Society, Caste ?

v) Namboodripad-Jyoti Basu-Nayanar

The Left parties are domesticated by the upper castes who 'use' socialistic jargon as a smokescreen for their oppression. Tell me, will the CPM allow (the backward caste) Mrs Gowri to come as Chief Minister of Kerala in place of (the forward caste) Nayanar? Tell me if Jyoti Basu does not belong to the Bengali aristocracy? Why is it the CPM dominated by leaders who come from highly affluent families, such as EMS Namboodripad?

— *The Illustrated Weekly of India, 16.2.1991*

vi) Janata Dal

The Janata Dal has a big hand in *Zulam, Zyadti* and *Dadagiri* (*Zulam*-oppression, *Zyadti*-excesses, *Dadagiri* — muscle power).

In fact, they may well be number one in this regard. It is as casteist as the Congress. We do not see much difference. But there are more feudal elements in the Janata Dal and they are more rustic, more crude. This is what we think.

— *India Week, 15.12.1989*

If the Congress is dominated by Brahminism, the Janata Dal is ruled by both Brahminism and feudalism. If Congress is corrupt, then the Janata Dal will be super corrupt.

— *Current, 28.10.1989*

vii) VP Singh, Devi Lal, Chandra Shekhar

VP Singh

This man (VP Singh) talks of clean politics and of ushering in new political culture but just to win the Allahabad by-election he threw all his principles to the wind. How can you talk of morals and yet align with fundamentalists like Shahabuddin, Bokhari, RSS and the Bajrang Dal?

— *The Free Press Journal 20.9.1989*

VP Singh cannot conceal his true identity. A man is known by the company he keeps. His most ardent supporters are the BJP and the RSS.

— *Current, 11.6.1988*

VP Singh is a good talker and not a doer.

— *The Telegraph, 16.3.1991*

He is full of contradictions. I feel he is not sincere to himself or to his ideologies.

— *Current, 6.4.1991*

The leader of the Janata Dal party should act in a responsible manner like a captain who is strong and firm. But VP Singh has behaved like a referee, doing patch work. This provides a very poor picture of the man.

— *Sunday Mail, 26.8.1990*

We did not support VP Singh and Chandra Shekhar because we feel one is *naagnath* and the other is *saapnath.*

— *India Today, 15.2.1991*

Why should we be with VP Singh? VP Singh was part of the Congress culture and during his tenure as Chief Minister of Uttar Pradesh, our people were persecuted. Or take the Moradabad riots, for instance, which took place during his time. Two thousands Muslims died but the pig which was cause of the trouble is still alive.

A man is known by the company he keeps. Two things are against him. One, he has been in Congress for 25 years and his record as the Chief Minister of UP is the most discussed, so far as the backward communities are concerned. Today he is trying to change, but he has got notorious company. VC Shukla, Arun Nehru, they are all corrupt people. Another thing is that he is a Thakur. Thakurs are very enthusiastic about him. If VP Singh speaks about equality and brotherhood, then the Thakurs will desert him.

VP Singh is a "first class hypocrite".

— *The Illustrated Weekly, 23.3.1991*

Devi Lal

Could a combination of Brahmins and Baniyas have made you a leader? They would and they did use you as a mere ladder not as leader.

— *National Herald, 10.8.1990*

Devi Lal wanted to become Prime Minister. He wanted to speak from the ramparts of the Red Fort. But the jats are to be found in only 20 of the 450 districts of India. Devi Lal cannot become the Prime Minister of India with only jat support. He wanted to broaden his constituency, which is why he started to bring up the concept of the brotherhood of the weaker sections and the kisans, the jats and the jatavas.

The jats were the first to rebel against Brahminism. Pakistan was not created by Jinnah, but by the large mass of jats who converted to Islam after 1880. The majority of the populace in Punjab today are also jat—they want Khalistan. The jatavs are also rebelling against Brahminism. What is more natural than to join hands to oppose Brahminical oppression?

— *The Sunday Observer, 12.8.1990*

Chandra Shekhar

Actually I am happy that Shekhar is a puppet. Shekhar could not have become Prime Minister without being a puppet.

— *Current, 19.1.1991*

Shekhar is doing fine. People had expected too much from VP Singh while they do not expect anything from Shekhar.

— *Current, 19.1.1991*

viii) Mandal Commission

VP Singh tried to put the cart before the horse in the sense that he promised reservation in jobs but he did not announce anything regarding education.

— *The Hindustan Times, 19.1.1991*

Implementation of Mandal Commission Report

I have been struggling for years to get the recommendations accepted. And I cannot discontinue my struggle yet, because this announcement is actually VP Singh's way of duping the people. It is a good beginning, but that's all. It is not a question of bread and butter or jobs for us. We want to be part of governance of the Land. They are trying to hoodwink us by giving the impression that they have done the needful but there are many areas lying untouched. What about reservation in the educational field — in Medical and Engineering colleges, what about Agriculture trade and commerce?

The Government has said that the castes which are mentioned in both the Mandal report and the States' lists, would be taken up first. But the State's lists are so sketchy that this amounts to duping the people.

It is only right and proper that we, who constitute the backward majority of 85 per cent rule over the other 15 per cent. A certain percentage of the district magistrates (DM) in certain areas must be from Scheduled Castes—that is our aim.

— *The Sunday Observer, 12.8.1990*

ix) BJP

We like the BJP Advani is a Cobra. I need not tell my people beware of the BJP. Everybody in my party recognizes this hooded cobra.

— *Current, 19.1.1991*

We stand for social transformation and the BJP stands for maintenance of the status quo. We want change, the BJP wants things to continue as they are.

— *Sunday Mail, 26.8.1990*

x) BJP-VHP-RSS

They are not an answer, they are a question. They are a problem. They have no economic approach. That's why they have been diverting the public attention.

— *Current, 19.1.1991*

xi) Shiv Sena

Other than me, for instance, no body can crush the Shiv Sena. Any time I come to Maharashtra I will finish them. The violence of the Shiv Sena will end. Who are the members of the Shiv Sena who burn and destroy? They are four castes: (1) Agari (2) Bhandari (3) Koli (4) Chamar. They are Scheduled Castes, Scheduled Tribes and most backward communities. As soon as I touch Maharashtra, these people will instantly come with me.

— *The Illustrated Weekly, 8.3.1987*

xii) About Advani Rath Yatra

I have been always against mixing politics with religion whether it is Advani or Sikhs or Muslims or Christians. But we fought tooth and nail against the Advani Yatra. I had warned VP Singh not to allow it and at the Madras National Integration Council meeting I had taken the same stand. We had told him either he should convince Advani of the disastrous consequences or take administrative action. On 17th October 1990 the Rath reached Delhi and again I told V P Singh to take some action because Advani was openly saying that he was proceeding to Ayodhya to demolish the mosque. He was preparing the masses to commit that crime. Why did V P Singh allow him?

Should I tell you the truth? He was hand in glove with Advani. His intention was that you go ahead with 'Ram' so that 'Rahim' will automatically come to me—Rahim and Mandal. It was conspiracy between V P Singh and Advani, and I had told V P Singh in so many words. The two between themselves divided 'Ram' and 'Rahim'. When I told him he refuted my contention. I told him we are so much worried and he was relaxed. Why was he so relaxed? A lot of damage had been done, a lot of enmity had been created between the two communities and he was relaxed. I was really surprised at his attitude and then I concluded that he must be in league with Advani.

— *Current, 19.1.1991*

xiii) Ram Janmabhoomi-Babri Masjid Controversy

We have been saying from the very beginning that we should abide by the court decision. It should not only be a Court's decision, but justice should be done. If it is possible to arrive at a decision politically, then we will be happy. But if that is not possible, then the court decision should be acceptable.

— *The Telegraph, 3.12.1989*

We are not interested in Mosques, Temples, Gurdwaras nor Churches. We do not interfere in religious matters. Our main concern is social transformation and economic emancipation. As far as this particular controversy is concerned, our view is that the courts should decide.

— *The Sunday Observer, 1.10.1989*

xiv) Punjab Problem

If talks could be held with 'boys' in Mizoram and Assam what is the hitch in negotiating with boys of Punjab? Government should have dialogue with Punjab militants to solve the problems.

— *Indian Express, 30.3.1990*

xv) Other Opposition Parties

To my mind, all parties represent the forces of status quo. For us, politics is the politics of transformation. The existing parties are the reason for the status quo. That is why there has been no upward mobility for the backward communities.

The communist parties have become the biggest stumbling block in this regard. They keep talking about change, but work for status quo. The BJP is better, they never talk about change. So people never feel duped.

Parties like the Congress and Communists talk about abolishing poverty but work towards keeping people poor. It the poor are not kept poor, these people cannot remain in their seats.

— *The Illustrated Weekly, 8.3.1987*

All the opposition parties are irrelevant. Now that we have arrived on the scene all the parties have become irrelevant.

If Congress is a snake, the Janata Dal is a serpent. Both are essentially poisonous. Whoever wants to come closer to us must first shed its poison. The BJP infact, is our best ally and vice versa. We cut into the low castes votes while they into the upper castes votes. We hate them, they hate us.

— *Current, 3.6.1989*

9

Poll Reforms

BEFORE CAMPAIGING FOR the hustings for Eleventh Lok Sabha were to start, the Election Commission had given strictures for the contesting parties on what should be model code of conduct for campaignings, and thereby how the parties should behave. The structures, interestingly, became the first of its kind in the history of Free India whereby they became the trend-setters for the future generation electioneering. As it is, they are imperative for all political parties today.

Keeping that in mind, the new government, of the United Front reached a consensus among its constituents on what should be the common code of conduct in their conception towards hustings in future. In order to put things into rational shape, the Government has passed the Reforms proposal successfully which are known today as a POLL REFORM CAPSULE that would stay.

- Delimitation on the basis of 1991 Census.
- Enhancement of punishment.
- Disqualification.
- Observers.
- Reduction in campaign period to 14 days.
- Restriction on nomination (not more than two seats).
- Substantial increase in deposits.
- Arrangement to permit the name of political parties (national) first in the ballot papers followed by the

regional parties and the Independents.

- Non-countermanding of election in case of death, including provision of changing the registered party candidate.
- Election Commission empowered to countermand the election without a report from the returning officer.
- Statutory backing of model code of conduct.

10

Common Minimum Programme of the Eleventh Lok Sabha

The ELEVENTH Lok Sabha is now in its office. The stroms over the democratic process and obligations are now settled, hopefull for five years from now (1996). Times is come, therefore, to work to build up the nation. As we have already come to learn, the 1996 Lok Sabha elections resulted in a mandate in favour of secular and democratic forces by and large, though the clear-cut absolute majority was still wanting. The largest party, BJP, which was called by the President of India for forming the government, however, was unfortunate to muster enough support to prove its majority, as required by two-third of the members present and able to vote in the House for rule within the stipulated period. The second largest party had to combine with 12 more to form a united front of group of parties.

The United Front reached among its constituents a consensus on A Common Approach To Major Policy Matters And A Minimum Programme.

According to the 13-party United Front group of parties, the Lok Sabha mandate was in favour of secular and democratic forces. Three out of four voters, on an average, have voted against sectarian and communal parties. Also, the total percentage of voters, voted for such number of parties, including national and State level ones have formed a ratio of 3:4. It is broadly considered that the mandate is for principles of probity, responsibility, accountability, geniuses and transparency in all decision-making. The UF, therefore, interpret the verdict as one for formation of secular, liberal and democratic qualition Government at the Centre. It is only such a Government today that can reflect the pluralistic nature of our society, it is largely believed today.

The UF represents the diversity of India in substantial measure. The Front hence pledges to:

> represent the people of India in preserving the secular nature of their heritage;
>
> to give them a Government truly representative, responsible and responsive;
>
> to represent the will of Indians to strengthen forces of political federation, that means, a strong Centre, strong States, and viable local bodies;
>
> to give them a higher standard of living, a better quality of life through faster economic growth and enhanced social justice.

UF will not be a replacement of one set of people by another. Its basic administrative norms will be on an alternate model of federalism, decentralisation, accountability, equality and social justice, eco-politico reforms, respect for human freedom, openness and transparency, ensuring dignity of both the nation and individual citizen.

Following are the aspects of the Common Minimum Programme that would be strictly followed by the new Government during its tenure; these aspects are based on secularism, stability, development and distributive justice:

a) Stability
b) Social Justice
c) Empowered
d) Secularism
e) Towards Just & Humane Society
f) Economic Policy

g) Agriculture
h) Poverty Alleviation
i) Industry
j) Public Sector
k) Industrial Sickness
l) Labour
m) Infrastructure
n) Public Investment
o) Fiscal Management
p) Price Stability
q) Drinking Water; Primary Health Care & Housing
r) Education
s) Science & Technology
t) Clean Administration
u) Jammu & Kashmir
v) Assam & North-East
w) Foreign Policy
x) International Bodies & Treaty Obligation
y) Prasar Bharati Act; and
z) Environment.

Stability and Federalism

The United Front is committed to giving a stable government at the Centre for full term of five years. In any coalition, there will be differences, but what is important is the manner in which these differences are aired, discussed and resolved. During its term of office, the United Front Government will advance the principles of political, administrative and economic federalism. In each of these sphere powers will be devolved and authority will be decentralised. The Last Review Centre-State relations was undertaken by the Sarkaria Commission which give its report over ten years ago. Since then, there has been a sea-change in both the politics and economics of the country. There has also been a new articulation of States' rights and the need for greater powers to the States to meet the aspirations of their respective States.

Hence, the United Front Government intends to pursue a two-track policy. On the first track, the recommendations of the Sarkaria Commission on which there is already a broad consensus will be implemented through legislation and administrative action as appropriate. The United Front believes that it is possible to take immediate action, legislative and/or administrative, on the following matters:

i) to give greater autonomy to States in determining their priorities in developmental programmes;

ii) to give States greater freedom to draw their State plans within the broad framework of the National Five-Year Plans;

iii) to transfer most Centrally sponsored schemes to the control of the State Governments;

iv) To grant assent promptly to Bills passed by State Legislatures on matters which are within the legislative powers of the State Legislatures.

On the second track, the United Front Government will immediately appoint a High-Level Committee to review and update the recommendations of the Sarkaria Commission. The Committee will be requested to also look into the vital question of devolution of financial powers from the Central Government to the State Governments. The Committee will be required to give its report within three months. The report of the Committee will then be made public so that there is an informed public debate before final decisions are taken.

Besides, the United Front Government will reactivate and energise institutions like the National Development Council and the Inter-State Council.

The scope of Article 356 of the Constitution has been interpreted and circumscribed by recent decisions of the Supreme Court. Article 356 will be amended to reflect these decisions and to prevent the misuse of that Article.

Elections have been held in most States to Panchayats and, in some cases, also to the Nagarpalikas pursuant to the 72nd and 73rd Amendments to the Constitution. The process will be taken further to ensure devolution of administrative and financial powers to Panchayats and Nagarpalikas in all the States. Step will be taken to ensure that regular elections are held according to the prescribed frequency.

Social Justice

The United Front is committed to the empowerment of the under-privileged and deprived sections and communities. One-third of the elected membership in Parliament and State Legislatures will be reserved for women. Legislation, including an amendment to the Constitution, if necessary, will be introduced to reserve one-third of all posts in Government for women. The United Front Government will take all possible measures to promote and ensure gender equality. All laws will be reviewed to remove provisions which discriminate against women.

The policy of reservation in public employment for Scheduled Castes, Scheduled Tribes and Other Backward Classes will continue and will be implemented vigorously. The benefits of reservation will be extended to dalit Christians. Special courts will be set up under the Scheduled Castes and Scheduled Tribes (Prevention of Atrocities) Act to ensure quick justice to victims of atrocities.

Artisans, craftspersons, tradespersons, weavers and fishermen are among the most neglected sections of society. Special programmes will be devised to enhance their skills, give them modern tools and more credit facilities and make their products and services more marketable so that they will earn living wages.

The United Front Government will urge the State Governments to take up, on a priority basis, the question of conferring ownership rights on slum dwellers in respect of the land on which they live with suitable provisions for slum improvement, public or private group housing to replace *kutcha* shelters and allotment of alternative sites in case it becomes necessary to relocate slum dwellers on grounds of public interest.

Empowerment of Scheduled Tribes, Scheduled Castes and Other Backward Classes

Scheduled Tribes are found in many parts of India and dwell in the most difficult and inhospitable terrains. There is growing dissatisfaction among Scheduled Tribes because of lack of security, alienation of their lands, exploitation of the mineral wealth, deprivation of their rights to forest produce and wealth and despoiling of their environment. The United Front Government will appoint a High Level Commission to enquire into and report on the status, problems and aspirations of the members belonging to the Scheduled Tribes. The United Front Government will also study the conclusions contained in the report of the Bhuria Committee on Scheduled Tribes made in 1995 and take necessary steps to implement the salient recommendations.

The United Front Government will urge the State Governments to make legislation for conferring ownership rights in respect of minor forest produce, including Tendu Patta on Scheduled Castes, Scheduled Tribes, Other Backward Classes and other weaker sections who work in the forests. The Central Government will consider extending some financial assistance to the State Governments which take up this responsibility.

A large number of members belonging to the Scheduled Castes and Other Backward Classes are dependent on their traditional occupations. On the one hand, the door of access to other occupations has been barred to them while, on the other hand, there is a sharp dwindling of opportunities and incomes in their traditional occupations. Despite the policy of reservation there is no true equality of opportunity. The Central Government and the State Governments have not addressed themselves comprehensively and consistently to measures which would bring economic freedom, educational equality and true equality of opportunities to these people. The United Front Government will carefully study the Dalit Manifesto formulated by the National Action Forum for Social Justice and implement its salient recommendations.

A number of cases are pending consideration for inclusion in the list of Scheduled Tribes. Decisions will be taken on these cases expeditiously.

Secularism

The United Front is founded on the plank of secularism and democracy. The United Front declares that secularism means that there should be separation of State and religion and also notes that it is this definition that has been accepted as correct by the Supreme Court in numerous decisions. Attempts by sectarian or communal forces to erode the multi-ethnic, multi-religious and multi-linguistic character of our society will be strongly resisted.

The contentious issue of Babri Masjid-Ram Janmabhoomi will be referred to the Supreme Court under Article 138(2) of the Constitution. Stringent steps will be taken to implement the Protection of Places of Worship Act.

The Constitutional rights to freedom of religion contained in Articles 25, 26, 27 and 28 of the Constitution will be respected and protected. At the same time, the United Front Government will not allow obscurantism and fundamentalism from any source and of any sort. The personal codes of different religious communities will not be altered unless and until a consensus has emerged in the religious community concerned for bringing about a change. Untiring efforts will be made to bring every section of the society together to build a strong, modern, forward-looking, liberal democratic society imbued with a scientific temper and an aspiration for material progress.

The United Front Government will review and, if necessary, enlarge the 15-point programme for the minorities and ensure the implementation of the programme. Special emphasis will be placed on finding solutions to the problems of the minorities in relation to education, employment and opportunities for economic betterment.

Towards A Just and Humane Society

The United Front Government will, in close cooperation with State Governments, take steps to build a just and humane society. The right to free and compulsory elementary education shall be made a fundamental right and enforced through suitable statutory measures. Special programmes will also be launched to take care of children and the disabled and to eradicate child labour in all occupations and industries.

The Indian Penal Code, the Criminal Procedure Code and all other penal laws will be reviewed and amended to make their provisions consistent with the sanctity of human rights. The United Nations Convention on Torture will be adopted. State Governments will be required to appoint Human Rights Commissions.

Economic Policies

Growth with social justice will be the motto of the United Front Government. There is no substitute for growth. It is growth which creates jobs and generates incomes. Self-reliance has been an article of faith since Independence and the United Front Government will adopt such growth-oriented policies that lead to greater self-reliance. The United Front is committed to faster economic growth. The country's GDP needs to grow at over 7 per cent per year in the next 10 years in order to abolish endemic poverty and unemployment. The Ninth Five-Year Plan is scheduled to be launched on 1st April 1997. The United Front Government will, within 6 months, bring out a detailed document that will articulate the priorities and programmes of the Ninth Plan.

Agriculture

The Agriculture sector cries out for reforms. No strategy of economic reforms and regeneration in India can succeed without sustained and broad-based agricultural development. The rate of investment in agriculture will be stepped up. All controls and regulations that are in the way of increasing the incomes of farmers will be reviewed immediately and abolished wherever found unnecessary. Controls on the movement of agricultural products and on the processing of agricultural products will be abolished. Measures will be taken to ensure that farmers receive fair and remunerative prices for their produce. Special attention will be devoted to augmenting rural infrastructure. A special plan for infrastructure development will be taken up in the 100 most backward and poorest districts of the country. The rural credit system will be restructured so as to double the flow of credit to agriculture and agro-industries, particularly to small and marginal farmers, within 5 years. A national policy on water sharing and water management will be devised in order to save farmers all over the country from recurrent floods and droughts.

Agencies that supply inputs to farmers will be professionalised and where found feasible converted into farmer-owned cooperatives. Agricultural research and extension organisations will be thoroughly overhauled. The most modern technology will be brought to the farm sector, e.g., bio-technology for livestock and cold storage for agro-processing.

A comprehensive law will be made by Parliament in respect of agricultural workers to guarantee them minimum wages and fair conditions of work, group insurance and other rights.

States will be encouraged to implement land reforms by plugging the legal and administrative loopholes. States will also be urged to make a law dealing with land records including record of tenancy rights. In cooperation with the States, larger funds will be allocated for irrigation and extension of cultivation.

Poverty Alleviation

A frontal attack on poverty is an important element in any development policy. This is the main rationale for anti-poverty programmes. Such programmes must be redesigned to ensure generation of more employment, creation of assets, imparting productive skills and raising the incomes of the very poor so that a significant number is brought above the poverty line every year and poverty, as we have known it, is abolished by the year 2005. The United Front Government will review all the anti-poverty programmes with a view to strengthening them and providing them with larger funds. A programme for guaranteeing 100 days of employment for every unemployed person will be implemented through Panchayati Raj institutions.

Industry

The key to faster economic growth is rapid, labour-intensive industrialisation. The United Front is committed to maintain a 12 per cent annual growth in the industrial sector. This will require massive capital and modern technology, apart from continuing the process of deregulation and decontrol as required. There is ample room for public investment as well as private investment. When it is required to face competition, domestic industry will be assured of a level playing field.

Suitable policies will be devised to stimulate domestic savings and capital formation. The bulk of industry's requirements will indeed come from within the country. However, at the margin, the country cannot do without foreign investment particularly if that foreign investment will also bring modern technology and management practices and create new markets for products manufactured in the country. The nation needs and has the capacity to absorb at least $10 billion a year as foreign direct investment.

Suitable credit and taxation policies will be devised to ensure that the bulk of new investments, both domestic and foreign, will be channelled into the core and infrastructure sectors. Entry of multinational companies into low priority areas will be discouraged through suitable fiscal and other measures. In order to promote even development, suitable incentives and policies will be devised to encourage new industries to locate in the backward districts of the country.

The United Front recognises the role of the corporate sector in building a strong and modern India. The corporate sector should create conditions in which the working class of the country is able to make its contribution with enthusiasm. The United Front Government in its dealings with the corporate sector will follow a policy informed by transparency and fair play and expects that the corporate sector will reciprocate by following the rules and conventions of a healthy market economy. The corporate sector should also keep in mind the paramount interest of the consumer and will be held accountable through an expanded network of consumer courts. The United Front Government will always be ready to engage in a meaningful and constructive dialogue with the corporate sector with a view to strengthening the Indian economy.

The progress towards the goal of bringing India's tariffs in accord with world levels will be measured and calibrated. An independent Tariff Commission will be appointed within three months to hear and determine tariff disputes as well as to recommend appropriate levels of tariffs for different products and different industries keeping in view the larger interests of the country.

There are a number of domestic industries which are essentially home-based or village-base requiring low skills and employing a large number of people. These industries will be given adequate protection and it will be ensured that foreign investment does not displace such industries.

The balance among large, medium and small/cottage industries will be restored. Small and cottage industries have the potential of creating large job opportunities. They are also more elastic in responding to changes in the market. Hence, special plans will be devised to promote small and cottage industries to achieve the twin objectives of growth and employment.

Public Sector

In the early decades of development, the public sector played a pioneering role. The public sector will continue to be an important component of Indian industry. The United Front Government will help to make the public sector strong and competitive. In a competitive and technology-driven economy, there is no room for monopolies and inefficiency. Public sector enterprises which are essentially commercial enterprises should conduct their business on commercial lines. They cannot be allowed to dissuave; they should show a healthy return on the capital employed. It is widely acknowledged that the public sector requires to be reformed and restructured. The United Front Government will identify public sector companies that have comparative advantages and will support them in their drive to become global giants. Other profit making and efficient public sector companies will be strengthened and their managements professionalised, and participation of workers in the management of these companies will be encouraged. Sick or potentially sick public sector companies will be rehabilitated through a menu of options that may include handing over the management to professional groups or workers' cooperatives.

The question of withdrawing the public sector from non-core and non-strategic areas will be carefully examined subject, however, to assuring the workers and employees of jobs security or, in the alternative, opportunities for retraining and redeployment. The United Front Government will establish a Disinvestment Commission to advise the Government on these steps. Any decision to disinvest will be taken and implemented in a transparent manner. Revenues generated from such disinvestment will be utilised in two vital areas, health and education, particularly in the poorer and backward districts of the country. A part of such revenues will be earmarked to create an investment fund which will be used to strengthen other public sector enterprises.

Industrial Sickness

A new law will be made to deal with industrial sickness and the Board for Industrial and Financial Reconstruction (BIFR) will be completed revamped. The law will also provide for a separate mechanism to deal with sickness in small industries. Efforts will be made to rehabilitate and revive sick industries and protect the interests of the workers.

Labour

Workers form the backbone of the industrial sector. Their rights are spelt out in a number of laws made by Parliament and State legislatures. The United Front Government will ensure that these laws are implemented in the spirit in which the laws were made. The rights of trade unions will be respected and recognition of trade unions will be required to be done by secret ballot.

Some laws have been made in respect of labour in the unorganised sector. These laws will be strengthened and, where necessary, new laws will be made to protect the interests of such labour particularly in the construction and beedi rolling industries.

Infrastructure

Investment in infrastructure has to be stepped up from the present 3.5 per cent to 4 per cent of GDP to at least 6 per cent of GDP in the next few years. The economy cannot grow and the needs of the people cannot be met without more capacity in power, oil, telecom, railways, roads and ports. The cumulative requirement of these sectors over the next five years is estimated to be $200 billion (Rs 7,00,000 crore) at the very minimum. Thus, there is ample room for all modes of investment — public and private, domestic and foreign. The United Front acknowledges that the State and public investment have a leading role to play in the development of infrastructure. The scope, functions and the procedures of the Foreign Investment Promotion Board will be reviewed in order to make it an effective and credible instrument to promote foreign investment in India. Transparent rules and regulations will be drawn up to attract foreign investment and for the award of contracts if any. Every decision on the award of large contracts will be made public together with the process by which the decision was arrived at.

There is a strong link between infrastructure development and financial sector reforms. Infrastructure needs long-term finances. The United Front Government will carry out further reforms of the financial sector so that the flow of both domestic and foreign funds to the infrastructure sector is enhanced substantially. There is room for public sector companies and private sector companies to co-exist and compete in the financial sector. We have gained considerable experience in the working of the banking sector. The said experience will be applied to the restructuring of the insurance industry but at the same time public sector companies like LIC, GIC etc. will be strengthened.

Public Investment

There is a crucial role for public investments particularly in social sectors like education and health. However, organisational and management changes in these sectors are as necessary as increased investment. Besides, there can be no compromise on efficiency and productivity. Public services and utilities must be made to deliver at the lowest cost. Where there is a need for subsidy, the subsidy must be closely targeted to benefit the really needy and the poor.

Fiscal Management

It is recognised world over that fiscal prudence is the key to low inflation, stable price levels and rapid growth. The United Front is committed to bringing the fiscal deficit to below 4 per cent of GDP. The management of the fiscal deficit will, therefore, enjoy the highest priority. The United Front Government will continue with tax reforms and take other steps to augment revenues legitimately due to the Government and to curb tax evasion. All inessential and unproductive expenditure will be eliminated. Subsidies will be targetted to the really needy and poor. Public borrowing will be severely restricted and, as far as possible, borrowed money will not be used for consumption expenditure. Growth in domestic debt will be slowed down and a portion of the debt will be retired in a phased manner. These principles of fiscal management will, however, not be followed at the cost of development or investment.

Prices Stability

The Public Distribution System will be strengthened to meet the twin objectives of price stability and making available essential articles to the poor. Special cards will be given to familiar below the poverty line and essential articles under the PDS will be sold to them at one-half of the normal issue prices. Access to the PDS will be barred for the affluent sections of the society. While the responsibility of supplying foodgrains and essential articles will remain with the Central and State Governments, the management of PDS shops will be entrusted to elected Panchayats and Nagar Palikas.

Foodstocks and foreign exchange reserves will be used imaginatively and purposefully to stabilise prices. Speculators, hoarders and blackmarketeers create havoc with availability and prices of essential articles. Preventive and punitive actions will be taken against them. Swift and severe punishment will be meted out to the offenders.

Drinking Water, Primary Healthcare and Housing

Although drinking water, primary healthcare and housing are subjects which fall under the purview of the State Governments, the Central Government also bears a responsibility to ensure that these basic human needs of every citizen are satisfied. Special plans will be drawn up during the Ninth Plan period to ensure that:

i) every habitation has access to potable drinking water;
ii) one primary health centre is established for a population of 5,000 people and it is efficiently managed; and
iii) the very poor have access to houses built under the public housing programme or to credit that can be utilised to build their own houses so that the goal of providing a shelter to every family is achieved by the year 2005.

Education

Six per cent of nation's GDP will be earmarked for education. This will be achieved by the year 2000. Of these funds 50 per cent will be spent on primary education. Substantial funds will be earmarked for imparting technical and vocational skills and training in order to turn out more employable and self-employed youth. The goal of the National Literacy Mission (NLM) to cover 10 crore adults will be achieved by the target year 1998-1999. The NLM will give special attention to the spread of literacy among women.

The United Front is also committed to making the nation fully literate by the year 2005. A special effort will be made in the States where there is very high incidence of illiteracy and constitute the bulk of educational deprivation. Weaknesses and loopholes in the implementation of the literacy programme will be identified and removed.

The mid-day meal scheme will be implemented in all the States to ensure regular attendance and retention in primary and middle schools. In every initiative that is taken to promote the spread of education, the girl-child will be a special focus of attention.

Science and Technology

Science and Technology are engines of change and growth. A nation can ignore the advances made in science and technology only at its peril. All-out efforts, including the provision of adequate funds, will be made to promote research and development and to strengthen the nation and other laboratories. The United Front Government will adopt and implement a forward looking policy on science and technology which will help build a modern and self-reliant society on the foundations of a rational outlook, scientific temper, creative work and material progress.

Clean Administration

The United Front is committed to a corruption-free and clean administration. A Bill to set up the Lok Pal will be introduced in the first Budget session of the Eleventh Lok Sabha. The Bill will cover the office of Prime Minister as well. All Members of Parliament will be required by law to declare their assets annually before the Lok Pal.

The Official Secrets Act will be reviewed and amended keeping in tune with the need for openness and transparency in governance. A Bill on Freedom of Information will be introduced within six months to give the people access to information at all levels.

Discretionary quotas, hitherto enjoyed by Ministers, will be abolished. In areas where it is necessary to make a small number of out-of-turn allotments, such allotments will be made by a Committee and in accordance with published rules and guidelines. All exercise of discretionary powers in this behalf will be made public quarterly through a suitable publication equivalent to the gazette.

A Bill on electoral reforms reflecting the consensus already arrived at will be introduced in the first Budget session of the Eleventh Lok Sabha.

A Bill on judicial reforms will be introduced within six months in order to expedite trial of cases and to eliminate delays.

In consultation with the Chief Justice of India and the Chief Justices of High Courts, steps will be taken to dispose of all pending cases within a period of three years.

The United Front Government is committed to fight corruption, particularly corruption in high places, and will take such steps as are necessary and in accordance with the law to restore the confidence and credibility of the offices and institutions of the State.

The people of the country are greatly exercised by the growing emergence of a nexus between politicians, civil servants, businessmen and criminal elements which has been eloquently illustrated by the report of the Vohra Committee. The United Front Government will disclose to Parliament the relevant facts and materials which formed the basis of the report of the Vohra Committee. It will also set up a statutory authority with adequate powers to go into these facts and circumstances and make suitable recommendations to identify and punish the guilty with a view to eliminate the role of the "parallel government."

Jammu and Kashmir

The State of Jammu & Kashmir and its people are an inalienable part of India. The resolution of the problem of Jammu and Kashmir can only be through consulting the wishes of the people. The elections held recently from Sixth Lok Sabha constituencies is a first step in the process of consultation. The United Front is committed to hold elections to the Jammu and Kashmir State Legislative Assembly as soon as possible. Respecting Article 370 of the Constitution as well as the wishes of the people, the problem of Jammu and Kashmir will be resolved through giving the people of that State the maximum degree of autonomy.

Assam and the North-Eastern States

The problem of influx of foreigners into Assam will be resolved on the basis of the Assam Accord to which the Central Government is a signatory. The resolution of the issues relating to ULFA and Bodo Security Force also lies only through a political dialogue.

The United Front Government will take up special programmes for the economic development of Assam and the North-Eastern region. The recrudescence of insurgency in Manipur, Mizoram and Nagaland is a cause for concern and will be met with a firm resolve to enforce law and order.

Foreign Policy

There is a large measure of consensus on foreign policy which is based on our traditional values and on the experience gained during the freedom struggle and in the post-Independence era. Non-alignment is the cornerstone of our foreign policy. The United Front Government will closely adhere to the consensus.

Good and friendly relations with neighbouring countries will receive the highest priority. The SAARC forum and

SAPTA leading to SAFTA will be the principal instruments through which close and friendly relations will be forged between India and her South Asian neighbours.

China is a neighbour of India. Important steps were taken in recent years towards cordial relations and harmony between India and China. Further steps will be taken in this direction.

The United Front Government will work to strengthen the Non-Aligned Movement. It will also actively participate in the deliberations of UNCTAD so that the organisation and the member countries are able to articulate the views of the developing countries.

India has taken many initiatives to become a partner in many multilateral arrangements e.g. the Indian Ocean Rim, APEC and ASEAN. These initiatives will be pursued.

While India has good relations with all countries of the world, it has especially warm relations with the United States and Russia as well as Japan and many countries in Central Asia, South East Asia, the European Union, the Middle East, Africa and Latin America. These warm relationships will be emphasised while strengthening relations with all countries of the world.

The United Front Government will continue the South-South dialogue in order to make South-South cooperation an important plank of multilateral efforts taken by the developing countries.

The United Front Government will continue to work for universal nuclear disarmament and will retain the nuclear option till this goal is achieved. It will press India's case for permanent membership of the Security Council.

Economic and commercial relations are now important components of our foreign policy. Foreign economic relations will be based on the principle of mutual cooperation and benefit through bilateral and multilateral arrangements.

International Bodies and Treaty Obligations

India has been an active member of the United Nations since its inception. India is also a founder of many international bodies and organisations. These organisations will play an important role in an increasingly interdependent world. The United Front Government will assert India's rights and interests in these organisations. It will also mobilise other developing countries to fight for their rights. In forging international or multilateral agreements, the United Front Government will continue to ensure the interests of the country's agriculture, leading sectors of industry and our genetic resources.

Prasar Bharati Act

The Prasar Bharati Act will be reviewed and amended in the light of the recent judgments of the Supreme Court and implemented without further delay.

Environment

The United Front is committed to protecting and preserving the environment and the adoption of green policies in every walk of life. A massive programme for afforestation, wasteland development and revegetation of degraded forests will be launched through Panchayati Raj institutions.

The United Front Government's policy on environment will be consistent with the need for rapid and sustainable economic development. Stern measures will be taken against pollution and polluters. The interests of the workers will be safeguarded when it becomes necessary to relocate polluting industrial units. The displacement of communities as a result of developmental activities will be avoided as far as possible and, in any case, rehabilitation of the displaced families will be made an integral component of any developmental plan.

Millions of young men and women are imbued with idealism. The United Front Government will harness the energies of the youth. They will be recruited in Development Corps and deployed in a large number of public works like afforestation, repair and restoration of canals, waterways and irrigation systems etc.

Conclusion

India today is in the midst of a major transition in its economic, social and political life. This is a transition period which will be guided by the need to strengthen the principles of democracy, secularism, federalism and social justice. The ethos of our humanist tradition and the aspirations of the Independence struggle inspire the United Front Government to carry out the above programme. In the building of this new India of equality, justice and fraternity, we seek the fullest participation of all citizens. The hallmark of the United Front Government's approach will be the greater and greater involvement of our people in all its endeavours.

India in 1996 has fallen into a transition period which continued its hustings for the Eleventh Lok Sabha. The nation sincerely felt that it has to be guided by different principles, different from influences of Nehru family and entirely on its own well-conceived goals uplifting democracy, secularism, federalism and—what the 13-party combine has expounded—on established norms of social justice. The ethos of humanist tradition and aspirations of the Independence struggles, now quite muzzled up by and large, would continue to inspire again the Government. This country now seems destined to be run by the United Front Government, all set to implement its above mentioned Common Minimum Programme. In building the new India of equality, justice and fraternity, the parties in power sought the fullest participation of all citizens. The hallmark of the new Government's approach will be greater involvement of our people in all its endeavour.